Anthropological Research

SUNY Series in Advances in Applied Anthropology
Erve Chambers, Editor

Anthropological Research

Process and Application

Edited by

John J. Poggie, Jr.
Billie R. DeWalt
William W. Dressler

State University of New York Press

Published by
State University of New York Press, Albany

© 1992 State University of New York

For information, address State University of New York Press,
State University Plaza, Albany, N.Y., 12246

Production by M. R. Mulholland
Marketing by Bernadette LaManna

Library of Congress Cataloging–in–Publication Data
Anthropological research : process and application / edited by John J.
   Poggie, Jr., Billie R. DeWalt, William W. Dressler.
        p.   cm. — (SUNY series in advances in applied anthropology)
   Includes bibliographical references and index.
   ISBN 0-7914-1001-3 (CH : acid-free). — ISBN 0-7914-1002-1 (PB :
acid-free)
     1. Applied anthropology.   2. Ethnology—Methodology.
3. Anthropology—Research. 4. Pelto, Pertti J.   I. Poggie, John J.
II. DeWalt, Billie R.   III. Dressler, William W.   IV. Series.
GN397.5.A564   1992
301'.072—dc20   91-16528
                                                                        CIP

10 9 8 7 6 5 4 3 2 1

To Bert
From all of us out here
First, second, and third generations

Contents

Tables and Figures

Preface

We set out on the task of preparing this book because we share a common underlying assumption about anthropology. The assumption that both guided and motivated us is that replicable and systematic procedures of data collection and analysis are essential requirements for building useful cultural theory. We view cultural theory as an aid both to understanding sociocultural phenomena and in changing existing social conditions.

Besides this overall approach of the volume, there are five specific themes which we consider to be very productive and which are used to organize the book's chapters. These themes represent a set of principles for conducting research and consist of the following: (1) the importance of intracultural variation; (2) the blending of qualitative and quantitative approaches; (3) the search for micro/macro levels of generalization; (4) the innovative matching of methodology to research problems; and (5) the practical or applied merit of systematically generated and evaluated theory.

The intent of this volume is to contribute to scientific applied anthropology and to honor an anthropologist who has been a leading figure in this enterprise. Pertti J. Pelto has been a lifelong champion of the cause of science and practical application in the discipline and one of the first to propose and utilize the principles stressed in this volume. This book is therefore appropriately dedicated to him.

Bert's book *Anthropological Research: The Structure of Inquiry* (coauthored in the second edition by Gretel H. Pelto) has greatly influenced a generation of anthropologists and other social scientists. It sets out a clear, common-sense rationale by which our thinking and research about cultural and behavioral phenomena can be structured. The papers that are assembled here have been influenced by and derived explicitly from the approach that Bert and Gretel pioneered.

Many of the authors represented in this book also had the good fortune to have been at one time, students of Bert's. Many of us know anthropologists who are great scholars or who are great teachers. Bert embodies that rare combination; he has been able to make significant contributions to the field and, at the same time, to communicate his love and ability for anthropology to a large number of others. He has done this in his teaching career at Cornell University, the University of Minnesota, the University of Connecticut, and most recently, in the National Science Foundation Summer Methodology

Camps at the University of Florida. Bert has supervised dozens of master's theses and doctoral dissertations. He has helped (even forced) many of us to structure our thinking and research. We are grateful for the time and effort he has put into this and for the friendship that has accompanied it. The role in anthropology that Bert chose for himself was not an easy one, but it is one that has made a difference. For his courage and for his steadfastness we are truly grateful.

It is sad to write that one of our authors, John M. Roberts, died before his paper, coauthored with Ronald Carlisle, appeared in this volume. Jack Roberts was a great methodologist and a wonderful friend. We acknowledge his contribution to scientific anthropology and feel enriched by having shared some time with him. We thank Ron Carlisle for his generous effort on the Roberts and Carlisle chapter. Carrying on the work is a fine tribute to the memory of his coauthor.

In addition to the authors of the chapters, a number of people and institutions have helped to project this volume into print. We are grateful for the helpful, positive suggestions for revision of the first version of this manuscript that we received from Erve Chambers and Robert T. Trotter II. Jeffrey Johnson made very helpful suggestions for refining the second draft. Erika R. Poggie helped greatly in the numerous editorial tasks involved in putting together a manuscript with 19 different authors and three editors. For her help we are greatly appreciative. Rosalie M. Robertson, our editor at SUNY Press, gave us encouragement and support, and we thank her. John Poggie and William Dressler wish to thank the University of Rhode Island and the University of Alabama respectively for support of this work. Billie R. DeWalt expresses his appreciation to the University of Kentucky for support in his work on this manuscript by a University Research Professorship.

I

Anthropological Research:
Process and Application

Introduction

The social sciences are currently marked by substantial controversy within the disciplines. This controversy concerns fundamental questions such as: What are the relevant questions to be asked? Is there an objective reality "out there" that can be perceived and studied? What are the appropriate methodologies that should be used in studying social phenomena? On one side are those researchers and practitioners who see social phenomena as subject to systematic regularities and therefore discoverable through systematic procedures of data collection and analysis. On the other side are those who question whether "objective" or, more precisely, "intersubjective" study of social phenomena is possible, arguing that the appropriate role of researchers should be to engage in careful analysis of the interplay of the observer and the observed, and of how the understanding of cultural phenomena is generated by that interaction.

In anthropology, the current debate over appropriate epistemologies, theoretical perspectives, and approaches harks back to many previous divisions. Indeed, the discipline of anthropology still straddles the fence that exists between the humanities and social sciences.

The approach advocated in this volume is certainly that replicable and systematic procedures of data collection and analysis are a requirement for the building of useful cultural theory, cultural theory that is an aid both to understanding social phenomena and in changing existing social conditions. At the same time, it is our contention that conventional social scientific procedures—those exclusively relying on the social survey or on ethnographic techniques—are not as productive as is needed for building cultural theory. Rather, a theoretical and methodological approach that is eclectic in its orientation is likely to be more useful, as Pelto argued some twenty years ago (Pelto, 1970). We have brought together in this volume the work of anthropologists who are committed to using appropriate and innovative methodologies to build better theories. Also, in keeping with the notion that "nothing is more useful than a good theory," this body of work is relevant to the application of ideas. These essays are forward-looking in terms of their contributions both to methodology in anthropology, and to efforts in formulating public policy. Before examining the theoretical and methodological themes unifying these papers, we will briefly put them in the context of discussions of methodological issues in anthropology.

A Historical Perspective

The history of anthropological research has been characterized by periods of intense interest in the methods by which that research is conducted, as well as by periods in which methodology has generated little thought or debate. Methodological debates were important in the development of anthropology early in this century. In response to what he saw as the excesses of armchair anthropology, represented by such people as Lewis Henry Morgan and Edward Tylor, Boas (original 1896, reprinted 1973) argued forcefully for the collection of primary field data in anthropology. He maintained that it would only be through the careful and systematic collection of primary ethnographic data that anthropologists could inductively arrive at lawlike statements concerning social and cultural processes, which in turn could be used to explain cross-cultural regularities.

Malinowski (original 1922) also was critical of a lack of systematic methods in ethnography. He stated:

> The results of scientific research in any branch of learning ought to be presented in a manner absolutely candid and above board. No one would dream of making an experimental contribution to physical or chemical science, without giving a detailed account of all the arrangements of the experiment. . . . In Ethnography, where a candid account of such data is perhaps even more necessary, it has unfortunately in the past not always been supplied with sufficient generosity, and many writers do not ply the full searchlight of methodic sincerity, as they move among their facts but produce them before us out of complete obscurity. (Malinowski, 1961:2–3)

Later in this same work Malinowski, in opposition to an inductive logic, argues that the ethnographer is best prepared for work in the field by a thorough grounding in theory, for "problems are first revealed to the observer by his theoretical studies" (1961:9).

This vision of a scientific anthropology was not universally shared or adopted. Throughout this century there have been anthropologists who have argued that the discipline cannot—indeed, should not—be regarded as representative of the natural sciences, but rather is better regarded as a humanistic endeavor. Evans-Pritchard (original 1950, reprinted 1973) represented this point of view. His basic objection to the natural science model was that it led ethnographers to force their observations into rigid and inappropriate categories, in an attempt to generate the lawlike statements of science. Rather than formulating their observations to fit inappropriate models, Evans-

Pritchard argued that ethnographers should be immersed in the "social reality" (his term) of the culture studied, to understand it as completely as possible without reference to other natural law or generalization. Foreshadowing more recent writings in phenomenological sociology, Evans-Pritchard pointed out the paradox in his suggestion:

> The concepts of natural system and natural law, modeled on the constructs of the natural sciences, have dominated anthropology from its beginnings, and as we look back over the course of its growth I think we can see that they have been responsible for a false scholasticism which has led to one rigid and ambitious formulation after another. Regarded as a special kind of historiography, that is, as one of the humanities, social anthropology is released from these essentially philosophical dogmas and given the opportunity, though it may seem paradoxical to say so, to be really empirical and, in the true sense of the word, scientific (Evans-Pritchard, 1973:368).

In other words, by giving up the false illusion that anthropological research can be conducted along lines similar to those employed in physics, biology, or even psychology, ethnographers will in part become more scientific, being freed to pursue social reality in the way best fitted to the particular context studied.

In the 1960s there was a remarkable spurt of interest in the development of more reliable and systematic methods for anthropological research. One source of this interest was ethnoscience or ethnosemantics, in which emphasis was placed on reliable techniques for eliciting culturally acceptable linguistic categories. It was also in this decade that explicit attempts to bring together anthropological methods in single sources were made, including Naroll and Cohen's (1973) handbook of methods, and Pertti J. Pelto's *Anthropological Research* (1970; Pelto and Pelto, 1978). These works differed from earlier contributions (e.g., *Notes and Queries on Anthropology* [Royal Anthropological Institute of Great Britain and Ireland] and the *Outline of Cultural Materials* [Murdock et al., 1982]) that were mainly collections of the kinds of topics that ought to be addressed by anthropology.

Both the Naroll and Cohen volume and Pelto's work were explicit in detailing a philosophy of social science that acknowledged the unity of scientific inquiry. Also, both were explicit in recommending a blending of the traditional strengths of anthropological inquiry—ethnographic methods—with quantitative methods.

Despite these positive moves, there was a countervailing trend in anthropology to reject a natural science or—to use a term that has gained the logical status of ethnic slur—positivist model of research in favor of an approach that emphasized not the formulation of lawlike or causal statements, but rather the uniqueness of human cultures, an essential noncomparability resulting from the creative expression and manipulation of symbols by members of society. There are actually many varieties of this orientation, which could be labeled symbolic, interpretive, hermeneutic, phenomenological, deconstructivist, or even postmodernist anthropology. Whatever the label, there is a tendency, variably doctrinaire in its expression, to reject a natural scientific model of inquiry in favor of a human scientific, or even literary approach.

The degree to which the natural science and symbolic approaches can be opposed is exemplified by two articles, both published in the 1980s, by two distinguished anthropologists. Clifford Geertz, in the published version of his 1983 Distinguished Lecture at the American Anthropological Association, takes the concept of cultural relativism as a vehicle for making clear his mission for anthropology. His aim is not to defend cultural relativism, but rather to criticize what he terms anti-relativism approaches in anthropology. His main criticism is of orientations that seek to illuminate regularities in human behavior across cultures—orientations that employ notions of "human nature" or the psychic unity of mankind. He characterizes these approaches, in the published authors chosen by him as representative, as assuming a kind of neofunctionalist view of human behavior and society. Any kind of functionalist theory assumes a structure, or a set of elements and the relationships among those elements. At least a portion of the relationships can be described as functional, in the sense of contributing to the continued integrity of the system. These functional relationships regulate the values of system parameters within broad limits, and can be described in terms of central tendencies and deviations from those tendencies. Inputs to and outputs from the system—in this example a human social system—can be described in causal terms. The theoretical orientations criticized by Geertz employ concepts of "human nature" and the psychic unity of mankind as limiting conditions on the range of diversity in human social systems.

Geertz argues forcefully (and always eloquently) that these approaches represent a return to an outmoded view, one which violates the very essence of a human science.

"Looking into dragons, not domesticating or abominating them, nor drowning them in vats of theory, is what anthropology has been all about . . . We have, with no little success, sought to keep the world off balance; pulling out rugs, upsetting tea tables, setting off firecrackers. It has been the office of others to reassure; ours to unsettle . . . Merchants of astonishment" (Geertz, 1984:275). In other words, it is far from the job of anthropology to search for lawlike regularities that describe human behavior within and between cultures. It is, rather, the job of anthropology to make explicit how much and how far cultures diverge, and to revel in that which is novel.

Melford Spiro (1986) also uses the concept of cultural relativism as a point of departure in an important article discussing the future of anthropology. He begins by distinguishing several varieties of descriptive relativism. A moderate form holds that cultures are indeed different and that all cultures can be regarded as equivalent in some evaluative sense. Spiro refers to this as the familiar Boasian form of normative relativism, one that is consistent with a science model. In the 1960s there developed a strong form of descriptive relativism that Spiro terms epistemological relativism, which serves as the foundation for symbolic anthropology.

"Epistemological relativism, by contrast, not only espouses the theory of wholesale cultural determinism, but it also holds a maximal view of cultural diversity; a combination, so it contends, that precludes both nonvacuous cultural generalizations as well as the axiom of psychic unity. Hence, that combination . . . constitutes its character for the claim that anthropology is an interpretive ('hermeneutic'), not an explanatory ('scientific') discipline" (Spiro, 1986:265). In other words, because human behavior is both widely culturally variable and totally culturally determined, as anthropologists we can only describe and interpret, rather than explain in causal terms, that behavior. Spiro goes on to argue that this view is misplaced, that the fact of cultural diversity is what makes genuine causal ("scientific") explanation truly possible. Therefore, it is not the fact of cultural diversity, or even a strong form of cultural determination, that precludes a scientific anthropology; rather, it is a prescriptive rejection of scientific approaches. He concludes the article with a systematic examination of the principles on which the hermeneutic critique of a scientific anthropology is based—principles that he shows are logically unsound.

It is worth noting here that although we have phrased this debate in the terms chosen by Geertz and Spiro, which are specific to the discipline of anthropology, there is no necessary reason to do so. The interested reader is referred in this regard to recent discussions by the French sociologists Raymond Boudon (1988) and Pierre Bourdieu (1988). Taking slightly different tacks on the subject, these sociologists agree that a fundamental issue dividing social scientific researchers is an "objective-subjective" dichotomy; that is, Can social science reach objective knowledge of social reality in research, or is it by its very nature forced to provide descriptive accounts of what various players in the game (researchers and research subjects) offer as accounts of reality, with no hope of verifying any account? Boudon concludes that, for some problems, an objectivist, hypothesis-testing, quantified social science is appropriate. Bourdieu concludes that a truly useful social science (useful at least in terms of theory building) must incorporate both of these perspectives.

The important point, however, is that although the debate can be centered around cultural relativism in anthropology, this is but one manifestation of a larger epistemological issue in social science in general.

In a nutshell, this is the modern history of a discipline in which some practitioners say that anthropology is a natural science, whereas others say that not only is it not a science, but indeed it should not be one. If this strikes the reader as a fairly quaint conclusion, that is because it is. This debate is obviously of long standing, and no clear resolution appears to be at hand. The terms in which the dispute is carried on have gained considerably in sophistication, but it remains a continuation of previous disagreements.

Our aim in this volume is not to resolve this controversy, for the simple reason that it cannot be resolved. Rather, our aim is to contribute more grist for the mill, but in such a way as to clarify some of the issues involved. All of the contributors to this volume come down on the scientific anthropology side of the debate. Furthermore, all of the contributors have been influenced in one way or another by the specific methodological approach advocated by Pelto and Pelto (1978). By providing a series of empirical examples of the use of that approach in a variety of substantive areas, we hope to show what the nature of a scientific approach in anthropological research really can be. This is no small contribution. By providing these examples, we show that the "positivist" characterization of explanatory/causal approaches in anthropology is the classic case of the straw man. It would be far beyond the scope of this essay to attempt an in-depth analysis of that term; it will suffice to note that, as used by many social scientists, "positivism" denotes a theory of knowledge in which social facts exist as objects, independent of social actors, their meanings, and the action of the observer. Explanation consists of creating propositions relating those objects, which in turn can be subjected to empirical verification. A truly positivist approach would consist of the development of objective measurements that could be used at all times and all places. All theoretical statements would then be verified by the use of those objective measurements, much as survey research is construed by some in sociology. Such a program has rarely been proposed in anthropology, but examples do exist (Moles, 1977).

Ethnography is the classic corrective to a proposal that a research program of this type should be instituted in anthropology. Familiar examples of how behaviors thought to represent one domain (e.g., religion) turn out actually to represent another (e.g., population regulation) abound. Therefore, what the critics of a scientific anthropology like to label as "positivism" is something we eschew as a naive empiricism. Instead, we seek to probe the limits of our own naiveté by the systematic integration of the ethnographic methods that represent the traditional strengths of anthropology with quantitative methods and formal research design, which will enable us to refine our theories in every substantive area. This was the promise of the methodological programs proposed by Pelto and Pelto (1978), Naroll and Cohen (1973), and others (Johnson, 1978; Bernard, 1988). The papers assembled in this volume exemplify the partial realization of that promise, and can serve as guides to future work.

The Contributions of This Volume

The papers in this volume are unified not by technique or even by method, but by a more abstract bridge that might be called "approach." The approach used in each paper is fundamentally problem-oriented. A question is raised, a puzzle is posed, and it becomes the task of the analyst to arrive at an explanation for that question. This question may involve the psychosocial risks of depression in a specific setting, or how to understand the determinants of successful fishing. Whatever the issue involved, it is first formulated as a question for which an explanation, causal in form, can be constructed.

One important advance in understanding social processes that has come out of anthropological theory is the awareness of how causality cuts across levels of system integration. Very often the behavior of particular individuals in specific communities is influenced in a very real and direct way by corporate decisions or cultural fads occurring half a world away. The incorporation of this understanding of macro-micro linkages has been an important step (see DeWalt and Pelto, 1985).

Once a problem has been formulated or a question asked, it then must be translated into operational terms. This is perhaps where interpretive and explanatory approaches diverge most completely. What is the point of operationalization? The simple point is that operational definitions enable the analyst to distinguish instances from noninstances of some phenomenon of interest (e.g., heart attacks, religious rituals, or fishing success). In other words, instances and noninstances can be compared. As Spiro (1986:265–69) notes, given the extreme relativism demanded by an interpretive approach, such comparisons, even of individuals within a single culture, are precluded. The extreme assumption of epistemological relativism holds that each individual's organization of knowledge and experience is unique, a result of his or her own biography. Under this assumption, at best we can interpret individual instances of belief or behavior, but without recourse to comparative examples related to different forms of experience, causal explanation can never be formulated. This same argument applies across levels of system integration, be it the individual, the social group, or the culture.

There are two crucial issues here. First, fundamental non-comparability flies in the face of the biocultural facts of life. Human beings did evolve as a single species. Culture evolved in tandem with, and interacting with, evolving human biology. It seems illogical to presume, then, an extreme form of cultural determinism, because certain limits on the variability of human behavior, including "cultural" behavior, are built into the mechanism, so to speak. Cultures and human behavior are highly variable, to be sure. But that fact aids in the development of causal explanation, rather than hindering it. Causal explanations can be formulated precisely because there is so much variability in human behavior, not in spite of it. We only need assume that behavior varies within certain wide limits that enable us to define operationally that behavior, or those beliefs, or those forms of social interaction (Spiro, 1986:265–71).

Second, an assumption of noncomparability can be viewed as applying not to the phenomena under investigation, but rather to the analyst. This really is the familiar "Martian observer" argument. Suppose, the argument goes, that a Martian ethnographer arrived on earth to study human behavior. He/she/it would be unable to understand the behavior because of Martians' inability to comprehend the meaning of that behavior. The argument goes that the Martian could not comprehend a genuflect before a religious icon because of an inability to grasp the meaning of that behavior. As Rudner (1966:5–7) points out, however, this is not an assumption about scientific methods, but rather a hypothesis about Martian observers. If the Martian ethnographer were able to formulate a hypothesis about genuflection, then that hypothesis certainly could be tested by operationalizing terms and using the agreed-upon canons of scientific logic. We are not sure about the psychology of Martian ethnographers, but human ones have shown themselves to be remarkably creative in proposing explanations for human behavior. Indeed, symbolic anthropologists are among the most creative, and their interpretations are fundamentally complex systems of hypotheses arising from the context of discovery of scientific research. The next step in the process is to formulate these hypotheses in systematic terms to be tested in the context of validation, a step not taken by symbolic anthropologists.

This blend of the interpretive and explanatory, of the qualitative and the quantitative, of the context of discovery and the context of validation, holds enormous potential for future research in anthropology. It is a truism in the philosophy for future research in anthropology. It is a truism in the philosophy of science that there is not a logic of discovery. One only need recall Watson's phenomenologic reconstruction of his formulation of the double helix to understand why. At the same time, however, discovery processes can be systematic, and the hypotheses derived in those systematic processes can in turn be scrutinized with the agreed-upon logic of validation. The blend of qualitative and quantitative methods can be viewed in this way. By being sensitive to local context and local knowledge, the anthropological researcher is more likely to arrive at valid contructs of relevance in a particular setting, and in turn to be able to formulate valid operational definitions for key terms and creative hypotheses relating those terms. Using this strategy, systematized by anthropological methodologists (Naroll and Cohen, 1973; Pelto and Pelto, 1978; Johnson, 1978; Bernard, 1988), the range of cultural diversity again opens itself as a fertile field in which to explore theories of human behavior.

How does this work in practice? Or even, *can* this work in practice? The papers in this volume have been assembled as evidence of how, employing this approach, key contributions to anthropological theory and to the application of anthropological understanding to the solution of policy issues can be made.

Beyond what we have referred to as "approach," there are five specific themes to which these chapters are addressed. These five specific themes represent a less abstract set of principles for conducting research than the general scientific approach described previously. These themes include: (1) the blending of qualitative and quantitative approaches; (2) the search for micro/macro levels of generalization; (3) the importance of intracultural variation; (4) innovative solutions to research problems; and (5) the practical or applied merit of systematically generated and evaluated theory. These principles were first proposed by Pelto and others, and it is our conviction that systematic application of these principles will carry anthropological research forward in a new and fruitful period of theory construction and testing.

The systematic integration of qualitative and quantitative techniques for gathering data holds considerable potential at several different levels of the hierarchy of theory and method. First, it should be made clear that in many instances, these forms of data collection lie on a continuum. In many cases the collection of data in the field consists primarily of talking to people. When data are collected in a manner such that each individual is asked the same questions in the same order, and the responses are constrained to a finite set, we refer to the information as quantitative data. When information is collected in such a way that each individual interview is treated as separate from each other, and the focus of analysis is on the specific content of utterances, we refer to the information as qualitative data. In short, the information itself is the same; it is how we as analysts treat it that varies.

An obvious way to integrate the two is from the standpoint of operationalizing variables. What precise verbal utterances can be construed as an instance of a variable of interest? Careful qualitative work is a prerequisite for quantitative work in many situations. On the other hand, in most cases the results of a quantitative analysis are reliable, valid, and frustratingly opaque. As we struggle to understand the theoretical significance of a correlation matrix, it is often useful to be able to turn to a description in words from an informant of the same reality described by a correlation matrix. Qualitative data can serve as an invaluable adjunct in interpreting quantitative results. There is thus theoretical as well as methodological value in interweaving these forms of data collection throughout a research project. There are, of course, other advantages to the use of multiple methods of data collection, which will be discussed in more detail in specific contributions that follow.

The integration of microlevel and macrolevel data and the systematic search for theoretical statements that cut across these levels is a second theme of this volume. Even a cursory examination of this notion of levels reveals the combined theoretical and methodological importance of the concept. In one sense, the notion of level is a purely methodological issue. In macrolevel data analysis, some aggregate of individuals, whether it is a county, a village, or a whole society, is the unit of analysis. This is a favorite form of analysis for policy scientists, since official statistics often come packaged in this form. In microlevel data analysis, the unit of analysis in usually the individual, but sometimes even smaller units (e.g., body movement). If this were the only difference, this would be an uninteresting and unfruitful distinction; but as Robinson (1950) originally pointed out with his concept of the "ecological fallacy," what patterns exist in the aggregate are often not evident in individuals, and vice versa (see also Schweder, 1973). But clearly the individual and the aggregate are not some completely different order of phenomena. Therefore, the relationship between individual level phenomena and aggregate level phenomena assumes theoretical as well as methodological importance. This relationship of levels of phenomena is something familiar to ethnographers as their attention turns from the most isolated and self-contained communities to those communities linked in systematic ways to supracommunity power structures. New emphases such as dependency theory or world systems theory also alert us to the fact that causal influences in the lives of individuals at the local level often emanate from social and economic institutions far removed from that local level. The challenge for theory and method is to develop concepts and measurements that enable us to model those linkages in systematic, not impressionistic terms, a challenge taken up by several contributors here.

A third theme addressed in these papers is the need to pay close attention to the intracultural diversity (Wallace, 1970; Pelto and Pelto, 1975). It is often thought that by intracultural diversity only individual variability is meant, but this is a false equation. As originally formulated, the concept of intracultural diversity was intended to balance the simplistic cultural uniformist notions in anthropology. Stated boldly, a cultural uniformist orientation presumes that there is one culture (i.e., a single set of rules and assumptions) within a collectivity, and that deviation from that culture occurs because, for example, some people do not know their culture very well, or perhaps because some people are deviants in the sociological sense of the term. In short, variability is treated as noise in the data.

Few people would acknowledge that kind of uniformist thinking these days, but there is still a lack of appreciation of how a single culture can come in different versions, as it were. That is, within a single community that can be described as a single culture in any generally accepted sense of the term, there may be systematic differences in the organization of knowledge and beliefs leading to patterned nonsharing, which in turn is distributed on social structure. If we wish to study some dependent variable and the predictors related to it, it seems likely that any statistical model will be badly misspecified if we attempt to fit it uniformly across these contexts of intracultural diversity. If, on the other, we recognize this patterned diversity within a culture and fit parameters to the model to partition the variance generated by that diversity, the fit of our model will be enhanced. Examples of this approach occur in several chapters here.

Every fieldworker, especially those employing more formal sorts of research design, will have run into these seemingly insolvable problems. It appears as though the data to operationalize a key concept or to test a particular hypothesis simply do not exist; or, if the data do exist, access to them is curtailed by any number of obstacles as various as the social settings we investigate. It is here that the creative and innovative solutions in research come into play. Like the formulation and generation of a hypothesis, these innovative solutions cannot be programmed into use. But the answers provided by other fieldworkers can often stimulate our thinking and lead us to consider a new avenue in research design and analysis, and this again is a theme addressed by the authors here.

The fifth and final theme that unifies this volume is that a systematic and competently evaluated theory will have implications for application. Although not all the contributors to this volume necessarily think of themselves primarily as applied anthropologists, all of them share the conviction that in order to have any salutary effect on the world, any social intervention must be guided by theory that has been tested and found to be empirically useful. Indeed, there is now too much of a division of labor between pure and applied research, between basic science and the policy sciences, between analysis and advocacy. We do not, of course, suggest that if we understood the world better we would automatically change it. Obviously, a refined understanding of the world can only be useful if the mechanisms and energies for application are available and in place. But unfortunately, as many examples attest, the mechanisms and energies for application are impotent if we fail to understand, in precise, measurable, valid, and replicable terms, the substantive phenomena we seek to change. The contributors to this volume take the business of understanding social phenomena seriously precisely because that understanding may or will be used to alter the lives of individuals.

In summary, this volume is intended for all students of anthropology, no matter what their status (undergraduate major or full professor), as a set of concrete examples of how a set of methodological principles can be applied in diverse settings and to diverse topics to improve our understanding of social phenomena, and our ability to influence those phenomena.

II
Intracultural Variation

Introduction to Part Two

In recent decades we have come to realize more and more that intra-cultural variability is to be expected in even the most ostensibly "traitlike" features of culture. For example, peoples' folk taxonomies of plants and the content of folktales are now considered to be as varied as social rank and material style of life. This conceptualization is in marked contrast to the assumption of cultural homogeneity that characterized anthropological reports before the 1950s. This assumption of variability requires the anthropologist to use a different logic of inquiry than has been employed in the past.

The three papers in this section derive much of their explanatory power from the analysis of intracultural diversity. By considering psychocultural characteristics as variables with distributions that are measurable, Dressler, Robbins and Kline, and Poggie are able to relate variables to one another in the context of cultural systems. Even though these authors are dealing with different constellations of variables, the underlying logic of inquiry follows a similar pattern. Variables are carefully measured and then empirically and statistically related to other variables in the logical context of a theory. This logic is compatible with the general conceptualization of culture as a complex system of interrelated components and is vastly different from the now-outmoded notion of culture as a shared set of common beliefs, values, and traits.

1

Culture, Stress, and Depressive Symptoms: Building and Testing a Model in a Specific Setting

William W. Dressler

Pelto (1970; Pelto and Pelto, 1978) has been prominent among anthropologists advocating greater methodological rigor in ethnographic research. Increased emphasis on methodology is necessary for advances in anthropologic understanding for two reasons. First, in terms of descriptive or hypothesis-generating studies, the careful definition of concepts in operational terms substantially increases the quality of primary data construction. Second, with respect to hypothesis-testing or theory-building research, careful attention must be devoted to research design in order to reliably evaluate a system of hypotheses, especially in the systematic elimination of alternatives.

Much, or perhaps even most of anthropological research has proceeded in a hypothesis-generating mode. In this mode the investigator approaches the study of a community (or some other collectivity) with a general theoretical orientation that directs him or her to consider certain broad classes of variables as relevant (e.g., kinship, religious behaviors, economic exchanges). He or she employs an initial period of ethnographic data gathering to understand how these relevant factors are manifest in that specific cultural contest. This often serves as a period of (at least) implicit model building; this model building provides the investigator with a set of hypotheses to be evaluated near the end of his or her field research, or serves to structure the data gathering for the next field trip. The results of these tests of hypotheses then stand as evidence for or against more general propositions about human behavior that must be integrated with similar research from other cultures in the continuing revision of general theories of human social life.

This scenario is research from the ground up, which is generally the bias in anthropology. The difficulty with this approach comes at the point of synthesis; if research on a particular topic within a particular culture has proceeded without the systematic inclusion of factors identified as important in models generated in other contexts, then it is unlikely that this culture-specific test will contribute much to the synthesis of general theory. These points seem to be painfully obvious, yet I would argue that this problem currently afflicts cross-cultural research in psychiatric epidemiology. There has developed a very specific and useful general model of the social and psychological risks for psychiatric symptoms, based on research in the U.S. and Western Europe (Dohrenwend and Dohrenwend, 1981; Cohen and Syme, 1985). Unfortunately, there has been little or no attempt to test, and hence refine, this general model in research in diverse cultural settings.

Pelto (Pelto and Pelto, 1978:251–87) has discussed some of the issues involved in testing general theories in specific contexts. Here I would like to describe an example of theory testing in anthropological research, focusing specifically on the psychosocial risks for psychiatric symptoms. Two of Pelto's methodological emphases are particularly important here: the careful operationalization of terms, and the appropriate specification of relationships among variables in the context of intracultural diversity. Before proceeding to a discussion of the specific application of these methodological principles, the model guiding the research will be described.

Psychosocial Risk Factors and Psychiatric Symptoms

The model to be tested in this research is the social stress/generalized susceptibility model developed by Lazarus (1966), Scott and Howard (1970), Cassel (1976), and Syme and Berkman (1976). In this model, "stress" is conceived of as a dysjunction between the demands placed on an individual and that individual's resources for coping with or resisting the effects of those demands. Where the individual is simultaneously taxed by environmental demands, referred to as "stressors," and has few resources for resisting those stressors, he or she is under "stress." This latter term is thus descriptive of the entire process, rather than analytic. Furthermore, this stress process creates a generalized susceptibility to disease, rather than causing any specific disorder. The person under stress may develop any one (or more) of a set of chronic or acute, organic or functional, infectious or degenerative, disorders. Specific stress outcomes will be influenced by the specific genetic, physical, chemical, and personality attributes of the individual.

For the purposes of this paper, the stessor dimension of the model will be the sole focus.[1] Two broad sets of stressors have been identified as important in research in the U.S. "Acute stressors" are sudden and oftentimes unpredictable events in the social environment that place increased adaptive demands on the individual (Rahe and Arthur, 1978). These acute stressors may be cataclysmic events such as a natural disaster, but most often are more mundane events that nevertheless are of considerable salience for individual well-being. The latter include death of a spouse or other close family member, divorce, loss of a job, and similar events. "Chronic stressors" are ongoing strains or difficulties that serve as more or less continuous adaptive demands (Pearlin, 1982). These chronic stressors are generated within the typical social roles performed by the individual, such as spouse, worker, parent, and others. Empirical research indicates that the combination of acute and chronic stressors increases the risk of psychiatric symptoms, especially the symptoms of depression (Pearlin et al., 1981; Aneschensel and Stone, 1982). (A complete model of the stress process requires the inclusion of the resistance resources that lower the risk of illness associated with stressors; space will only allow here for a discussion of the risk or stressor dimension.)

My aim was to examine the nature and effects of these stressors in a specific sociocultural context, an Afro-American community in the rural South of the U.S.[2] Doing so required paying close attention to two methodological principles discussed by Pelto.

The Content of Stressors

A major issue in specifying a model of the psychosocial risks for psychiatric symptoms involves the measurement of stressors. Can we use what are regarded as appropriate stressor measures in American society in other cultures? This bears on the issues of operationalization, and especially on the emic-etic debates in anthropology. A nearly unassailable assumption in research on the stress process is that relevant stressors are not inherently (or universally) problematic, but become so because they are imbued with this meaning from particular cultural perspectives. Thus, the death of a family member may be regarded as culturally stressful in some societies, but not in others. Furthermore, individuals will differ from one another in the extent to which the occurrence of a stressor will be regarded as personally meaningful.

An extreme response to this dilemma would be the argument that every individual must be studied intensively to determine what he or she regards as stressful, and then to relate the occurrence of those events and circumstances to symptoms. This extreme relativist position (combining cultural and individual relativism) is untenable, however, because it flies in the face of what we know about cultural sharing or the social patterning of meaning. An event or circumstance can be regarded as potentially stressful *not* because of its idiosyncratic meaning, but precisely because its occurrence signifies something of *cultural* salience. This is not to say that very special meanings may not be attached to events, the occurrence of which may precipitate illness; on the contrary, psychiatric journals regularly print case reports in which these unusual and rare etiologies are prominent. But this is precisely the point. These *are* rare and unusual occurrences, and need not detain us in developing an understanding of the *shared* meanings of events and circumstances that precipitate illness. From an epidemiologic, as opposed to clinical, point of view, it is precisely that shared perspective that is important.

Given that we will investigate events and circumstances culturally regarded as potential stressors, how do we compare the effects of stressors across cultures? Pelto and Pelto offer the following general guidance:

> Anthropologists are frequently in a position where they must ask questions, and note information about research communities, in terms derived from cross-cultural ethnological theory and from their own special research hypotheses. In these cases fieldworkers do not wait to extract native categories of experience through full emic processes. They assume that for purposes of testing theory and hypotheses, *some* of the outsiders' definitions of significant actions or cultural categories are useful. They do not, on the other hand, ignore completely the question of the local insiders' definitions and categorizations of behavior . . . the only useful test of our classifications is in the successes and failures of hypothesis testing and theory building. (Pelto and Pelto, 1978:65–66)

The application of this advice in the research described here was facilitated by the fact that the community studied was an Afro-*American* community. Black people in our society have been subject to cultural influences both from the larger society and from the unique Afro-American culture that developed in the Southern U.S. as a result of the diaspora, manumission, and the oppression effects of economic marginality. Therefore, many of the social processes examined in the larger society will be applicable in black communities; at the same time, however, the history of research in the black community is littered with examples of facile and jejune analyses resulting from the failure to recognize Afro-American cultural distinctiveness.

It was assumed here that stressors studied in other American communities would be culturally salient in this Afro-American community, but that there would also be special meanings attached to particular events and circumstances. This was evident in preliminary ethnographic studies. When the question of what was stressful was raised in key informant interviews, people generally spoke of economic difficulties, but in two distinct ways. First, they spoke in terms of the specific event of losing a job, or unemployment. The state of being employed is of obvious relevance for providing economic resources to a household. But a related issue concerns the moral component of employment. In this traditional, conservative black community, indolence is seen as a moral transgression; hard work and faith in God are the essential elements of the right way of living. Therefore, the loss of a job assumes a special meaning in the community.

Second, people spoke of economic difficulties in terms of the chronic, day-to-day problems of living. These concerns revolved around problems of paying bills, obtaining adequate health care, having the financial opportunity for leisure, and above all, the issue of race and finances. It was repeatedly emphasized that black people are "the last hired, the first fired"; that black people are not paid as well as whites in comparable jobs; and that black people are passed over in terms of promotions.

Generally speaking, other kinds of stressful events (such as marital dissolution) and circumstances (such as chronic marital problems) are seen as stemming from these basic kinds of economic difficulties. These culturally salient stressors are consistent with those studies in other American communities (Tausig, 1982; Ilfeld, 1977). There is, however, an important difference. This is clear in the way in which people separate out unemployment from other kinds of life change events. In standard inventories of stressful life events unemployment would be considered to be equivalent to other events (e.g., divorce, death of a child). In scoring an individual's level of exposure to this risk factor, the occurrence of these events would contribute equally to the overall risk score. In the black community, however, unemployment is of such cultural salience that it deserves to be treated by itself as a separate measure of risk. There thus become two inventories of acute stressors: unemployment, treated as a single dichotomous event; and other, primarily noneconomic, life change events.

Similar reasoning applies to the measurement of chronic stressors. Other investigators, studying majority communities in the U.S., have found it useful to combine separate measures of chronic role stressors into summary indices of chronic stressors (Ilfeld, 1977; Aneschensel and Stone, 1982). Because of the salience of chronic economic stressors in the black community, however, it seems appropriate to treat this as a distinct stressor. Other forms of chronic difficulties (marital, parenting, job, and others) can be combined into an overall scale of chronic stressor load.

These stressor or risk measures have been derived from the combination of theory and ethnography. One final stressor measure will be introduced, derived primarily from theory. This is what has been referred to as "lifestyle stress" (Dressler et al., 1987), but for which I now prefer the term "lifestyle incongruity" (Dressler, 1988). This is a measure of the discrepancy between style of life (assessed as the accumulation of consumer goods and the adoption of behaviors indicative of greater articulation to the larger culture), and the individual's economic resources for maintaining that style of life (economic resources assessed as occupational status). In developing communities this factor has been found to be a potent predictor of poorer health status, and was anticipated as important in the black community. No informant spontaneously mentioned this discrepancy as problematic, although several observed that a new kind of "consumerism" had settled into the black community.

To summarize: five separate measures of stressors or psychosocial risk factors have been developed for studying psychiatric symptoms in the black community. All are derived from theory, from ethnographic observation, or from a combination of the two. The acute stressors are: (a) unemployment; and (b) noneconomic life change events. The chronic stressors are: (a) lifestyle incongruity; (b) economic stressors; and (c) role stressors.

Model Specification

Having arrived at a culturally appropriate set of stressors or risk factors for psychiatric symptoms, it now becomes necessary to correctly specify a model of their effects. In most cases, whether the analysis is bivariate of multivariate, a model of simple linear effects is assumed. In the present case this would involve predicting symptoms from the set of five stressors in a multiple regression analysis. Two considerations indicate, however, that this would be inappropriate.

First, there are good theoretical reasons to anticipate intracultural diversity in the effects of stressors. Pelto (Pelto and Pelto, 1978:275–76) notes that the recognition of intracultural diversity and the exploitation of that diversity in research design is an important methodological strategy in building theory. Most often intracultural diversity is equated with individual variability. The latter notion simply means that any variable assumes different values for different individuals; this is variability by definition. The more interesting sense of intracultural diversity is one in which there can be anticipated variability in cognitive sharing between subgroups within a society. These diverse subgroups may be generated by any number of processes. It is the task of the analyst to identify the major processes and to suggest where diversity can be anticipated. Then, having identified population subgroups in which variables of interest may take on different meanings, specific models can be formulated for each group.

This latter sort of diversity is evident in the specification of a model of high blood pressure in the context of economic development (Dressler, 1985). In that research it was found that socioeconomic differentiation in the process of development led to a divergence of groups along social class lines. In the lower social class blood pressure elevation was predicted by the struggle to maintain a higher status lifestyle, or the process of lifestyle incongruity as described previously. In the upper social class, blood pressure elevations were predicted by stresses as perceived by the individual. It was argued that the lower-class person was involved in a struggle to establish a valued social identity, as measured by lifestyle. The upper-class person, having superior resources for establishing that social identity, experienced threats primarily in individual, psychological terms. Put another way, lower-class persons were affected primarily by objective stressors, whereas upper-class persons were affected primarily by subjective stressors.

Second, there are good ethnographic reasons to anticipate intracultural diversity in the meanings and effects of psychosocial risk factors. The black community has traditionally been differentiated along class lines. Some argue that this differentiation began during the period of slavery, but it is clearly visible in the classic studies of Southern black communities (Frazier, 1966; Powdermaker, 1939). The vast majority of the black community has been lower-class, but historically there has been a small group of business persons and professionals in the community. Most often these were teachers, ministers, health professionals, and business persons who served the needs of the community. They were distinguished from the majority of the black community by style of life, demeanor, and, historically, physiognomy.

Social change over the past forty years has not diminished this differentiation. It has changed the mobility potential for particular sets of individuals, but economic circumstances have not made it such that vast segments of the black community have become middle-class (Farley, 1985). Upward mobility is a greater possibility, but only for a relatively small segment of the community, hence reinforcing traditional divisions.

The past forty years have brought about a second source of differentiation within the black community, however. This is age, or perhaps more accurately, generational status. Black people born prior to World War II grew up in an entirely different world, a world of apartheid. It was a world in which freedom of movement did not exist, in which many events were completely unpredictable because so much was not under one's control. The civil rights movement, generated by the new experiences associated with the Second World War and the great Northern migrations, fundamentally changed the world in which black people lived. Although it was (and is) a slow, painful, and tortuous process, black people achieved some measure of social and political equality for the first time in three centuries. Persons socialized under these differing conditions are likely to have fundamentally different perceptions of the world and their own chances in it.

Therefore, there are good theoretical and ethnographic reasons to anticipate differentiation within the community along the lines of age and social class. Different stressors are likely to assume different meanings for individuals, depending on their age and social class, and hence to have different effects on psychiatric symptoms.

Testing the Model[3]

The dependent variable chosen for study here is a ten-item scale of depressive symptoms (see Table 1.) Consensus is growing that depressive symptoms are particularly sensitive to the occurrence of social and cultural stressors (Paykel, 1979; Turner, 1981). The frequency of occurrence of the following ten psychological and physical symptoms of depression in the week prior to the interview was recorded on a four-point scale: loss of appetite, loss of interest in things, loneliness, loss of sexual drive, sleep disturbances, feeling downhearted, loss of energy, suicidal ideation, frequent crying, and feelings of hopelessness. The scale shows acceptable reliability in terms of internal consistency (alpha = .79).

The independent or stressor variables were assessed as follows.

1. Lifestyle incongruity—A twenty-one-item scale of style of life, including ownership of material items and adoption of cosmopolitan behaviors, was developed (alpha = .79) and standardized to a mean of 50 and a standard deviation of 10. A measure of economic status was formed by summing occupational ranks for employed persons in the household, also standardized to 50 (±10.0). Lifestyle incongruity was operationally defined by subtracting economic status from style of life, large positive scores are thus indicative of a life-style in which material consumption patterns exceed economic status (M = 0.00, s.d. = 10.5) (see Dressler, 1988).

2. Noneconomic life change events—This is a fifteen-item inventory of the occurrence of events that are primarily noneconomic in nature, such as getting married or divorced, residency changes, birth of a child, death of a loved one, and others. The number of events experienced in the year prior to the interview were counted (M = 0.89, s.d. = 1.35).

3. Unemployment—This was coded as a dichotomy. Those persons who had lost their jobs in the year prior to the interview were given scores of 1 (17.4 percent). This represents an unemployment rate of approximately 27 percent (Dressler, 1986).

4. Economic stressors—This eight-item scale assesses chronic economic problems such as difficulty in paying bills, worrying about money, and racism in financial matters. Respondents rated each item on a four-point scale of its frequency, and total scores were derived by averaging across the items. Reliability (alpha = .69) is acceptable (M = 2.36, s.d. = 0.70).

5. Role stressors—A series of scales, adapted from prior research (Ilfeld, 1977) and revised to be culturally appropriate, assessed chronic difficulties in the following areas: neighborhood, job, conjugal relationships,

TABLE 1

Items Measuring Depressive Symptoms

In The Past Week How Often Did You:	Never Or Almost Never (%)	Once In A While (%)	Much Of The Time (%)	Almost Always (%)
1. Have a poor appetite	77.1	15.4	5.6	1.8
2. Feel bored or have little interest in things?	59.2	33.3	6.3	1.1
3. Feel lonely?	64.9	24.6	8.8	1.8
4. Lose sexual interest or pleasure?	89.1	5.3	3.2	2.5
5. Have trouble getting to sleep or staying asleep?	61.7	28.1	8.4	1.8
6. Feel downhearted or blue?	64.5	29.1	3.5	2.8
7. Feel low in energy or slowed down?	53.3	35.4	8.1	3.2
8. Have any thoughts about possibly ending your life?	98.2	1.1	0.7	0.0
9. Cry easily or feel like crying?	72.9	19.3	6.3	1.4
10. Feel hopeless about the future?	76.8	16.1	5.3	1.8

parenting, retirement, and unemployment. Each consisted of eight to twelve items, scored as (4). Each showed acceptable reliability (alpha >.70). Each was dichotomized at its median, and the number of social roles in which the respondent was experiencing above-average difficulties was counted (M = 0.96. s.d. = 1.0).

In addition to these independent variables, age, sex, household structure (nuclear vs. nonnuclear), and a multivariate social class measures (the first principal component of occupational status, employment status, amount of employment in past year, and household income) were included as covariates.

Finally, as already argued, differences in the effects of stressors can be anticipated along the lines of age and social class. This model was specified using the variable set method described Cohen and Cohen (1975). The five stressors were conceived of as a single set; to determine whether the effects of these stressors varied as anticipated, further sets of cross-products were formed between stressors and age; stressors and social class; and stressors and age and social class. These cross-products (i.e., stressors multiplied by age and social class) test the hypothesis that the effects of stressors vary according to the values assumed by the modifying variable. A multiple regression analysis was conducted in which the following sets of variables were entered: (a) covariates; (b) stressors; (c) stressors x age; (d) stressors x social class; and (e) stressors x age x social class. The total variance explained (R^2) can then be partitioned into components explained by each of these five sets, and the relative contribution of each can be tested for significance by calculating an F-ratio. For set (a) this ratio would have four degrees of freedom in the numerator, whereas for each other set it has five degrees of freedom in the numerator (and N-K-1 for the denominator). The entire method is described by Cohen and Cohen (1975) in detail.

The results of these tests are presented in Table 2. Each of the variable sets accounts for a statistically significant portion of the variation in depres-

TABLE 2

Summary of Hierarchical Regression of Depressive Symptoms

	Variable Set	Cumulative R^2	F	df
1)	Covariates	.143	11.63***	4,277
2)	Stressors	.281	13.27***	4,273
3)	Class × stressors	.326	3.59**	5,268
4)	Age × stressors	.350	2.45**	4,264
5)	Class × Age × stressors	.410	5.23***	5,259

NOTE: *p < .05   **p < .01   ***p < .001   n = 282

sive symptoms. This is most important for the final set of three-way inter-actions. What this test tells us is that indeed, these stressors have different effects on depression, depending on the age and social class of the respon-dent. Put differently, there are different models of depression for different seg-ments of the black community.

Following this sort of demonstration of reliable intracultural diversity, it becomes appropriate to divide the sample into subgroups for the development of more specific models. Here the combination of theoretical and ethno-graphic insight becomes essential, because there obviously are a large num-ber of logical alternatives for dividing the sample. Since age is the logically prior variable, it seems reasonable to start there. As argued earlier, it was the new experience provided by the Second World War and related migrations that began to substantially alter views of the world in the black community. Therefore, the sample was dichotomized between those persons age forty or younger, and those persons over the age of forty. Since the bulk of our inter-viewing was done in 1982, this identifies persons who were born during the war and presumably more influenced by the civil rights movement than those persons well past their formative years during these major social changes in the U.S.

Next, within each age group, persons were divided into groups on the basis of social class. As argued previously, social class distributions are skewed toward the lower end of the scale in the black community; however, in order to maintain sample sizes sufficient for within-groups analyses, it was necessary simply to dichotomize the age subgroups at age-specific medians. These operations resulted in four groups: younger, lower-class persons; younger, upper-class persons, older, lower-class persons; and older upper-class persons. There are approximately fifty cases in each of the younger groups, and approximately ninety cases in each of the older groups.

We are now in a position to specify models of intracultural diversity in the social and psychological risks of depression by examining the effects of the five stressors within each of the subgroups. These analyses are shown in Tables 3 and 4. (Sex was included as a covariate within groups in order to adjust for gender differences in the reporting of symptoms.)

For younger, lower-class persons, depressive symptoms are related to lifestyle incongruity and life events. For younger, upper-class persons, depres-sive symptoms are related to economic stressors and role stressors. For older, lower-class persons, depressive symptoms are related to life events and un-employment. For older, upper-class persons, depressive symptoms are related to role stressors. Two comments regarding the goodness of fit of these models are in order. First, in three of the four groups the models explain between 40 percent and 50 percent of the variance. Adjusting the R^2 for the number of variables does not substantially alter these figures; also, the variance

TABLE 3

Effects of Stressors on Depression (Age <40)
by Economic Class: Younger Age Group

	Age < 40	
	Low Economic Class	High Economic Class
Sex	−.17	−.18*
Lifestyle incongruity	.39**	−.14
Life events	.24**	−.24*
Unemployment	.18	−.01
Economic stressors	.21	.60**
Role stressors	.17	.21*

R = .64**   R = .72**
R^2 = .41 R^2 = .51
*p < .05   **p < .01

TABLE 4

Effects of Stressors on Depression (Age ≥ 40)
by Economic Class: Older Age Group

	Age ≥ 40	
	Low Economic Class	High Economic Class
Sex	−.16	−.39**
Lifestyle incongruity	−.13	−.02
Life events	.21*	−.17*
Unemployment	.29*	−.01
Economic stressors	.10	.06
Role stressors	.05	.47**

R = .47**   R = .65**
R^2 = .22 R^2 = .43
*p < .05   **p < .01

explained in the older, lower-class group is artificially low because the measure of unemployment is a skewed dichotomy. Second, when standardized residuals were analyzed within each subgroup, the residuals were approximately normal and no outliers were detected. Both of these observations indicate a substantially good fit of these models to the data.

Discussion

As noted earlier, the real evidence for the utility of one versus another orientation in the study of human behavior rests on explanatory efficacy. The orientation put forth here appears to have some merit in this respect. The conceptualization of stressors or psychosocial risk factors is consistent both with major theory in the area and with the ethnographic realities of this black community. The specification of the model of psychosocial risks again represents a compromise between theory on the one hand (especially in terms of the generation of intracultural diversity along social class lines), and ethnographic realities on the other (primarily in terms of the recognition of age or generational status as a cross-cutting source of diversity).

The final within-groups models of depression are consistent with a theoretical model presented earlier (Dressler, 1985), and, indeed, extend that model. It was proposed in that model that stress-related health outcomes are mediated primarily by threats to the individual's self-concept. To the lower-class individual, the significant self-concept is primarily the social identity, that self projected to and known to the social environment. This is why lifestyle incongruity has the effect it does, because it represents the continuing or chronic threats associated with the attempt to maintain a socially valued style of life in the context of meager economic resources. To the upper-class person, having established an appropriate social identity, the significant self-concept is primarily the personal identity, that self experienced phenomenologically by the individual. Worries and anxieties over the performance of the self represent major threats to the individual, and this accounts for the major effects of these kinds of perceived stressors among upper-class persons.

The results obtained here extend this model by showing that, within the black community, age determines the precise meaning of factors, and hence which combinations of stressors will have effects in particular age–social class groupings. Within the younger, lower-class group, the struggle to obtain the visible symbols of success in American life is of paramount importance, but of course their ability to do so is severely hampered by their economic position.[4] The occurrence of life events within this group, even ostensibly positive events, is also likely to be problematic, primarily because of the drain on economic resources many of these events entail. In a real sense, the fundamental issue of identity in this group is establishing and maintaining a course of upward mobility, and the stressors influencing depressive symptoms are those comprising that social trajectory.

Within the younger, upper-class group, these mobility issues are not of concern; some degrees of upward mobility, whether acquired or inherited, exists. Therefore, the issue of identity revolves around the question: "How well am I doing in the performance of my social roles?" And, given that younger

persons have fewer other roles established and that they have been more exposed to the increasing emphasis on personal wealth in American culture (the
"bumpies," or black, upwardly mobile professionals), the answer to that
question of adequacy of role performance revolves around financial or economic adequacy. Those persons who feel more conflicted in this area of life
are more likely to feel depressed.

Within the older, lower-class group, the issue of social identity again
looms large, but because of their age, the definition of that identity is different. It may be that, through time, an adequate style of life can be achieved;
or, it may be that this older group is less susceptible to the new consumerism
in the black community. What is significant in the prediction of depression,
however, is unemployment. In this older age group people are beginning to
assume positions of leadership in their extended families and community.
They have the moral obligation to lead socially significant lives—lives
which, we have seen, require gainful employment. The loss of a job in this
age group, along with all it entails in terms of financial hardship, involves a
fundamental loss of social identity, especially given the cultural orientation
toward work in the black community.

The older, upper-class group represents the historical middle class in
the black community. Stably employed, they are the leaders in the community. Threats to their personal identities are again the primary mediator of depressive symptoms. With older age they have established many different
social roles, and the more roles in which they perceive themselves to be performing less than adequately, the more likely they are to be depressed.

One note of qualification concerning these within-groups models is in
order. A glance at the beta weights will indicate that for some groups, if there
were larger within-group sample sizes, and hence more statistical power, additional stressors would become statistically significant. This would do no
particular violence to the argument presented here, however, because the real
issue is the relative magnitude of the effects of stressors, not the significance
(or lack thereof) of specific variables. In other words, even if, with a doubling
or tripling of the sample size in the younger, lower-class group, the effect of
economic stressors were significant, the effect of lifestyle incongruity would
remain twice as large, supporting the model.

It is also worth noting that objective and subjective stressors have quite
independent effects. Lifestyle incongruity, unemployment, and life events all
fall into the former category, and are so defined because they do not depend
on any report of tension, worry, or problematicness on the part of the respondent. The subjective stressors—economic stressors and role stressors—all
depend on the self-perceptions and definitions of strain by the respondent.
These results lend further weight to the suspicion of the "mentalistic bias" in
research on the stress process (Dressler et al., 1987).

In the final analysis, these results point to the value of testing general theories of human behavior in varying contexts. There is, however, more to it than simply testing hypotheses. Rather, these results point to the need to carefully specify models of human behavior in particular cultural contexts. Without the ethnographic specification of the model, for example, it could be concluded that all of the psychosocial risk factors, excluding lifestyle incongruity, have significant, but very small, effects on depression (from regression analysis including only main effects). The more complete model presented here has an obviously better fit with the observations, and this model could only have been developed by assuming the importance of cultural diversity in generating particular configurations of stressors. Once that assumption was made, ethnography and the anticipation of intracultural diversity led to the detection of the observed results. A very important implicit assumption here is that individual variability is constrained by sociocultural variation. It is this variation, within and between societies, that places boundary conditions on propositions about human behavior. Once it is assumed that these boundary conditions exist, then the attempt to specify a model within a particular cultural context can begin. To the extent that this specification is guided by the judicious mix of ethnographic observation and hypothesis-testing research; to the extent that intracultural diversity as generated by links between macrolevel social processes and microlevel behaviors is explored; and to the extent that the careful operationalization of terms, with respect both to theory and to local systems of meaning, is carried out, then the potential for contributions to general theories of human behavior is enhanced.

2

Pattern Probability Models of Intracultural Diversity: Tobacco Smoking Among Shrimp Fishermen[1]

Michael C. Robbins and Annette Kline

This paper illustrates the relationship between tobacco smoking and occupational stress through an intracultural study of shrimp fishermen along the Gulf coast of Alabama. Presented is a pattern probability algorithm for classifying shrimp fishermen according to smoking status by combinations of personal and occupational characteristics.

Since the Surgeon General's report in 1964, there has been an overall decrease in cigarette consumption in the United States. This decline in smoking prevalence is largely attributed to an increase in the cessation rate, especially among adult male smokers (Remington et al., 1985; U.S. Department of Health and Human Services, 1985). Despite this, 33 percent of the adult male population in the United States in 1985 continued to smoke (McGinnis et al., 1987; U.S. Department of Health and Human Services, 1986). A recent report of the Surgeon General, for example, states, "Because cigarette smoking usually begins between the ages of 12 and 25 . . . the prevalence of smoking among people 25 years of age or older is determined in large part by the rate by which they stop smoking (or die)" (1985:33).

Research has shown that smoking is closely associated with type of employment, with the highest prevalence in blue collar occupations, and the lowest in white collar jobs (Sterling and Weinkam, 1976, 1978; U.S. Department of Health and Human Services, 1985). More precisely, research suggests that tobacco use is related to the nature of one's job. A higher prevalence of smoking exists in jobs where workers experience feelings of powerlessness and suffer occupational stress (Wesnes et al., 1984). It has been shown that individuals more exposed to stress smoke more than those less exposed. Also, smokers smoke more during periods of work stress than at other times (Wesnes et al., 1984; Westman et al., 1985).

In general, although it is safe to say that most, if not all, occupational roles engender some degree of stress, differences in the nature of blue and white collar jobs, and their associated social status, are profound. Overall, the white collar worker has more personal control over his or her work situation, higher attendant social status, and far fewer physical demands than the blue collar worker (Siegrist, 1985).

Occupational roles expose people to a number of mental, physical, and psychosocial stressors or stress-producing factors to which they must adapt in order to maintain themselves in the workforce. Following Kasl and Cobb (1983:252) we define a stressor as the perceived imbalance between demand and capability. The inability to meet demands produces pathological stress responses.

Smoking has been identified as an adaptive behavior, or psychophysiological tool, that can be manipulated to meet environmental demands (Ashton and Stepney, 1982; Pomerleau and Pomerleau, 1984; Westman et al., 1985). Numerous self-reports of smokers show that smoking helps them think, concentrate, and remain alert when tired; and relax when tense (Ashton and Stepney, 1982; Dunn, 1978; Gilbert, 1979; Ikard et al., 1969; Spielberger, 1986; Wesnes et al., 1984). Subjectively, smoking can thus be viewed as beneficial for occupational stress reduction, a motive for its continued use.

A large amount of research has shown that indeed, tobacco smoking does possess a number of beneficial properties that can be recruited to enhance job effort and performance. For example, tobacco smoking: (1) *enhances pleasure and relaxation*, e.g., it provides a time-out and filler; is a distractor; has a palatable taste, etc. (cf. Ikard et al., 1969; Kleinke et al., 1983; Spielberger, 1986); (2) *enhances task performance*, e.g., increases efficiency in reaction time and accuracy of signal detection tasks through sustained vigilance and alertness; improves concentration and selective attention; facilitates rapid audio and visual information processing; aids learning, memory, and problem solving, etc. (cf. Ashton and Stepney, 1982; Elgerot, 1976; Warburton and Wesnes, 1978; Wesnes and Warburton, 1978, 1983); (3) *facilitates social relations*, e.g., communicates social roles and images; reinforces positive exchanges; aids composure, etc. (cf. Ashton and Stepney, 1982; Black, 1984; Clark, 1978; Dredge, 1980; Eckert, 1983; Feinhandler, 1986; Polivy et al., 1979); (4) *reduces stress and negative affect*, e.g., reduces the disruptive effects of anxiety, anger, irritability, and tension, etc. (cf. Ague, 1973; Ashton and Stepney, 1982; Cherek, 1981, 1985; Cohen et al., 1983; Dunn, 1978; Gilbert, 1979; Ikard et al., 1969; Spielberger, 1986; Wesnes et al., 1984; Westman et al., 1985); (5) *reduces somatic problems*, e.g., pain, hunger, and muscular tension, and increases energy when fatigued (cf. Ashton and Stepney, 1982; Bowers and Allen, 1984; Fertig and Pomerleau, 1986; Gilbert, 1979; Grunberg, 1985; Pomerleau et al., 1984; Russel, 1976; Silverstein, 1982; Wack and Rodin, 1982).

In sum, research suggests that tobacco smoking can be beneficial both directly, by improving occupational role effort and performance, and indirectly, by reducing emotional stress reactions. Those in occupations with the most to gain from continuing to smoke, such as fishermen and other blue collar workers, would therefore be expected to be less likely to quit. And indeed, the statistics support this.

Research Community and Sample

Research was conducted in a single Gulf Coast fishing community located south of the city of Mobile, Alabama. According to the 1980 U.S. Census, this community had a population of 2000. Current estimates of the population are about 2800. The community's economy is highly dependent upon the seafood industry of the area. It currently ranks in the top fifteen of most valuable commercial fishing ports in the U.S., and among the most important seafood producers along the Gulf of Mexico (Thomas, 1986). Because the community is a center for national and international seafood production, the fishing economy and supporting industries (boat building and petroleum) are estimated to generate as much as $124 million annually. The 1984 shrimp landings alone in the community were valued at $41 million (Thomas, 1986).

Ethnographic fieldwork and social survey research was conducted during 1985 and 1986 among a sample of 149 male shrimpboat captains selected randomly from an official list. The captains were an average age of 38.5 years, of whom 82 percent were married. They spent an average of 180.3 days at sea per year, and worked an average of 83.2 hours per week. The survey instrument consisted of questions concerning the technology of shrimping vessels, equipment, specific job tasks, economics of shrimping, income, values, personal history, demographic characteristics, and so on. Information was also collected on cigarette, alcohol, and coffee consumption.

Fishermen's Stress Syndrome

Fishing is a dangerous and high-risk occupation that demands self-direction, responsibility, skill, and flexibility (Maril, 1983; Norr and Norr, 1978; White, 1977). For fishermen, the maritime environment is uncertain, offering no control over weather or catch (Aronoff, 1967; Norr and Norr, 1978). Most fishermen work long hours on crowded boats, isolated from home. At home, the fisherman's family is forced to adjust to recurrent absences of a father/husband during daily activities. For many fishermen and their families, more time is spent apart than together (Acheson, 1981; Danowski, 1980; Poggie and Gersuny, 1974). These work load stressors (and the engendered stress) will be referred to collectively as the "fishermen's stress syndrome."

Eight major stressors in the shrimp fishermen's occupational environment have been identified.

Overload. Fishermen in general work a larger number of days and hours per week than the typical land-based worker in a forty hour per week job. Shrimpers may work up to twenty-five days in a row at sea; up to thirty-six hours straight without rest; they average eighty-three hours per week at sea. Work often involves the continuous scanning of visual and auditory equipment, requiring sustained attention, concentration, and memory, to say nothing of the arduous physical labor. The lack of sleep and mental and physical overload result in sore muscles, fatigue, sleep disturbances, vigilance decrements, and irritability (Acheson, 1981; Poggie and Gersuny, 1974; White, 1977). As one shrimpboat captain remembered:

> I've done my time offshore. I'll tell you, "offshore" is a young man's business. With a little age on you, you haven't got the stamina it takes to work an offshore boat . . . and then they get old quick . . . Your body can't put up with the twenty-four hours a day, and just one or two hours off . . . They think that those air-traffic controllers have it bad, they ought to put an air-traffic controller on a Gulf boat!

Underload. Fishing tasks can be simple, repetitive, and monotonous, resulting in a need for stimulation (Acheson, 1981; White, 1977). As one captain observed:

> If you're sitting there in that chair at night, and you start doing this [nodding], it's time to quit because you aren't at your peak . . . I learned a long time ago when I shrimped in the Gulf, if I ever owned my own boat, whenever I got tired, I was going to stop. I wasn't going to punish myself anymore.

Shiftwork. Three general work patterns characterize the shrimp fishing occupation: daywork, nightwork, and "clocking," which requires shrimpers to work literally "around the clock" (Acheson, 1981; White, 1977). To quote one shrimper,

> I've had blood run out of my fingers for working so long; just around the clock, never stopping.

Migration. Fishing requires frequent alternation from land to sea; from workplace to family. As a result, fishermen experience worry about the welfare of their families and crew (Acheson, 1981; Danowski, 1980; Maril, 1983; White, 1977).

Social interaction. There is an essential need for camaraderie and group solidarity among shrimpers on a boat. They must depend upon each other and work together in order to produce shrimp and avoid disaster. The interdependence of the crew is required to maintain coordination and prevent accidents (Acheson, 1981; Maril, 1983; Norr and Norr, 1978; Poggie and Gersuny, 1974). As a case in point, one captain reported that:

> . . . they were letting the anchor drop out, and it just started falling out the chute (and boy, it does!). That rope threw out real fast, and the kid, he reached up there (first trip he had ever made on a boat) . . . He was going to throw that loop out of that rope, and when he did . . . that thing snatched around his wrist and snatched him up in that anchor chute and pulled his arm off. The other deck hand went into shock. The captain couldn't leave the wheel. It was rough!

Working conditions. When at sea, there is always the threat of storms, accidents, and mechanical failure, because of open machinery, close quarters, and environmental and chemical exposure. Mental and physical fatigue develop, increasing the probability of injury from hooks, knives, fish scales, and the cold, wet conditions (Acheson, 1981; Norr and Norr, 1978; White, 1977). As one captain warned:

> . . . bad weather, you could fall overboard, or something could hit you in the head, or you could drown . . . you just have to be careful. When you're picking up and setting overboard, make sure you don't get wrapped up in the winch. In the engine room, checking the clutch or the stuffer box, make sure you don't fall in the front end and get wrapped up in any of the belts . . .

Organizational role. Captains bear responsibility for the safety and welfare of the crew and for producing a catch for self, owners, and the crew members (Aronoff, 1967; Norr and Norr, 1978). Commenting on this, one captain complained:

> It's the captain's responsibility. You have to make enough to keep him (deckhand) satisfied and keep him going . . . Sometimes pieces of equipment are needed, and they give them junk. You know, like as far as they need a new pair of doors, the doors are falling apart, they're not working up to par. The owners, instead of buying some new ones, will try to make the old ones work; and the captain's not able to use equipment that's worn out.

Career development. It is the case that captains must overcome strong competition and work many hours consistently to obtain sums large enough to buy a boat, an important career goal (Acheson, 1981; Jepson et al., 1987; Norr and Norr, 1978). One captain remarked:

> Work! W-O-R-K! That's the only way I know how to put it. You just have to work . . . You know I'm an ambitious person, so I drag as long as I can. Go till I can rest. And go some more. You know, if you live with ten or twelve thousand a year . . . fiddle around, not do anything . . . fine with me, but you know, I want to do better for myself. I figure, I've always been taught the only way to do better is to work. That's what I try to do, is work.

It is clear that many of the benefits of tobacco smoking mentioned previously (e.g., providing a time-out, increasing vigilance, reducing emotional stress, etc.) can be useful for ameliorating the "fishermen's stress syndrome." Recent work, for example, reveals that when asked "When do you smoke the most?" 50 percent of those working at sea (n = 131) say while "watching the wheel," a task that requires sustained attention and concentration. Another 15 percent say "when working" or "dragging" (J. S. Thomas, personal communication).

These shrimp fishermen, as is true with most blue collar workers, have maintained a high prevalence rate of smoking compared to white collar workers.[2] It is postulated that in large part, stress mitigation accounts for the persistence of the comparatively high smoking prevalence rate among shrimp fishermen. This evidence suggests that smoking provides physical, psychophysiological, and social benefits that can reduce the physical, emotional, and psychosocial stresses of this occupation.

In our research we discovered that two major features distinguish shrimp-boat captains from each other: *type of captain* (hired vs. owner), and *type of shrimping* (offshore vs. inshore). About half are hired captains (50.7 percent); 49.3 percent own their own boat. The hired captain works an average of 190.2 seadays per year (with an average of ninety-three worker-hours per week). Sixty-five percent of the hired captains shrimp offshore, and thirty-five percent shrimp inshore. The owner captains work an average of 174.9 seadays per year (with an average of eighty-six worker-hours per week). Only 33 percent of the owner captains shrimp offshore, whereas 67 percent shrimp inshore.

With regard to type of shrimping, offshore captains compose 49.3 percent of the total sample population. Offshore captains spend an average of 222.4 seadays per year, either working days and nights, or "clocking." These captains work an average of 109 worker-hours per week while at sea. Offshore captains are 67 percent hired and 33 percent owner. Fifty-one percent of all captains are inshore and work an average of 143.9 seadays per year, with an average of seventy worker-hours per week while at sea. The inshore captains are 35 percent hired and 65 percent owner.

These features (type of captain and type of shrimping) distinguish shrimpboat captains from each other in terms of occupational demand. Hired captains work more seadays and worker-hours than owner captains. Most hired captains work offshore in deeper, more hazardous waters than those who own their boats. Competition among hired captains is fierce, and those who do poorly are given the older, worn-out boats. More important, hired captains have less control over work routines and boat operations. Hired captains are also younger than owner captains (34.3 years vs. 48.9 years). Number of years as a captain (or experience) is regarded highly in this occupation in terms of success and safety. Captains who own boats have a higher average number of years experience (17.8 years) than hired captains (10.7). It should be noted that a higher proportion of owner than hired captains are married (39 percent vs. 76 percent).

Offshore captains, like hired captains, work in hazardous waters. Offshore captains spend much of their work time at night and clocking, requiring much time away from their families and home.

In sum, older, married, owner, and inshore captains have several advantages over younger, single, hired, and offshore captains: more experience, a family support group, fewer working days and hours in safer waters, and more control over their economic plight and personal career.

Research Methodology

Since the objective of the present study is to examine tobacco smoking as an occupational role adaptation among shrimpboat captains, we hypothesized that where occupational stressors are the greatest, the utility of smoking for mitigating stress will be the highest, and it is here that the preponderance of smokers will be found. Our research strategy is thus an example of an intracultural analysis as described by Pelto and Pelto (1978:275). The variables we consider to be most important in this regard for shrimpboat captains are: type of shrimping, ownership, marital status, and age. These variables will be incorporated in the construction of a pattern probability model for identifying and optimally classifying shrimp fishermen according to smoking status.

The pattern probability model to be presented is an algorithm for selecting from among a set of smoking status categories the one category most

TABLE 1

Smoking Status by Personal and Occupational Characteristics

	Smoke		Nosmoke	
	N	p	N	p
Young	46	.61	29	.39
Old	29	.39	45	.61
Single	14	.64	8	.36
Married	61	.48	66	.52
Hired	51	.69	23	.31
Owner	24	.32	51	.68
Inshore	32	.42	44	.58
Offshore	43	.59	30	.41
Total	75	.503	74	.496

likely associated with a particular pattern combination of personal and occupational characteristics. It is formulated by estimating the conditional probability that a shrimpboat captain with a particular pattern is in each smoking status category and then allocating him to the category for which the conditional probability is the greatest (Birnbaum and Maxwell, 1961).

Let m denote the number of smoking status categories to which a shrimpboat captain can belong; and let k be a generic label for the categories, $k = 1, 2, \ldots, m$. Then $p(k) \approx N_k/N$ is the estimated, a priori probability that a randomly selected shrimpboat captain belongs to category k; N_k is the number of captains in category k, and N is the number of shrimpboat captains. In this case, $k = 1$ (Smoke), and $k = 2$ (Nosmoke). Furthermore, $p(1) \approx 75/14 = .503$, and $p(2) \approx 74/149 = .497$.

Next, let j denote the number of personal and occupational characteristic patterns logically possible (given the measurement procedures) and let i be a generic label for the patterns $i = 1, 2, \ldots, j$. Then $p(i/k) = N_i \div N_k$ is the conditional probability of pattern i, given category k where N_i/k is the frequency of the pattern i in category k. Table 1 presents the number and proportion of smokers and nonsmokers according to each of the four personal and occupational characteristics separately. Table 2 lists the sixteen shrimp captain characteristic patterns and associated frequencies of smokers in each of the status categories. Table 2 provides the conditional probabilities ($p(i/k)$) of each pattern, given a particular status category.

From Bayes' Theorem in elementary probability theory, it follows that $p(k/i)$, the conditional probability that a randomly selected shrimpboat captain with personal and occupational characteristics with pattern i belongs to status category k, is given by:

(1)

$$p(k/i) = \frac{p(k)\ p(i/k)}{p(i)}$$

where
$$p(i) = m$$
$$\sum_{k=1} p(k)\ (p(i/k)$$

It may be inferred from Bayes' Theorem, therefore, that a shrimpboat captain is most likely to belong to that category k for which the quantity $p(k/i)$ is largest. However, since $p(k/i)$ is proportional to $p(k)\ p(i/k)$, the relative magnitudes of the $p(k/i)$s can be used without computing the denominator $p(i)$. Table 3 lists the "weighted probability," $p(k)\ p(i/k)$, according to which each pattern has been allocated to a status category.

FIGURE 1

Shrimpboat Captain Smoking Status Categories Allocated by Numbered Pattern

	HIRED		$\overline{\text{HIRED}}$		
YOUNG	1 S	3 S	9 N	11 N	
					OFFSHORE
$\overline{\text{YOUNG}}$	2 ?	4 S	10 ?	12 N	
YOUNG	5 S	7 ?	13 N	15 ?	
	6	8	14	16	$\overline{\text{OFFSHORE}}$
$\overline{\text{YOUNG}}$	S	N	?	N	
	SINGLE	$\overline{\text{SINGLE}}$	SINGLE	$\overline{\text{SINGLE}}$	

"$\overline{\quad}$" refers to "not" feature

Overbar means "not."

TABLE 2

Relation of Fishermen Characteristic Patterns to Smoking Status

Number (i)	Hired	Offshore	Single	Young	Smoking Status p(k)	
					Smoke	Nosmoke
1)	1	1	1	1	7	2
2)	1	1	1	0	+	+
3)	1	1	0	1	21	4
4)	1	1	0	0	9	5
5)	1	0	1	1	2	1
6)	1	0	0	0	3	0
7)	1	0	0	1	6	6
8)	1	0	0	0	3	5
9)	0	1	1	1	0	1
10)	0	1	1	0	+	+
11)	0	1	0	1	3	6
12)	0	1	0	0	3	12
13)	0	0	1	1	0	2
14)	0	0	1	0	2	2
15)	0	0	0	1	7	7
16)	0	0	0	0	9	21
Total					75	74

*1 = yes; 0 = no; + = no entries

TABLE 3

Probabilities of Fishermen Pattern Given Status p(i/k)
and Weighted Probabilities for Status p(k) p(i/k)

Pattern Number (i)	p(i/k) Smoke (S)	p(i/k) Nosmoke (N)	p(k) p(i/k) Smoke	Pattern Nosmoke	Allocation*
1	.093	.027	.047	.013	S
2	0	0	0	0	?
3	.28	.054	.141	.027	S
4	.12	.068	.06	.034	S
5	.027	.014	.014	.007	S
6	.04	0	.02	0	S
7	.08	.081	.040	.040	?
8	.04	.068	.02	.034	N
9	0	.014	0	.007	N
10	0	0	0	0	?
11	.04	.081	.02	.04	N
12	.04	.162	.02	.081	N
13	0	.027	0	.013	N
14	.027	.027	.014	.013	S
15	.093	.095	.047	.047	?
16	.12	.284	.06	.141	N

*based on highest weighted probability;
"?" indicates questionable allocation

Thus, on this basis, a decision rule can be formulated to allocate a shrimpboat captain to a status category k, as follows, if:

(2)
$$\frac{p(1)\ p(i/1)}{p(2)\ p(i/2)} > 1$$

Then allocate the shrimpboat captain to category $k = 1$ (Smoke); otherwise allocate the shrimpboat captain to category $k = 2$ (Nosmoke).

Using this decision rule and the information from Table 3, Figure 1 displays the final assignment of status categories on a map of personal and occupational characteristics.

In order to facilitate the use of this model, the information in Figure 1 can be systematically reduced to construct the decision flow chart in Figure 2. This chart enables the analyst to classify the most likely smoking status category to which a shrimpboat captain belongs simply by observing the following rules:

Nonsmoker:
1. If a shrimpboat captain owns his own boat, he is most likely a nonsmoker.
2. If a shrimpboat captain is hired, married, and inshore, he is most likely a nonsmoker.

Smoker:
3. If a shrimpboat captain is hired and single, he is most likely a smoker.
4. If a shrimpboat captain is hired, married, and offshore, he is most likely a smoker.

In order to assess the accuracy of this model, the number of correct classifications achieved with its use was compared to the number of incorrect classifications. This information appears in Figure 3.

Using this model, eighty-nine shrimpboat captains, or seventy-five percent of the total number, are correctly classified (see main diagonal in part A). Matrix B in Figure 3 displays the conditional probability that a correct (or incorrect) classification will be made according to smoking status. For example, the probability that someone classified by the model as a smoker is, indeed, a smoker is .78.

Conclusions: Theoretical and Practical

In sum, the results are consistent with the general proposition that where occupational stressors are most severe, the utility of tobacco use for the

FIGURE 2

Flow Chart for Identifying Captains' Smoking Status

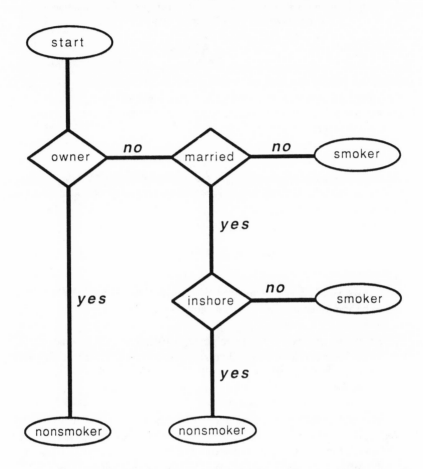

mitigation of engendered stress is the greatest, and tobacco smokers are to be found among those most exposed. More specifically, these results demonstrate that intracultural variation in smoking status is related to the nature of occupational roles and attendant tasks as they interact in concert with personal characteristics.

We think the specific model we have presented for identifying smoking status according to personal and occupational traits merits further consideration and may be helpful in other kinds of studies. For example, with refinement the model could be of some practical value in identifying individuals

FIGURE 3

Number of Fishermen Correctly and Incorrectly Classified (A)
and Conditional Probability of Correct and Incorrect Classification
Given Status (B) from Pattern Probability Model

(A)   **ACTUAL CATEGORY**

		SMOKE	NOSMOKE	TOTAL
	SMOKE	42	12	54
PREDICTED CATEGORY FROM PATTERN				
	NOSMOKE	18	47	65

(B)   **ACTUAL CATEGORY**

		SMOKE	NOSMOKE
	SMOKE	.78	.22
PREDICTED CATEGORY FROM PATTERN			
	NOSMOKE	.28	.72

exposed to severe stress and in need of remedial interventions. Clearly, it needs to be improved and tested again, among both members of this population and others.

We should also add that a large genre of pattern probability models exists and has been applied to such diverse research topics as: diagnosing and classifying psychiatric patients (Overall and Williams, 1963); determining wealth categories (Ugalde, 1970); and identifying social status levels (Thomas and Robbins, 1985, 1988).

Although smoking as a customary behavior is currently becoming outmoded in our society, and may be viewed as a "deviant" behavior (Troyer and Markle, 1983), its use is still prominent in certain social groups. This probably reflects its value as an adaptive coping mechanism for those in stressful situations (Wills and Shiffman, 1985). One implication is that unless stressful conditions at work (and elsewhere) are reduced or an acceptable alternative is found, tobacco smoking will probably continue to be widely used.

3

Intracultural and Intrasocial Variability as a Tool for Policy Making in Fisheries Development and Management

John J. Poggie, Jr.

The notion of incorporating social and cultural considerations into fishery policy making has received considerable support in government circles around the world. In the United States, for example, the Fisheries Conservation and Management Act of 1976 mandates that U.S. fisheries be managed for "optimal sustainable yield" (OSY), which means for some combination of biological, economic, and social goals. In conversations with government officials in several developing countries, maritime anthropologists have encountered considerable appreciation for the idea of a holistic approach to fisheries development and management. The stumbling block to enacting this approach is not at all that the idea is rejected, but that there is the unanswered question of how to do it.

Biologists and economists seem to have found a way to understand each other by means of the "Schaeffer curve" and a bioeconomic model based on that curve (Schaeffer, 1954). This model relates production to effort by means of a symmetrical convex upward curve with a maximum. The concepts of maximal sustainable yield (MSY) and maximal economic yield (MEY) are points on the curve that represent biological and economic maximizations vis-a-vis effort. The goal of fisheries development and management policy, if viewed from this model, is to bring effort in line with MSY or MEY. If production is below MSY or MEY, as in the case of an underutilized fishery, effort can be increased. This increased effort could be actualized by establishing specific policies such as loans to introduce more productive technology into the fishery. If current production is above MSY or MEY, effort can be reduced. For example, the suggestion is often made that this can be accomplished by means of a policy to limit entry and/or landings.

These theoretical approaches to fisheries management and development do not work well in the real world, and the theory of common property resources (Gordon, 1954; Hardin, 1968) is often invoked as an explanation of why fishermen tend to exceed MSY or MEY and vigorously (sometimes violently) oppose management policies. The theory of common property resource proposes that fish represent a common property neither belonging to nor controlled by anyone, so that it is not in the interest of the individual producer to reduce effort because others, so the argument goes, will simply take what he or she does not and thus increase their incomes at the expense of the conservor.

Some social scientists have challenged the very notion as well as the unstated assumptions of the theory of common property resource, and have pointed out the threat that these assumptions place on the fishermen and their families (Acheson et al., 1980; Acheson, 1981; Marchak et al., 1987; McCay and Acheson, 1987; Brox, 1990). Empirical studies conducted in New England and elsewhere, which looked closely at the motivations of fishermen, show that individuals in the occupation of fishing are characterized by diverse motivations, among which income is not always the most salient for entering into or continuing in the occupation (Pollnac and Poggie, 1988; Smith, 1981; Apostle et al., 1985). The latent assumption of the theory of common property resource and its associated bioeconomic model is that increased income potential is the prime motivation of fishermen.

Although the findings from the several studies of the motivations of fishermen may not apply to all fishing populations, they clearly document the undeniable importance of understanding and taking into account relevant social and cultural features of any fishery in which development and/or management schemes are contemplated—be they in developed, developing, or underdeveloped economies. This argument is one that is readily accepted by most behavioral scientists and by many biologists and economists, all of whom wish to improve the outcome of fishery policy efforts. The problem is that social and cultural considerations cannot be readily interjected into the Schaeffer curve. Although efforts have been made to accomplish this by reducing the social and cultural domain to a monetary cost, there is no satisfactory way to draw "OSY" on the curve and address biological, economic, and the diverse sociocultural aspects of management and development simultaneously (cf. Smith, 1981; Anderson, 1980; McConnell and Sutinen, 1979; Gordon et al., 1973; Stevens, 1969). All this brings us back to the question of utilizing sociocultural information in policy making and the question of what type of sociocultural information to use.

Theoretical and Practical Significance of The Cultural-Ecological Approach

For the policy-oriented anthropologist, the problem thus changes from whether there should be a sociocultural component to fishery management and development, to the kinds of social and cultural information and/or models that can be used in conjunction with biological and economic information and models in developing more effective policy in this domain.

Rather than search for ways to integrate sociocultural variables into a quantitative bioeconomic-social model of fisheries system, and thus be constrained by the dominant models of economics and biology, we need to provide an approach that draws on the theoretical strengths of sociocultural studies. This approach should be a pragmatic one that is both theoretically acceptable and applicable to all societies. Of course, it needs to be one which is readily understandable by non-specialists and nonbehavioral scientist policymakers and which can be incorporated into policy decisions. Finally, the approach must be one that can deal with the social and cultural diversity that is characteristic of individuals, social groupings, communities, and populations in regions everywhere, for much of fishery policy is directed toward regions, and characteristically affects and is affected by individuals, groups, communities, and populations.

The cultural-ecological-theoretical perspective from anthropology fits the requirements of this context very well. This perspective sees individuals and groups of individuals adapting through variable characteristics (mixes) of the overall sociocultural context in which they operate. The perspective rejects the assumption of sociocultural homogeneity at the individual and group levels. In place of the assumption of homogeneity is a purposeful focus on intracultural and intrasocial diversity and the methodological requirement of rigorous empirical documentation of the distribution of socio-cultural characteristics. The analytical side of the perspective looks at how different individuals and groups adapt to their total environments by means of combinations of behaviors, technologies, beliefs, structures, and organizations that make up the total "sociocultural pool" in which they operate (cf. Pelto and Pelto, 1975).

The current proponents of this approach in anthropology have taken themes put forward by Branislaw Malinowski and by Julian Steward and have refined and expanded these themes more recently into an inclusive and pragmatic approach that has been widely and productively applied in the complexity of today's sociocultural world environments (cf. Malinowski, 1931, 1939; Steward, 1963; Bennett, 1969; Wood and Graves, 1971; Pelto and Poggie, 1974; Pelto and Pelto, 1975; DeWalt, 1979, to cite but a few users of this approach).

In this paper I will illustrate the usefulness of the cultural-ecological perspective, particularly because of its emphasis on intracultural and intrasocial variability, in fishery policy matters. The focus of my empirical analysis will be on an organization—a fishermen's cooperative in Costa Rica—and on a case of technology transfer to fishermen in Puerto Rico. The purpose of this paper is to illustrate by specific examples how relevant intracultural and intrasocial information derived by way of the cultural-ecology approach provides a very useful and available tool for addressing the elusive sociocultural component in policy making. Of course, the cultural-ecology approach is not restricted only to fisheries policy making, since it has been and can be useful in other types of applications.

Case Study I

Cooperatives have been viewed by government officials and other individuals in institutions that deal with fisheries policy as an excellent mechanism to consolidate the efforts of dispersed small-scale producers into more efficient economic units. By consolidating individual small-scale fishermen into groups, many of the recurrent problems of small producers can be alleviated. Problems such as quality of product, postharvest loss, obtaining competitive selling prices, marketing, transportation, obtaining loans, and procuring supplies and equipment are the most frequently mentioned ones for small-scale producers. Also, cooperatives are considered to be potentially useful avenues for carrying out management of fisheries in both developing and developed regions. There is no doubt that if they work well, cooperatives can be beneficial to the producing fishermen, to consumers, and to the long-term interests of whole nations.

The selected case study of cooperative operation is an analysis of fishermen's perceived benefits of belonging to a cooperative set up to serve four communities in the Gulf of Nicoya and the northwest region of Guanacaste Province in Costa Rica. One of the features of the development program promoted by the Costa Rican Presidential Office of Planning, beginning in the early 1970s, was the establishment of a small-scale fishermen's cooperative centered in Puntarenas to serve the Gulf of Nicoya and the northwestern coastal region of the country. The purpose of the cooperative was to "develop" the fishery in this area by increasing production, improving quality of the product, and cutting costs to producers and consumers while at the same time raising incomes to producers.

A regional cooperative (with headquarter in Puntarenas) was formed, but it did not meet the expectations of government and other planners. Overall, it functioned poorly, but with more success in some locales than in others. The cooperative, although still in existence at this time, was a failure as it was envisioned by government planners. During the last decade there was considerable economic inefficiency and loss because of the disappointing way the cooperative functioned. My interest in this case was to understand, while the cooperative was still in existence in 1974, some of the sociocultural factors that contributed to its poor performance. I did this by focusing on local perceptions of cooperatives and analyzing what factors contribute to these perceptions. To do this I set out to measure among individuals the patterns of perceived benefits of cooperatives, as well as sociocultural factors that relate to these perceptions in the populations of fishermen in the four communities serviced by the cooperative. By understanding the small-scale fishermen's perceptions and some of the reasons for these perceptions, it might be possible to identify some of the causes of the lack of overall success of the cooperative. From this analysis, factors that could be addressed in policy decisions regarding cooperative formation should emerge.

Preliminary participant observation fieldwork in the four communities revealed considerable social and cultural variability, and it was my assumption that this diversity needed to be understood and incorporated into policy decisions aimed at improving the function of the cooperative. Ideally, of course, this knowledge would be most effectively employed at the beginning stages of policy making and institution building, rather than after the institution had been established.

Systematic data were obtained from a total sample of 186 small-scale fishermen from the four communities serviced by the cooperative.[1] Two communities, Puntarenas and Costa de Pajaros, are located on the eastern shore of the Gulf of Nicoya, whereas the other two, Playa del Coco and a cluster of several small settlements (jointly referred to here as "the North") in the Cuajiniquel Area, are located on the Pacific coast. The geographical distance from the southernmost of the four communities (Puntarenas) to the northernmost is approximately 125 kilometers.

By means of an interview schedule, sampled fishermen in each community were asked in an open-ended question to express what they consider to be the benefits of belonging to a fishermen's cooperative. Benefits of belonging to a cooperative is the dependent variable in this analysis. Participant observation ethnographic data were also obtained on social structural and economic features of each community. Ethnographic data suggested that the number of private fish dealers (middlemen) in each community was especially important in understanding perceptions of cooperatives. Thus "number of fish dealers" became one of the independent variables in the systematic analysis. Other independent variables, also identified by ethnographic observations, were systematically measured by means of direct response to questions in the interview schedule. The independent variables in this analysis were selected because of their demonstrable importance from other research and middle-range theory on the sociocultural adaptations of small-scale fishermen in Central America and elsewhere, and because of my observations in the preliminary ethnographic phase of my work (cf. Poggie and Gersuny, 1974; Pollnac, 1974). The twelve independent variables in the study are: (1) age; (2) years of fishing experience; (3) number of kinsmen who fish; (4) boat ownership. (5) number of kinsmen who fish with the respondent; (6) hours fished per trip; (7) days fished per week; (8) current self-perception of socio-economic position; (9) years of formal education; (10) whether father is/was a fisherman; (11) whether father is/was a farmer; and (12) number of fish dealers in the community.

Analysis

Table 1 shows the community level patterns among these variables. The variables are sufficiently different among the four communities to justify further intracommunity analysis of the relationship of the dependent and independent variables.

Data from the open-ended question concerning the dependent variable—the benefits of cooperatives—were systematized into nine categories by means of content analysis. For each of the four communities, frequency of first response of perceived benefits of belonging to a fishermen's cooperative are presented in Table 2. These findings support the conclusion that there is considerable diversity of perceived benefits of cooperative membership.

In the Puntarenas sample, 48 percent of respondents felt that there are no benefits to belonging to a cooperative; 16 percent said they did not know what the benefits would be, and an equal percentage thought that it would bring mutual help to fishermen. Nine percent thought it would bring better income. Other categories of response accounted for the remaining responses, but all were under 5 percent of the total. In Costa de Pajaros, 52 percent said they did not know what the benefits would be; 20 percent saw no benefits, and 16 percent of the total saw the advantage in mutual help or other miscellaneous positive benefits. Six percent saw a chance to participate in a savings plan as the main advantage, while 4 percent and 2 percent cited better income and loans, respectively.

Responses in the northwestern region were different in pattern from those in the two Gulf of Nicoya communities. At Playa del Coco the most frequent response (31 percent of total) was "equipment/supplies," while "don't know" was second most frequent with 28 percent of the total. "No benefits" accounted for 10 percent of the total, and "better income," "other positive," "selling point/marketing" each accounted for 8 percent of the total. "Mutual help" and "loans" accounted for 5 and 3 percent, respectively. In the North community "don't know," with 52 percent of the responses, was the most frequent response, and "equipment/supplies" was the second, with 32 percent of the total. "No benefits" and "mutual help" had 6 percent each, whereas "savings plan" had 3 percent of the total.

As the next step in the analysis, we note the relationship between patterns of responses to perceived benefits of cooperatives and a community level variable. Variable 12 (Table 1) is the number of middlemen in each community. As seen in Table 3, there is a perfect positive rank order correlation

TABLE 1

Community Level Differences on Independent Variables

Variables	Puntarenas	Costa de Pajaros	Playa del Coco	North	Probability
1. Age $\overline{X}$	32.8	27.6	27.6	28.7	<.05
2. Years fished $\overline{X}$	12.4	11.8	11.8	5.9	<.01
3. No. of family who fish $\overline{X}$	1.9	7.1	4.9	2.4	<.001
4. Own boat (%)	30	50	33	45	>.05
5. No. kin fish with $\overline{X}$	.43	1.0	.82	.48	<.01
6. Hrs. fish/trip $\overline{X}$	10.5	5.2	9	17	<.001
7. Days fish/week $\overline{X}$	5.6	5.5	6.2	6.1	<.001
8. Scale level $\overline{X}$	4.7	4.1	5.0	4.9	>.05
9. Education $\overline{X}$	4.1	3.2	6.2	4.4	<.001
10. Father Farmer (%)	24	28	41	58	<.01
11. Father Fisherman (%)	40	68	28	9	<.001
12. Number of fish dealers per community	17	6	1	.75*	——
N =	66	50	39	31	Total 186

*Four communities with three dealers.

TABLE 2

Benefits of Belonging to a Fishermen's Cooperative

Category	Puntarenas		Costa de Pajaros		Playa del Coco		North	
	(f)	Percent	(f)	Percent	(f)	Percent	(f)	Percent
1. Better income	6	9	2	4	3	8	—	—
2. Saving Plan	2	3	3	6	—	—	1	3
3. Loans	1	1	1	2	1	3	—	—
4. Equipment/supplies	—	—	—	—	12	[31]	10	32
5. Mutual help	11	16	4	8	2	5	2	6
6. Other positive	3	4	4	8	3	8	—	—
7. No benefits	32	[48]	10	20	4	10	2	6
8. Don't know	11	16	26	[52]	11	28	16	[52]
9. Selling point/marketing	—	—	—	—	3	8	—	—
	66	100	50	100	39	100	31	100

[ ] = highest frequency response in community.

between number of middlemen and response category 7 (no benefits), and a perfect negative rank order correlation between response category 4 (supplies/equipment) and number of middlemen. This relationship will be discussed further.

The next step in the analysis is to determine how the dependent and other independent variables are related to each other. Because "lack of knowledge" about the benefits of cooperatives formed the single most frequent response in two of the communities, a new variable "knowledge vs. no knowledge" (K/NOK) about the benefits of cooperatives was created and tested against independent variables 1 through 11. Table 4 shows the results of this part of the analysis. In each community (K/NOK) was significantly related to at least one of the independent variables.

In Puntarenas and Costa de Pajaros boat owners had more knowledge about cooperatives than nonowners. In Costa de Pajaros and North, the more kinsmen individuals had fishing with them, the less knowledge they had about the benefits of cooperatives. In Playa del Coco the interrelated variables of age and years of fishing experience are related to (K/NOK). In that community, the older and more experienced a fisherman is, the more likely he is to have knowledge about the benefits of cooperatives. Also in that community, individuals with fathers who were fishermen had more knowledge about cooperatives than individuals who had fathers with other occupations.

Discussion

The overall results of this analysis show that there is considerable variation from community to community regarding perceived benefits or lack of benefits of belonging to a fishermen's cooperative. Both situational and individual factors help to explain this variation. A systematic relationship exists between the number of fish dealers in a community (situational variable) and

TABLE 3

Relationship of Variable 12 and Response 7 and 4

	Rank		
Variable	Variable 12 Number of Fish Dealers Per Community	Response 7 No Benefits	Response 4 Supplies/Equipment
Puntarenas	1	2	3.5
Costa de Pajaros	2	2	3.5
Playa del Coco	3	3	2
North	4	4	1

TABLE 4

Knowledge of Cooperatives vs. Independent Variables

Variables	Puntarenas			Costa de Pajaros			Playa del Coco			North		
	K	NOK	P	K	NOK	P	K	NOK	P	K	NOK	P
1. Age $\overline{X}$	33.5	29.1	>.05	29.6	25.8	>.05	29.9	21.8	<.05*	29.7	27.7	>.05
2. Yrs. fished $\overline{X}$	12.7	10.6	>.05	12.8	10.9	>.05	14.4	5.4	<.05*	6.5	5.4	>.05
3. No. of family who fish $\overline{X}$	2.0	1.5	>.05	6.5	7.7	>.05	5.9	2.5	>.05	2.1	2.8	>.05
4. Own boat (%)	34	9	<.05*	63	39	<.05*	39	18	>.05	53	38	>.05
5. No. kin fish with $\overline{X}$	.40	.50	>.05	.67	1.35	<.05*	1	.4	.05	.2	.8	<.10*
6. Hrs. fish/day $\overline{X}$	10.3	10.7	>.05	4.8	5.6	>.05	7.3	4.8	>.05	15.7	19.8	>.05
7. Days fish/week $\overline{X}$	5.6	5.6	>.05	5.6	5.4	>.05	6.4	6.0	>.05	6.0	6.1	>.05
8. Scale level $\overline{X}$	4.7	4.7	>.05	4.0	4.3	>.05	5.0	4.9	>.05	4.5	5.2	>.05
9. Education $\overline{X}$	4.1	4.5	>.05	2.5	3.8	<.05*	6.1	6.5	>.05	5.0	3.9	>.05
10. Father Farmer (%)	27	9	>.05	29	27	>.05	36	54	>.05	60	56	>.05
11. Father Fisherman (%)	39	46	>.05	67	69	>.05	39	0	<.001*	7	12	>.05

* = significant
relationship
alpha = .10

perceived lack of benefits of belonging to a cooperative, as well as with perceived benefits in the form of supplies and equipment.

Besides the obvious point of supplying a selling point, middlemen also serve the important function of obtaining supplies and equipment for fishermen. In fact, as reported by Pollnac (1985), Costa Rican middlemen carry on a variety of important functions besides purchasing of fish for resale to others. Pollnac cites providing loans, picking up parts, and providing other help as some of the other functions of middlemen. It would appear that where there are sufficient middlemen in a community who compete with one another to supply a variety of functions to fishermen, perceived benefits of a cooperative are low. Where there are not enough middlemen in competition to supply the needs, then the perceived benefits of cooperatives increase. Perceptions of fishermen reflect the differing cultural-ecological context in which they live.

Some might argue that the high negative evaluation of coop membership in Puntarenas is due to the fact that the headquarters of the regional cooperative is located there; and thus this is where cooperative weakness and shortcomings are most visible. Respondents there would then generalize to all cooperatives from their local experience. However, the data do not support this alternative view. There was a branch of the cooperative in Playa del Coco that did not function at all well and eventually closed down just before the data reported here were collected. Yet it is in Playa del Coco that we find the highest total positive responses (63 percent) concerning the benefits of belonging to a fishermen's cooperative. This suggests that the "negative visibility issue" is not a valid alternative explanation.

Regarding knowledge or lack of knowledge about benefits of belonging to cooperatives, we note that in each of our four communities different combinations of variables predict whether an individual will have or lack knowledge of the benefits of cooperatives. Although it is not possible at the present time to explain why these various combinations of variables are related to K/NOK, there is an important policy implication to the findings. This implication is related to other findings of the research that show that there is considerable diversity and complexity of beliefs, opinions, and knowledge, as well as their correlates in the four communities.

The Theoretical and Practical Nexus. It is clear from this analysis that programs related to cooperative formation must take into account the diversity within and between communities. Blanket policy decisions that disregard this diversity solely on a statistical basis are less likely to be successful than those that address the complexity. Policymakers must routinely deal with complexity not as an exception to the rule, but as a normal social and cultural feature of human life. It is, of course, impossible to deal with the social and cultural complexity unless studies are carried out as a prior step to policy decisions. In the case studied here, the sociocultural analysis would suggest that greater effort in cooperative development in communities with lower numbers of middlemen and efforts to adjust the cooperative's structure to the needs of the fishermen in communities with high concentrations of middlemen would have been useful in helping to ensure the success of the project.

Case Study II

The second case study in this paper focuses on small-scale fishermen's beliefs about success and economic development policy. Many attempts to enhance the economic well-being of poor fishermen throughout the world have been based on the transfer of more advanced technology to these producers. Various mechanisms such as equipment-oriented low-interest loans, grants, or the direct gift of new technology have been carried out. Policymakers may decide a priori that more productive technology in the hands of less successful producers will enhance their position; or, at times, the less successful are asked what they need to improve their position. These approaches often take the biological and economic factors of availability of fish stocks and market effects into consideration, and yet the outcomes of these attempts are frequently disappointing.

In Puerto Real, a Puerto Rican fishing community, informants reported that during the administration of Lyndon Johnson grants of money were given to less successful fishermen in the population with the stipulation that the money be used only to purchase fishing equipment. However, according to informants, the policy was unsuccessful, for although some fishermen upgraded their gear by means of this grant, a number of others purchased gear but then sold it and lived off the money for a time. This behavior negated the prospects of improving their long-term economic position, which was the goal of the policy.

In order to understand the sociocultural patterns that might be related to the failure of this policy, I set out to study the sociocultural correlates of being a successful fisherman in the population and to compare these empirical correlates of success with the beliefs about success on the part of successful and less successful fishermen. I hypothesized, based on cultural-ecological theory, that beliefs about success between the two groups (successful and less successful) would be different because they operated in very different sociocultural environments within the fishery. By understanding these hypothesized differences in beliefs and how they related to actual success, we would be in a better position to formulate more useful policy concerning how to match technology to its users and vice versa. My approach focused on the intracultural diversity of the population of fishermen and tried to measure a seemingly deterministic aspect of that diversity.

Analysis

Puerto Real, located on the west coast of Puerto Rico, has a population of about 2000 people, 10 percent of whom are involved in the fishing industry. In terms of landings and employment, it is the most important fishing port of the commonwealth. Data for this study were gathered in an interview schedule administered to a sample of fifty fishermen.[1] Qualitative and quantitative data were also obtained from unstructured and structural key informant interviews and participant observation.

Success of fishermen, the main variable in this study, was operationalized as a dichotomous variable by categorizing the sample of fifty individuals as at or above the median and below the median of the rankings of six key informants. With a split-half correlation of .97, the reliability of informants proved high. Convergent validity, as measured by the correlation of a field assistant's ranking after seven months of fieldwork with that of the key informants, was also fairly high at .67. I was also able to compare the rankings of the key informants with those of the sample of fifty fishermen who were asked to indicate who were the most successful fishermen in the community. Ten individuals were mentioned in the group of most successful, but some more frequently than others. The correlation of the key informants' ranking and the fifty fishermen's ranking for most successful was .98.

The individuals in the sample of fishermen were also asked to indicate why the most successful were so successful. While there was considerable agreement between the successful and less successful fishermen on the question of who are the most successful ($r = .73$, $p < .001$), the reasons they give for success are strikingly different. Successful fishermen's most frequent response to this question is that success comes from "fishing often" (46 percent of total responses), whereas the less successful cite "boats and equipment" as the single most important reason (29 percent of total responses). Table 5 shows the full range of responses, as well as the fact that these response patterns are statistically different from each other.

The second part of the design of this study was to compare the beliefs of the successful and less successful fishermen with the empirical correlates of success. By collecting data on variables that are part of the middle-range cultural ecology theory of fishing adaptation (cf. Poggie and Gersuny, 1974; Pollnac, 1974, 1986), it was possible to test the empirical correlates of success in this population. Three of the four variables that most differentiate the beliefs about success of the two groups were tested. These are as follows: degree of deferred gratification orientation taken to be the psychological substratum of the behavior of fishing often, years at the occupation as a measure of experience, and boat size as an indicator of technological level. Gratification orientation was measured by means of a content analysis of two hypothetical projective questions about utilizing "windfalls" (cf. Pollnac and Poggie, 1978). Boat size is actually a direct measure of "level of

TABLE 5

Successful and Less Successful Fishermen's Beliefs about Success

Beliefs	Success High*	%	Low*	%	Total
Fish often	23	46	12	17	35
Understanding and competence	11	22	11	16	22
Experience	0		8	12	8
Boats and equipment	7	14	20	29	27
Wealth	8	16	8	12	16
All equal, luck and contacts	1	2	10	14	11
Totals	50	100	69	100	109

$\chi^2 = 22.5$, df = 11, p < .05
*Defined as at or above the median and below the median respectively.

technology," in that boat size is related to level of complexity and productivity in this fishery. "Wealth" and "understanding and competence" do not differentiate the two groups and were, therefore, not analyzed. It was not possible to test the category "all equal, luck and contacts."

As seen in Table 6, all three independent variables are significantly correlated at the 20 percent or less level with success and are not significantly related to each other. When looked at in a multiple correlation model, the three variables with a multiple correlation of .58 account for 33 percent of the variance in the success variable, with deferred gratification accounting for 15 percent, boat size 8 percent, and years at the occupation 10 percent.

Discussion: Theoretical and Practical Connections

If we ask, "Who is correct?"—the successful or less successful fishermen—the answer is that they are both, in part, correct. Successful fishermen, who already have the more productive technology, see success primarily as the result of the frequent application of that technology. The less successful primarily see success as the result of having the technology. Thus, in each stratum, beliefs reflect realistic and necessary conditions for success as revealed in the analysis of the empirical correlates of success, but they do not reflect the full picture.

In development projects intended to enhance the economic well-being of the less successful we can see that neither the a priori transfer of technology nor the determination of what the less successful believe they need would address the range of empirical correlates of success. Both plans have "face validity," but would be unrealistic according to this analysis.

TABLE 6

Intercorrelations among the Variables

Variable	1	2	3	4
1. Deferred gratification orientation		.102	.014	.393**
2. Years experience			-.184	.298*
3. Boat size				.283*
4. Success[a]				

N = 50, * = $p < .05$, ** = $p < .01$.
[a] The full ranked variable is used here.

It is the task of the applied anthropologist to determine the distribution of diverse beliefs that people hold about success, as well as the sociocultural correlates of success, as a means to develop policy to better accomplish the aims of development schemes among the poor. Technology transfer by itself is not the solution. What is needed is a better match between technology and the people who will use that technology. In the case looked at here, perhaps the establishment of a policy for training in the basic skills of fishing with more advanced technology, as well as time and effort management, would have improved the outcome of this effort in technology transfer.

Conclusions: Theory and Application

I began this paper with the idea that there is the pressing need to develop a way to incorporate sociocultural information into the policy-making formula for fisheries development and management. Using the cultural ecology approach—with its emphasis on intracultural and intrasocial diversity—I illustrated the application of the approach in two case studies involving policy related to (1) fishermen's cooperatives, and (2) the transfer of technology. In these cases, knowledge of aspects of social and cultural diversity that resulted from differing ecological adjustments of individuals would have facilitated policy recommendations that were practical and realistic adjustments to help ensure desired outcomes.

The kind of information derived by this method does not fit neatly into the bioeconomic model of fishery functioning. However, there is no magic way to reduce the diversity of socio-cultural issues and systems into a single variable in an elegant, unified bioeconomic-social model. Each policy plan that utilizes sociocultural information will first require a general understanding of the social and cultural context so that highly salient issues vis-a-vis policy considerations can be identified, studied, and incorporated into the policy.

In order to use the sociocultural information in fishing policy, it is necessary to break from the constraints of the bio-economic model and adopt a much more inclusive and qualitative view of a fishery system. This approach will require decision makers to formulate policy that is complicated. There is a widely held view among administrators that good policy is simple policy. Trying to incorporate sociocultural information into policy frequently makes for considerably more than simple policy. Yet the trade-off is compelling. It seems to me that it is a trade-off between ease of administration and potential for success. We do not have to look far to see that we have not been very successful in fishery policy making in most parts of the world, and we know that a large part of our lack of success is due to our failure to deal adequately with the sociocultural issues involved. The change that will bring greater success to this important area of policy making is the realization and implementation of the notion that good policy is not necessarily simple policy. Good policy, at least in this realm of human activity, is complicated in that it must simultaneously address the bioeconomic parameters as well as the social and cultural diversity that is a known and deterministic part of all human populations. The cultural-ecology approach to that diversity provides us with a valuable methodological and conceptual tool to address this element of fishery policy making. Finally, there is the urgent need for policymakers to ensure that their deliberations are informed with the best information that the natural, economic, and anthropological sciences can provide.

III

Qualitative/Quantitative

Introduction to Part Three

"Qualitative and quantitative data inform each other and produce insight and understanding in a way that cannot be duplicated by either approach alone." H. Russell Bernard (1988:151)

Too often in social science research it is assumed that the more quantitative the study, the more "scientific" it is. Mindless quantification, however, is to be avoided as assiduously as mere description (thick or otherwise). The most productive research strategies, we believe, establish a dynamic, productive interplay between qualitative and quantitative data (see Pelto and Pelto, 1978:122).

In general terms, research goes through the following steps. Theory or observations (qualitative or quantitative) lead to insights that are expressed in words. These words must be translated into concepts that can be measured. The measurement process often involves an interplay of qualitative and quantitative thinking. Although observations, instruments, and tests are devised to measure the concepts, the researcher must constantly think about the reliability and validity of these measurements. Some measurements that are simple to get and easily quantifiable, for example, may have only marginal relevance to the concept in which the researcher is interested (e.g., the debate concerning IQ tests).

Most research does not begin or end with a single concept, however. We are usually interested in how concepts are related to one another, and these are most productively expressed in the form of hypotheses. Ideally, testing these hypotheses can be done through the collection of quantitative data to establish probabilistic statements about how closely the previous insights of the researcher approximate the phenomena being investigated. Usually, these quantitative data are collected using structured interviews or observations of behavior. Deviations from expectations, or further insight into the processes involved, may be explained by appeal to unstructured observations or additional information collected outside the context of the structured interviews. Sometimes, however, phenomena may be difficult to quantify. In these cases, the researcher must be able to muster qualitative evidence in support of his or her hypothesis. The procedures by which the observations, reports, or other qualitative evidence were collected should be described in sufficient detail that other investigators can evaluate the strength of the evidence and, should they so desire, attempt to replicate or disprove the results. Finally, the end result of this variable mix of quantitative and qualitative research will be explanation in the form of words, i.e., in qualitative terms (Bernard 1988:61).

The judicious mixing of quantitative and qualitative data for a variety of research objectives is illustrated by the chapters in this section of the book. Bentley et al. explore the important issue of child feeding during episodes of diarrhea in India. This research team investigated the relationship between beliefs expressed by people about food restrictions and compared these with actual feeding behavior. Their work combines ethnographic, survey, and case study methods. Rylko-Bauer examines one of the fastest-growing segments of the U.S. health care system—the use of freestanding emergency centers. Using quantitative and qualitative data, she proposed to determine the clientele of these centers, why this option for care is chosen, and what other segments of the medical care system are also used by these people. Westermeyer summarizes the results of his long-term research on opium dependency. He shows how analysis of data leads to insights that can then be incorporated in further data collection. In addition, while quantitative data can be collected on some aspects of opium use, qualitative research is the only feasible method of collecting other types of information.

4

Child Feeding During Diarrhea in North India: The Use of Complementary Methods

Margaret E. Bentley, Gretel H. Pelto, Lindsay H. Allen, Meenu Mathur, and Dijouratie Sanogo

There is widespread concern in the public health community about whether mothers change their feeding practices when children have diarrhea. In developing countries, where children often experience repeated and chronic diarrhea episodes, feeding practices may further exacerbate the nutritional problems associated with diarrheal disease (Committee on International Nutrition Programs, 1985). There is evidence to suggest that children who continue to be fed during diarrhea episodes are less likely to experience weight loss and growth faltering (Brown et al., 1988). This is especially true for children who are already malnourished.

Several studies have shown that approximately 25 percent of the growth deficit experienced by children in the developing world, compared to children from industrialized countries, can be explained by repeated diarrheal episodes (Brown et al., 1988; Martorell et al., 1975; Black et al., 1983; Rowland et al., 1988). Although there has been considerable study of the effects of diarrhea on child nutritional status and growth, we still have little understanding of the behavioral antecedents of the nutritional outcomes. Specifically, there is a dearth of information on the relationships among diarrhea, maternal feeding practices, children's food intake, and growth.

Medical anthropologists who have studied cultural aspects of diarrheal diseases commonly report the presence of beliefs that the quantity of food should be reduced during diarrhea, and that certain types of food should be restricted (Nichter, 1988; Coreil and Genece, 1988; Green, 1986; Kendall et al., 1984; Nations, 1982), as have nonanthropologists who rely on "KAP" (knowledge, attitudes, and practices) survey research (Kumar et al., 1985;

Khan and Ahmad, 1986; Srinivasa and Afonso, 1983). Few previous studies have attempted to document relationships between beliefs about food restriction during diarrhea and actual feeding behavior.[1] The lack of data on this issue is particularly unfortunate because there is a widely held belief among health professionals that food is deliberately withheld from a child experiencing diarrhea (Chen, 1983; UNICEF, 1985; Molla et al., 1983; National Academy of Sciences, 1981; Morley, 1973; Khan and Ahmad, 1986). In the absence of evidence to the contrary, the international medical and public health community appears to have developed a common mythology that inappropriate feeding behaviors are the norm in most cultures. When feeding practices during diarrhea have been systematically observed, however, widespread food withholding is not evident (Brown et al., 1987; Bentley et al., 1991). In fact, Nigerian mothers appear to force-feed their children more often when they are experiencing diarrhea, compared to nondiarrheal illness days (Brown et al., 1987; Bentley et al., 1991). Moreover, a recent study in Peru has shown, through use of structured observations, that children's acceptance of food scores are lower during diarrhea when compared to health, while at the same time, mothers' encouragement to eat scores are higher (Bentley et al., 1991). This implies that diarrhea-associated anorexia is an important limiting factor in dietary intakes during illness, and that maternal food withholding is not evident.

This paper presents data from rural North India on maternal beliefs and feeding practices when children experience diarrhea. The data were collected as part of an anthropological study of household diarrhea management, conducted in collaboration with the All-India Institute of Medical Sciences (AIIMS), New Delhi. The study was part of a larger oral rehydration therapy (ORT) intervention study undertaken by the Department of Pediatrics, AIIMS. The study was conducted in three villages, Tilpat, Palla, and Anangpur.

According to the AIIMS study design, oral rehydration packets were available to households in Anangpur, through a system of village ORT workers who trained mothers in the proper preparation and administration of the solution. Tilpat and Palla did not receive ORT, and were thus considered control villages. Fortnightly surveillance to establish morbidity and mortality was conducted in all three villages by AIIMS personnel. Results from the AIIMS study are presented elsewhere (Bhan et al., 1986).

The anthropological study reported upon here piggybacked on top of this larger intervention study and utilized the experimental design to compare the villages on a number of behavioral factors. Data for the anthropological component were collected over a twelve-month period during 1983–1984. A more detailed discussion of the anthropological study, and of the larger AIIMS intervention study, has been reported elsewhere (Bentley, 1987, 1988).

This paper will show how the use of complementary methodologies, drawn from both nutrition and anthropology, allow an interpretation that would not have been possible if only survey data had been collected. It will be argued that the use of both qualitative and quantitative methods, and the inclusion of ethnographic research, observational methods, and survey data, provide a unique opportunity to test specific hypotheses that have relevance for policy and program issues in public health.

The Ethnographic Setting

In order to understand infant feeding patterns and household diarrhea management among these villages, it is necessary to have a broad understanding of the ethnographic setting, and of the interrelated environmental, socio-economic, and cultural factors that influence the behaviors of interest.

Figure 1 shows a map of India and the location of the study villages. The villages are located approximately twenty-five kilometers south of Delhi, just across the Haryana state line. They are situated within five km of the highway that leads to Agra (site of the Taj Mahal). The villages of Tilpat and Palla lie on the eastern side of the highway, whereas Anangpur is located about four km west of the highway.

The villages are situated in the Faridabad Complex, which is a designated government industrial development area of Haryana state. Small factories line the highway and provide employment for men from the nearby villages. Farming is still practiced, but there is currently pressure on the land for suburban-style residential development. Two such housing developments with expensive houses are under construction. These homes, owned by urban commuters to Delhi and the nearby city of Faridibad, contrast sharply with the characteristics of poverty observed in the three villages of this study.

Land on the western side of the highway is flat and fertile. Of the two control villages, Tilpat is more fully rural, and agricultural work occupies more households than in Palla. Palla, which is located directly adjacent to the highway and factories, has attracted many new families and transients, including a sizable population of single men. Many of the families who own farmland have converted part of their lands into residential units to house the migrants. Palla is more peri-urban than rural, and the characteristics of urbanity—increased wealth, higher education, and smaller families—are more evident in Palla in comparison to the other two villages.

To reach Anangpur, one must travel a few kilometers down a side road that cuts through rather rough countryside. This land, which surrounds most of Anangpur, is full of rocks, boulders, and brush. Sections of the land are quarry areas, and have been so for several decades. The quarries are managed

FIGURE 1

Map of India Showing Study Sites

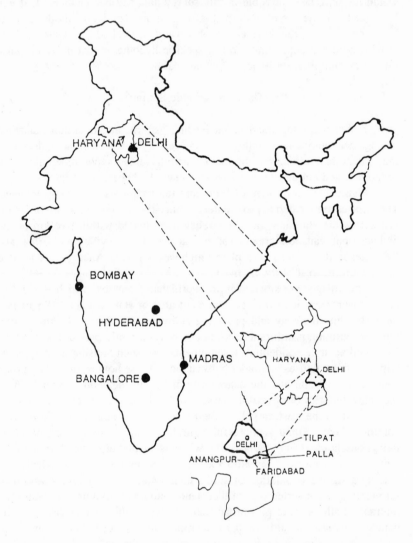

by wealthy local contractors, who compete for five-year leases of the land in auctions organized by the state government.

There is one fertile, flat stretch of agricultural land on the northwest corner of Anangpur. This land is owned mostly by Gujar families, a tribal majority of the village. About one-quarter of Anangpur men work in the quarries, but pay is low, irregular, physically difficult, and dangerous. Access to the factories is possible by bicycle, but only a minority engage in factory work.

The Agricultural Cycle

The study villages are situated on the fertile Gangetic Plain, south of the spectacular Himalayan mountain range. The Ganges River is the great waterway that serves the floodplain.

There are three seasons: (1) the rainy or monsoon season, from early July through September; (2) the dry, cooler season, from October to late February; and (3) the hot, dry season, from March through June, which peaks in May/June. The seasons are distinct and the climatic shift rapid.

The hot, dry season is characterized by extreme high temperatures, averaging 104–105 degrees Fahrenheit in April and May. During the peak of the hot season, temperatures of 110–115 degrees Fahrenheit are common. There is no measurable precipitation during that period.

Heavy rain marks the arrival of the monsoon season, and breaks the stifling heat. The bulk of precipitation (up to thirty-six inches) occurs during this season. Although temperatures are still in the high nineties, the air is humid and fresh. Nearly everyone welcomes the monsoon season, although floods, mosquitoes, flies, and various diseases accompany it.

The cooler season brings an end to measurable precipitation. Nighttime temperatures drop to the high thirties and low forties, and daytime temperatures average in the fifties and low sixties.

There are two major agricultural seasons in North India: summer (*kharif*) and winter (*rabi*). The summer season crops are sown in June–July, immediately before the rains, and harvested in mid-September through early November. The winter season crops are sown after the summer harvest, and harvested in mid-March/April. Sometimes a fodder crop is sown between the summer harvest and winter planting.

The major crops of the summer season include two kinds of millet (*jowar* and *bajra*). Wheat is the major winter crop, providing the staple food item, *roti* or *chapati* (unleavened flat bread). Mustard is grown and processed as a vegetable oil. Potatoes, rice, maize, fodder crops, tomatoes, and green vegetables are grown as less important crops during both seasons.

The Hygiene Environment

Sanitation in all three villages is poor. A combination of high-density housing; lack of piped, clean water, latrines, refrigeration, and sanitation drains; numerous animals and flies; and poor hygiene patterns all contribute to a high degree of contamination. Adults defecate in the fields, but young children and old people defecate within or near the compound, as do animals.

Nearly 25 percent of mothers report their small children defecate within the house, and another 45 percent report defecation takes place within the household compound. Fecal waste is usually cleaned with ash shortly after the child defecates.

Water source and availability vary among the villages. Twenty percent of households in Anangpur and one-third of the families in Tilpat and Palla have access to a handpump. The remainder of the households in all three villages secure their water from open, communal wells. These wells are an important source of fecal contamination. This is the place where water buffalo are watered down, where laundry is done, and where some men take their daily bath.

Caste and Social Stratification

The highly ordered social stratification system, known as caste or *jati* in several languages of Sanskrit origin, is an important factor in the social structure of the villages. Although all human societies exhibit some form of social stratification, caste in India has long been characterized as a social system that particularly emphasizes inequality (Mandlebaum, 1970). Despite economic progress and a "march to modernization" (Stevens, 1984), caste is still an important factor in Indian life.

In the research area, one observes a critical example of the influence of the Hindu concept of pollution and intercaste relationships on factors affecting diarrheal disease in the restrictions concerning water utilization—separate wells, designated for separate caste or ethnic groups, are the norm.

In Anangpur, the well for Harijans[2] is overused and contaminated (M. K. Bhan, personal communication). A walk to the Harijan side of Anangpur brings vivid images. A large, open well constructed of cement rises three feet above the ground. It is surrounded by mud, dung, and buzzing flies. Twenty to thirty persons are involved in diverse activities related to water use, such as washing clothes, themselves, or their buffalo. Women and young girls are seen pulling up buckets of water for household consumption, while dirty, soapy water spills over the edges and runs back into the well. In contrast, the multiple communal wells of Gujar[3] families on the other side of Anangpur are smaller and cleaner. The gradual shift to private, household handpumps within the villages is one answer to intergroup contamination of water sources.[4]

Caste structure in the three villages varies considerably, as shown in Table 1. Brahmin, Rajput, and Kshatriya are the higher caste groups within the Hindu stratification system. Brahmins are those born into the priestly caste, although in Tilpat nearly all are involved in agriculture and other occupations. Rajputs and Kshatriya are technically the same group (Kshatriya is the "varna" into which the Rajputs belong). Kshatriya were originally con-

TABLE 1

Social Organization in the Study Villages

	Percent of Households (n = 199)		
	Tilpat	Palla	Anangpur
Hindu groups			
Brahmin	54	17	1
Rajput/Kshatriya	4	31	1
"Service" castes	12	21	1
Harijan	18	21	39
Non-Hindu groups			
Gujar	0	0	50
Muslim	7	10	8
Other	5	0	0

sidered the warrior caste and are one step below Brahmins on the caste ladder. In Tilpat, the Brahmins wield political power and own more land than the other groups (Anangpur has very few households from these upper caste groups).

The service caste (*Shudra*) include both "clean" and "unclean" Shudras. Clean Shudras include barbers, *dobis* (washermen), carpenters, and the like. As seen in Table 1, in Anangpur there are few families in this grouping. Unclean Anangpur Shudras previously collected large, waxy leaves from a scrub tree, which they made into leaf bowls and sold in urban markets. They are now involved in other occupations, including the quarry work available to Anangpur residents, although some of them still collect the leaves seasonally to produce bowls.

The Harijan group includes all the unclean Shudras and untouchables. "Untouchables" are those directly associated with occupations involving dirt and filth (such as leathermaking, sweeping, or midwifery), and they fall outside the caste system. Strict rules governing personal and physical relationships between untouchables and other groups evolved, such as those just described concerning sharing of water. Similar restrictions surround the sharing of food and hearth.

Gujars do not belong within the Hindu caste system, but are a pastoral tribal group that has its origins in North India. Although Gujars originally were nomadic, they have become assimilated into predominantly Hindu villages in North India, although maintaining their ethnicity. In the state of Rajasthan, Gujar men wear colorful turbans and often have handlebar mustaches, and women wear bright, wide, knee-length skirts and tailored shirts, rather than saris. In Anangpur, Gujar men do not dress traditionally, but women do.

Animal husbandry is still an important activity for many Gujar families. This is true for the Gujars of Anangpur, who raise cows, water buffalo, and goats for milk and sale. Animal protein, especially milk, is an important dietary item for Gujars—unless the family is so poor that they sell their animal dairy products. Milk availability at the household level is an important factor in infant feeding behavior for this setting.

Muslims are a separate religious and ethnic group in India. The partition of the Indian subcontinent in 1947 led to a vast migration of Muslims from India to East and West Pakistan, and conversely, of Hindus to India. Presently Muslims make up about 15 percent of India's population. As a group they are a minority who suffer from a lack of political power. They are less educated and poorer than Hindus. Muslim women, in particular, are the least educated Indian women as a consequence of religious doctrine that restricts their roles. Muslims are considered unclean by orthodox Hindus because they are outside of the caste system and because they consume the meat of the sacred cow. In most villages they live in clusters separate from Hindus. This is true of Muslims in Tilpat and Anangpur, but not in Palla. The Muslim families in Palla are relatively new immigrants, more modern and more integrated into the economy, compared to Muslims in the other two villages.

Socioeconomic Status of Households Within Study Villages

Table 2 shows the distribution of values for various wealth indicators. The majority of families in all three villages own no land, which is the most important wealth indicator in India. The majority of landowners own less than five bighas. Only in Tilpat are there significant numbers of large landholders. As discussed earlier, Palla families are least likely to own any land.

Monthly income varies among villages. The standard deviations within all three villages are large, reflecting the two extremes of poverty and wealth. Incomes in Anangpur are significantly lower, even when adjusted for household number.

Household Structure and Composition

Traditionally, the joint or extended family has been the norm in India. Marriages are arranged, and potential husbands are sought from outside the daughter's village. Marriages are usually within a caste or ethnic group. When young women marry, they generally relocate to live in the household of their husband's family. Sons stay in the village of their birth, sharing hearth and home with their parents, grandparents, and brothers and their families. In India, the official definition of a joint family (for census purposes) is a group of family members who "share the same hearth"; that is, prepare food and eat as a group. Therefore, family members could share the same roof but cook separately, and so be classified as nuclear.

TABLE 2

Wealth Indicators in the Study Villages

Percent of Households

	Tilpat		Palla		Anangpur		Total	
Land Ownership								
No land	66		83		65		71	
< 5 bighas*	12		5		17		11	
5–10 bighas	5		2		6		4	
11–20 bighas	4		5		8		5	
> 20 bighas	12		5		4		7	
	$\overline{X}$	S.D.	$\overline{X}$	S.D.	$\overline{X}$	S.D.	$\overline{X}$	S.D.
Rupees/month	771	460	663	388	641	688	696	551
Per capita rupees/month	122	80	124	58	90	82	112	78
MSL scale score [1]	2.71	1.34	2.40	1.34	2.09	1.27	2.40	1.34

*1 bigha is about 1/5 of an acre

[1] A "material style of life score" (MSL) was attempted through use of the Guttman scale technique. Eleven variables were entered, including ownership of land, animals, radio, fan, sewing machine, television, bicycle, motor scooter, handpump, number of rooms, and household construction type. Eleven variables did not scale (i.e., lead to a satisfactory "reproducibility" coefficient). Several other combinations were tried, resulting in two scales with adequate reproducibility coefficients. They were (1) ownership of land, animals, and the number of household rooms; and (2) rupees per month (based on four levels), and the ownership of a handpump. Both of these scales had a "reproducibility" coefficient of > 0.9 for the total sample. In the regression analyses reported in this paper the second MSL scale was used.

Although joint families are the idealized household structure, nuclear families are more and more common and are related to growing industrialization and modernization (Kolenda, 1968). In part this development reflects the fact that employment opportunities are in cities away from one's native home, so that nuclear families are formed in the city. Thus, nuclear families represent a shift to a more urban and modern model.

The villages in this study, which are in close proximity to Delhi, are becoming more urban and less traditional, so it is not surprising to see that the nuclear family has overtaken the joint family as the main type of household structure. In all three villages, approximately two-thirds of households are nuclear, whereas the remaining third can be categorized as joint.

The presence of a mother-in-law within a household can be an important influence on decision making, especially in the realm of child feeding and care. In joint families, the mother-in-law technically holds domestic authority. In general, the daughter-in-law is directed in all her household activities by her mother-in-law (Freed and Freed, 1980), although there is, no doubt, much variation.

Slightly more than one-third of households in Tilpat and Anangpur report a mother-in-law present, compared with 10 percent in Palla. The low percent of households in Palla with a mother-in-law is related to the decreased prevalence of joint families and to a more transient population, compared to Tilpat and Anangpur.

Patterns of Child Care

Child care patterns are related to household structure. In large joint families, child care is shared among mothers, mothers-in-law, and older female children. Concerning male participation in child care, Minturn and Hitchcock (1966:108) state, "The role of the men in the care of infants is negligible, except for a few elderly men who are too feeble for farm work and have retired from active participation in the village political scene." This does not appear to be uniformly the case in the study villages. Although child care is primarily in the female domain, men were observed feeding and bathing their children. This was especially so in families where the female had extrahousehold work roles. In addition, men often participate in decisions about whether, when, and where a child is seen by a health care provider during illness. Men frequently took the child to a practitioner for treatment.

Child Nutritional Status in the Study Villages

This section provides a brief review of child nutritional status in the study villages, setting the stage for the dietary data presented later.

Table 3 shows variation in child nutritional status within the villages. Nutritional status of children from the villages of Tilpat and Palla is pooled in

TABLE 3

Nutritional Status of Children under Five in Three Study Villages

| Nutritional Grade* | Percent of Children Surveyed | | |
	Anangpur n = 554	Tilpat/Palla n = 598	Total n = 1152
Grade 0	26	30	28
Grade I	44	41	42
Grade II	20	22	21
Grade III	10	8	9

*Based on weight/age groups according to Indian Academy of Paediatrics, using 50th percentile of international values as the reference (Bhan, 1986)

the table, since the data derive from the experimental design of the All-India Institute of Medical Sciences oral rehydration therapy study.

The data show that slightly more than one-quarter of village children fall within the normal (Grade 0) nutritional status category. More than 40 percent are classified as suffering from mild malnutrition (Grade I). About one-fifth of children are moderately malnourished (Grade II), and about 10 percent are severely malnourished (Grade III), based upon the classification system. The data for the two control villages are not disaggregated, but it appears that the prevalence of malnutrition is equally distributed among the villages.

Study Methodology

Three complementary data-gathering techniques were utilized over a period of twelve months: (1) ethnographic interviewing and observation; (2) structured interviews with mothers and health practitioners; and (3) case monitoring of children during and after a diarrhea episode.

Maternal beliefs about feeding during diarrhea were collected using both unstructured and structured interview techniques. Data from the survey on maternal beliefs about feeding during diarrhea are compared to actual feeding patterns during the diarrhea episodes.

The data on feeding and dietary intake are derived from two sources: (1) twenty-four-hour dietary recalls for 195 weaned or partially weaned children (ages three to forty-eight months), which were collected in a cross-sectional survey; and (2) twenty-four-hour dietary recalls obtained during the case studies of fifty children with diarrhea, forty-five of whom were weaned.

Ethnography

The first weeks of the study were focused entirely on ethnographic research, and the ethnographic component continued for the duration of the study. During this phase, informal visits were made to a wide variety of households. Many different household members were interviewed, as well as village leaders, schoolteachers, and doctors. Although diarrhea and health care were the predominant topics of discussion, interviews were by no means restricted to health. In fact, information about socioeconomic characteristics and the social/political structure of the villages was actively sought because such information is known to be important to the decision-making process of illness management.

The informal interviews were often one-on-one, with mothers or mothers-in-law, or occasionally with fathers or grandfathers. Focus-group interviews also were conducted; in fact, they were difficult to avoid in large extended families.

As the general picture of village social stratification became obvious to us, care was taken to visit a number of households within each identified socioeconomic cluster. Particular attention was paid to variations in caste affinity. In the two control villages where livelihoods ranged from agricultural to industrial factory work, interviews were carried out in households engaged in different occupations.

During this process, several households were identified as those where repeated visits would be possible and where detailed information could be obtained. These households, representing a wide variety of socioeconomic strata, became key informant families.

Along with the goal of gaining trust, rapport, and general ethnographic information, initial qualitative data were collected concerning the knowledge, beliefs, and practices of diarrheal disease. This information was systematically recorded in our notebooks, and became important reference material for the design of the structured interview schedule. For example, during the ethnographic phase we learned that mothers could articulate cultural definitions and categorizations of diarrhea; they used a variety of home treatments; they were very much connected to the allopathic medical system and used a wide variety of drugs to treat diarrhea; and they had definite beliefs about feeding and fluid intake during diarrhea. Although at this stage we did not have a picture of the total variation in these beliefs and practices, we were able to identify the important questions to be included in the interview schedules.

Cross-Sectional Survey

A stratified random sample (based on socioeconomic status) of households from the larger AIIMS oral rehydration therapy intervention study was drawn for the anthropological study. No sample size was calculated, since estimates of variability for the behavioral data were unknown. A biostatistician/consultant recommended a total sample size of 200.[5]

Interviews were done with 199 women who had children between zero and forty-eight months old. The interview schedule was constructed after the preliminary ethnographic work, so that we had some knowledge of possible responses and the language to use for the instrument. Both closed and open-ended questions were included. The interviews required approximately sixty to ninety minutes to administer, but we often had informal discussions before, during, and after the structured interview. The interviews were conducted from June to August, 1984.

Case Studies of Diarrhea Episodes

The structured interviews with mothers provided qualitative and quantitative data on knowledge, beliefs, and practices of diarrhea management. It was not assumed, however, that what was reported by the mother was always an accurate reflection of her behavior. Many factors influence behavior, including cultural and material considerations. Therefore, the next logical step was to follow diarrhea cases that were in progress.

Case studies of diarrhea allowed the observation and documentation of a series of behaviors, such as feeding and fluid intake during diarrhea, ORT use, home treatments, health actions, and work roles of the mother. The results of this more intensive step are compared to the survey data on household diarrhea management.

The procedures adopted for the "case following" specified monitoring cases of diarrhea episodes that had begun no more than one or two days previously. Cases were identified through the surveillance workers in all villages. Visits were to be made daily or every other day until the diarrhea had stopped for two days. During each visit, a data sheet was completed and qualitative notes written on the afternoon of the visit, based on informal observation within the household. Logistical problems resulted in minor deviations in the case-monitoring protocol.

Fifty diarrhea episodes were monitored. Fifty percent of the cases were less than three days old when monitoring began, and 80 percent less than six days old. The range of episode duration was two–sixty days. In one case, the monitoring was terminated when the child was sent to the AIIMS hospital in Delhi. About 10 percent of the cases were protracted (more than fourteen days duration).

Dietary Intake Data

Twenty-four-hour dietary recalls were obtained during both the household interviews (for the youngest weaned child) and on each visit during the monitoring of diarrhea episodes, and for several children, on postepisode visits. The data were obtained by asking the mother which foods/drinks the child first consumed the preceding morning, which foods and drinks were next consumed (and at what approximate time), and so on until the child went to bed. Although we attempted to quantify protein and caloric intake, analyses of the data resulted in values we considered extremely low. They are not reported or used in the statistical analysis. (One possible explanation for the low nutrient values was the high contribution of unmeasured breast milk calories for those children still breast-feeding).

The purpose of the dietary recalls collected as part of the survey was to describe general dietary consumption patterns in the villages. These dietary intakes could provide a benchmark of normal intakes against which to compare dietary intakes during diarrhea. One limitation of the dietary survey data is that children who had diarrhea (or another illness) on the day before the interview (the day the food was consumed, for the twenty-four-hour recall) were not systematically identified. Therefore, some unknown percentage of food intakes derived from the twenty-four-hour recalls may not represent normal days.

Dietary intakes of children experiencing diarrhea were obtained for each visit throughout the episode and, for about 70 percent, on one or more postdiarrhea days. Thus, for those children who were consuming solids, and for whom we had both diarrhea and postdiarrhea recalls, the child is his or her own control (n = 28).

Scoring for Dietary Diversity

The concept of dietary diversity as a relative measure of nutrient quality has been developed by several investigators (Burke and Allen, 1981; Pelto et al., 1983; Cattle, 1976; Dewey, 1981). The theoretical premise is that a diet higher in variety is likely to be more adequate nutritionally.[6]

Scoring twenty-four-hour recalls of dietary intake can be a useful field method to determine the dietary quality of individuals or groups. In a situation where obtaining precise quantities is not possible, scoring diets for diversity can provide an inexpensive field method for a rough assessment of relative dietary quality.

The data were scored for dietary diversity, adapted from a method developed by Pelto and Bentley (Pelto et al. 1983). The procedure categorizes foods consumed into five food groups: cereals, dairy products, vegetables, fruits, and meat/legumes. Points are given for each category, and the total score is the cumulative counting of each food group. Thus, a child consuming milk and chapati (unleavened wheat bread) would receive one point in the dairy group (for milk) and one in the cereal group (for chapati), with a total dietary diversity score of two. A child consuming milk, *kichuri*, a banana, and milk tea would receive one point in the dairy group (for milk and tea), one in the cereal group (for the rice in kichuri), one in the meat/legume group (for the *dal* in kichuri), and one in the fruit group (for banana), with a total score of four. Dietary diversity, therefore, analyzes food items based upon their major components. The analysis can be done at the level of the food category, or of the cumulative food group score.

Breast milk is not counted in either score, nor are condiments, sauces, spices, or sugar. Breast-feeding patterns were monitored, but they are not part of the diversity scores.

Results

Dietary Patterns of the Study Children

In order to assess feeding patterns during diarrhea, it is necessary to understand how children are fed when they don't have diarrhea. Table 4 shows the frequency of food items consumed in the preceding twenty-four hours for all the children in the cross-sectional survey.

Chapati is overwhelmingly the staple food for young children, closely followed by vegetables, which are usually prepared as a mild curry dish. Between one-half and three-quarters of children in the three villages received milk from cows or water buffalo, figures that reflect the high degree of milk

TABLE 4

List of Foods Consumed by Weaned Children

Food Items	Percent of Children
Chapati/Roti	94
Vegetables (*Subzi*)	76
Milk (*Doodh*)	66
Milk Tea* (*Chaje*)	49
Lentils (*Dal*)	49
Biscuit	29
Yogurt (*Dahi*)	18
Lassi (Yogurt drink)	16
Rice (*Chavel*)	11
Bread (*double roti*)	13
Porridge (*Dalia*)	6
Fruit (misc.)	6
Kichuri (rice/dal)	4
Banana (*Kela*)	<1
Potato (*Aloo*)	<1
Egg (*Anda*)	1

*Generally served with milk and sugar
n = 195 Dietary Recalls

TABLE 5

Dietary Diversity Scores

Tilpat (n = 76)		Palla (n = 37)		Anangpur (n = 79)		Total (n = 188)	
$\overline{X}$	S.D.	$\overline{X}$	S.D.	$\overline{X}$	S.D.	$\overline{X}$	S.D.
3.1	(1.0)	3.4	(.79)	3.2	(.79)	3.2	(.73)

animal ownership in the area. Fruits are rarely offered to children, and are considered a luxury or therapeutic food item.

Table 5 shows the distribution of dietary diversity scores by village for the survey data, which represent normal (non-ill) intake.

The correlation between dietary diversity and socioeconomic status is positive and significant for the sample as a whole: $r = 0.20$, $p = 0.01$. The association between socioeconomic status and dietary diversity increases with age of the child, raising the correlation to $r = .37$ for children aged two years and older. This suggests that as children's diets more closely approach those of older family members, the effect of socioeconomic status on dietary complexity and nutrient adequacy becomes more apparent. There is also a significant positive correlation between fruit consumption and dietary diversity: $r = 0.27$, $p = 0.001$.

To investigate dietary diversity from a multivariate perspective, a stepwise multiple regression was done, as shown in Table 6.

Results of the multiple regression show that approximately one-third of variability of dietary diversity scores can be explained by the variables entered in the model. As can be seen, socioeconomic status and age of the child are important predictors of total dietary diversity score, although both Harijans and Gujars enter negatively. Boys are also more likely to have higher dietary diversity scores than girls.

Maternal Beliefs About Feeding During Diarrhea

In the survey interview mothers were asked several questions about the feeding of children during diarrhea; this information was elicited to provide the frame of reference for observations of feeding behavior during diarrhea.

Beliefs About Breast-Feeding During Diarrhea. Mothers in all three villages overwhelmingly believe that breast-feeding should continue during diarrhea: 95 percent answered in the affirmative, and the percent did not vary across villages. This finding supports results from other studies that show breast-feeding continues normally during diarrhea (Vijayaraghavan et al., 1985; Brown et al., 1985; Hoyle et al., 1980; Sarker et al., 1982).

TABLE 6

Stepwise Multiple Regression of Dietary Diversity

	DF	Sum of Squares	Mean Square	F	Prob
Regression	12	45.40	3.783	7.26	0.0001
Error	175	91.14	0.520		
Total	187	136.55			

R-Square = 0.332

Variable	Beta	Std Error	F	Prob
Intercept	3.494	0.003		
* Child Age	0.014	0.110	20.47	0.0001
* Child Sex	−0.391	0.110	12.58	0.0005
SES Group 3	0.147	0.150	0.96	0.3274
* SES Group 4	0.376	0.175	4.63	0.0329
* SES Group 5	0.598	0.186	10.36	0.0015
* Gujars	−0.810	0.258	9.82	0.0020
* Harijans	−0.901	0.220	16.73	0.0001
Brahmins	−0.383	0.203	3.53	0.0620
Muslims	−0.324	0.263	1.52	0.2190
* Anangpur	0.462	0.172	7.23	0.0079
Palla	0.225	0.151	2.22	0.1381
Mother-in-law	−0.141	0.133	1.13	0.2884

Beliefs About Child Appetite and Quantity of Food During Diarrhea.
Child appetite is hypothesized to play a role in nutrient losses during diarrhea, although there are currently no published qualitative or quantitative data on appetite loss during diarrheal illness. The data from this study provide an opportunity to examine this issue to some extent. Mothers were asked whether children with diarrhea are more or less hungry than when they are healthy. Forty-nine percent of mothers said a child is more hungry, 40 percent less hungry, 12 percent reported no change, and 4 percent said it depends on type of diarrhea.

Mothers were also asked whether children should eat more, less, or the same amount of food during diarrhea. Eleven percent said a child should receive more food, 63 percent less food, and 27 percent the same amount of food.

To examine the predictors of these responses, stepwise logistic regression was carried out, comparing the ''more food'' and ''less food'' groups. Socioeconomic and demographic factors were included in the model (see Table 7).

TABLE 7

Logistic Regression: Mothers Who Think More Food
Should Be Given During Diarrhea

Variable	Beta	Std Error	χ^2	P
Intercept	1.427	1.349	1.12	0.290
Maternal Age	−0.121	0.051	5.52	0.019

Only one variable is associated with holding positive beliefs regarding feeding during diarrhea; older mothers are less likely and younger mothers more likely to think a child should receive more to eat during diarrhea. This suggests that beliefs about food restrictions in diarrhea are traditional. It is extremely unlikely that beliefs about giving more food are associated with increased exposure to modern health care, however, because recommendations by the medical community have consistently been to restrict the intake of food during diarrhea. It may be hypothesized that younger mothers are less experienced and have had fewer encounters with individuals who recommend withdrawing foods during diarrhea.

Mothers were also asked the reasons for their beliefs. Of those who believe less food should be given (n = 122), the majority in all villages think less food will decrease the diarrhea: 62 percent (Tilpat), 64 percent (Palla), and 67 percent (Anangpur). About 25 percent report less food should be given because of loss of appetite.

In sum, these survey data show there are no universal beliefs about food restriction during diarrhea, and that perception of child appetite appears to be an important factor. Mothers are concerned with stool volume and duration of the diarrhea, and many of them believe less food should be given. This concern, however, is far from uniform.

Foods Considered Helpful or Harmful During Diarrhea. Mothers were asked whether there were foods they considered either helpful or harmful during diarrhea and the reasons for these beliefs. The question was open-ended, and respondents were free to list as many foods as they wished. Ninety-six percent of mothers believed some foods were helpful, whereas 85 percent listed some as harmful. Table 8 shows these perceptions.

Foods in the villages were considered helpful because of their (1) physical properties (e.g., light foods, such as rice and kichuri); (2) cooling abilities (e.g., *dahi* and *lassi*), which is related to the hot/cold humoral system; and (3) antidiarrheal properties (e.g., *isagbol* and bananas). Diarrhea, which mothers believe stresses the digestive process, requires foods that are light, or more easily digested. Diarrhea, which is considered a ''hot'' illness by the majority of mothers (and related to the hot season), requires cooling foods to

TABLE 8

Foods Considered Helpful or Harmful During Diarrhea

Helpful	No. of Mothers n = 192	Harmful	No. of Mothers n = 162
Kichuri	82	*Chapati*	55
Dahi (Yogurt)	62	Milk	43
Rice	31	Milk Tea	37
Banana	24	Potato	20
Lassi	24	Spices	16
Isagbol* &	7	*Jaggery*	15
Dahi		Vegetables	12
Bread	9	Sweets/sugar	8
Dalia*	6	*Moongdal**	8
		Masoor dal	4
		Fried Food	3
		Hot Breast milk	1

Isagbol (fleased husk) is manioc, which is purchased in the market and added to *dahi* (yogurt) as an extender; *dalia* is a wheat/milk porridge; and *moongdal* is a popular type of lentil.

achieve balance. Finally, since the overwhelming desire of mothers is for the diarrhea to stop, foods that are perceived to slow down or decrease the diarrhea (stool-thickening foods) are identified and recommended by mothers. Mothers in Anangpur were somewhat more likely to identify specific foods that will stop or decrease diarrhea, compared to the other two villages.

Chapati, the main staple of North India, tops the "harmful during diarrhea" list (n = 89). Chapati is an unleavened bread that resembles the tortilla of Latin America, but is made of wheat rather than corn. It is usually the main food for everyone, at all meals (in contrast to South India, where rice is the staple). Vegetable curries or chutney often accompany chapati, but chapati alone is the largest contributor of calories. Because of its major role in dietary intake, its withdrawal during diarrhea could have serious consequences if foods high in nutrient density were not substituted.

Jaggery is hard molasses, and is used as a sweetener in place of more expensive refined sugar. *Dal* and *masoor dal* are lentils that are widely consumed in the villages, often as an accompaniment to chapati.

There are differences and similarities among villages regarding beliefs about harmful foods during diarrhea. The high and uniform response across villages that chapati and milk are harmful is testimony to the traditional roots of these beliefs.

Foods are considered harmful during diarrhea because they increase diarrhea or because they are "hot," further aggravating a "hot" disease. Another, less frequently voiced concern is about consuming foods that are heavy and difficult to digest during diarrhea. Mothers in Anangpur are more likely to be concerned that harmful foods increase diarrhea and to believe helpful foods decrease diarrhea, compared to mothers in the other two villages.

Dietary Shifts During Diarrhea. The household interview data on beliefs about diarrhea and diet suggest the likelihood that during diarrhea mothers will change the diet of their children. The critical question is whether behavioral changes in feeding patterns do, in fact, occur, and if so, what they are. If mothers act in accordance with their beliefs, some of the shifts would involve some inconvenience and/or expense for the mother and the household. For example, bananas, which are considered helpful by about one-quarter of mothers, must be purchased, and in the villages of Anangpur and Tilpat this requires a visit to a town market. As was seen in Table 5, fruit is consumed by only a small fraction of children in the villages, and is considered a luxury food by most mothers. Also, *dahi* (yogurt), which more than half of mothers view as helpful, must be either purchased or prepared at a cost of time, money, or both.

Withholding foods during diarrhea has potential consequences for the mother and child. If chapati is withdrawn without adequate substitution, the child may be irritable and hungry (if appetite is not affected by the episode). If it is withdrawn and a substitution made, this may require extra time for the preparation of a helpful food.

Three separate analyses provide the evidence that a dietary shift occurs when children experience diarrhea. First, foods offered at some time during a diarrhea episode are compared to the twenty-four-hour recalls of dietary intake collected for weaned children in the survey. Thus, the helpful or harmful foods offered during diarrhea can be compared to ordinary dietary intakes. Second, dietary diversity scores from the survey and from episode monitoring are compared, with the former data representing normal intakes, and the episodes reflecting diarrhea intakes. Third, dietary diversity scores are compared both during and after diarrhea for the same children (based on the case study data).

Comparison of Household Interview Data and Dietary Recalls

Dietary items from the household interviews and diarrhea case studies were coded as helpful or harmful, based on their categorization by mothers. In the following analysis, twenty-four-hour recalls from the survey are defined as "normal dietary days." During the diarrhea episode monitoring, a total of 136 twenty-four-hour recalls were collected for forty-one weaned children. These are defined as "diarrhea dietary days." In Table 9, the recalls during illness are disaggregated into short duration (< 8 days) and long duration (> 7 days) episodes. A frequency distribution of food items offered in each of the categories allows a rough comparison of food patterns during normal (nonillness) days and during diarrheal illness.

In interpreting the table, it is important to recognize that these are intake days, not children, so that a smaller number of children contribute more days to the case study data than is the situation with normal days. In addition, the survey data were collected during June–August, 1984, whereas the monitoring of diarrhea episodes took place in September–November, 1984. It is possible, therefore, that there are some seasonal differences in diet.[7]

Table 9 shows that for many children dietary patterns continue normally during diarrhea, but in some cases a dietary shift occurs. The direction of the shift is both toward supplementation of the normal diet with helpful foods, and a reduction of some foods that are considered harmful. The shifts are much more pronounced in episodes of increased duration. A chi-square for trend test indicates that there were no statistically significant differences among the three groups.

In summary, there is some evidence of a dietary shift during diarrhea, but more important, an overall maintenance of normal dietary patterns is apparent. Of helpful foods, only bananas are frequently added to the diet of a child suffering from diarrhea. Of harmful foods, there is some reduction in the staple food items, which must involve a nutritional cost for the affected children. The reduction in these foods is much more evident in protracted diarrhea episodes.

Comparison of Dietary Diversity Scores of the Household Survey and Diarrhea Episode Data Sets

A comparison was made of the dietary diversity scores from the survey with the scores of case study children. The mean diversity scores for each data set were compared, using t-tests to assess significance. The case study data were compared at two points with the mean score from the survey data: (1) the last postepisode score for each child, representing more or less normal dietary intakes; and (2) the first diarrhea episode score, representing diarrhea intakes (see Table 10).

The normal intakes from the survey and postconvalescent normal intakes from the case studies are not different. Therefore, a comparison of the normal dietary diversity scores from the survey data can be made with the diarrhea diversity scores from the episode monitoring data set, as shown in Table 11.

There is no statistically significant difference in dietary scores for the two sets of data. Hence, we conclude there is no evidence of a reduction in

TABLE 9

Comparison of Helpful and Harmful Foods Consumed During Fifty Diarrhea Episodes
and from Survey Data (Weaned or Partially Weaned Children)

	Normal Diet n = 192 Nonilness Dietary Days	Percent of Days Food Was Consumed	
		Short Duration n = 36 Diarrhea Days (Episodes < 8 Days)	Long Duration n = 100 Diarrhea Days (Episodes > 7 Days)
"Helpful" Foods			
Banana	1%	5%	22%
Kichuri	4%	0%	12%
Yogurt (*Dahi*)	18%	5%	5%
Rice	11%	16%	13%
Lassi	16%	5%	5%
Misc. Fruits	4%	9%	11%
"Harmful" Foods			
Chapati	94%	89%	70%
Vegetables	77%	67%	57%
Milk	65%	44%	32%
Milk Tea	49%	67%	52%
Potatoes	1%	23%	28%

TABLE 10

Comparison of Dietary Diversity Scores
Normal Dietary Days from Survey
and Postepisode Case Studies

	N	$\overline{X}$	S.D.
Survey	192	3.17	.86
Postepisode Intake	31	3.00	.97

Student's t = 1.01
P = >0.2

TABLE 11

Comparison of Dietary Diversity Scores
Normal Dietary Intakes (Survey Data)
Compared to Diarrhea Day Intakes (Episode Monitoring)

	N	$\overline{X}$	S.D.
Normal (Nonillness)	192	3.17	.86
Diarrhea	35	3.26	.95

Student's t = −.56
P = >0.4

dietary diversity during diarrhea. The interpretation of the data, however, should acknowledge that these are different children.

Comparison of Diversity Scores During and After Diarrhea

A comparison of dietary diversity during and after diarrhea was made for the twenty-seven children in the case episode data set for whom both scores were available. A new variable was created, defined as:

Difference in dietary = Diversity score during diarrhea −
diversity   Diversity score after diarrhea
               (postepisode visit)

The first diarrhea observation visit for each child provided the score during diarrhea; the last postepisode observation visit provided the score for the postepisode period. Thus, the maximum distance between the intervals of diarrhea and postdiarrhea was obtained. This strategy assumes that the last postepisode visit has a greater probability of representing a normal rather than convalescent dietary intake of the child. The comparison, then, is of diarrhea and normal dietary days, and the child provides his or her own benchmark normal score.

If food is withheld, or refused because of loss of appetite during diarrhea, the dietary diversity scores for that period should be lower than scores during the postrecovery or normal period. The results show that for 19 percent of the children dietary diversity scores were higher during diarrhea. Scores were lower for 33 percent of children, and there was no change for 48 percent of children. In two-thirds of the cases the diversity scores were equal or higher during diarrhea, and in one-third the scores were lower.

Based on the two analyses comparing intakes during diarrhea and on normal days, it appears that dietary patterns during diarrhea generally continue normally, but in a minority of episodes—perhaps from one-quarter to one-third of episodes—there is a reduction in the diversity—and probably quantity—of food consumed.

Mothers' Perception of Child Appetite During and After Diarrhea

At each household visit during the case monitoring, mothers were asked if their child's appetite was more, less, or the same as it had been the previous day. Responses were classified as early (1–3 days) and late (4–7 days) in illness and postillness periods. The results are shown in Table 12.

Caution is required in the interpretation of these data because of the small number in some of the cells. In about 40 percent of diarrhea days mothers report that appetite is decreased, and this appears to be slightly more pronounced during the first days of diarrhea. For a nearly equal percentage of days appetite is unchanged, and in a minority, appetite is increased. During the first postepisode (or convalescent) days, child appetite is reported to return to normal (same) for 75 percent, or to be increased among 10–20 percent

TABLE 12

Child Appetite During Diarrhea and Recovery as Reported by Mothers

Appetite	Diarrhea		Recovery	
	Early	Late	Early	Late
More	15%	15%	19%	10%
	(4)	(5)	(8)	(1)
Same	41%	47%	75%	70%
	(11)	(16)	(31)	(7)
Less	44%	38%	5%	10%
	(12)	(13)	(2)	(1)

on observation days. In only a small percentage of early postepisode days is appetite reported to be less. In summary, appetite appears to be reduced during the early period of diarrhea in nearly half of the episodes, and children tend to regain their appetite during the early recovery period. These data accord with mothers' testimonies that appetite loss is a major concern during diarrhea.

Breast-Feeding During Diarrhea. As stated previously, more than 95 percent of mothers surveyed reported that they continue to breast-feed during diarrhea. In the case studies, mothers were asked whether they were breast-feeding the same, more, or less than the day before the visit. There were no significant differences in breast-feeding patterns during the diarrhea and postepisode visits. During diarrhea, 71 percent of mothers said they were breast-feeding normally, 22 percent less, and 7 percent reported more frequent feeding. The same percentages were given in the postepisode visits.

Comparison of Frequency of Feedings During Diarrhea and Health. To assess the effect of diarrhea on frequency of feeding foods and fluids other than breast milk, diarrhea and postdiarrhea observation days were compared using a rank order statistic. The results of a Mann-Whitney U analysis indicate that frequency of feeding is unchanged by diarrhea. However, as with dietary patterns, there is a minority of children for whom feeding frequency declines. This may be a result of changes in maternal behavior, child anorexia and refusal to eat, or both. This is an issue that deserves further study in future research.

Summary and Discussion

Mothers in rural North India hold a wide variety of beliefs about how children should be fed when they have diarrhea. Their cultural system includes ideas about foods that are helpful as well as foods that are harmful for the sick child. While a number of factors probably influence variations among mothers, it appears that older women are more likely to hold beliefs that may have negative consequences for child health. They are more likely to say staple foods are harmful and that children lack appetite and need less food when they have diarrhea. These attitudes may reflect greater adherence to traditional culture or older mothers' increased experiences with medical practitioners.

Analysis of actual dietary intakes during diarrheal episodes shows that for the majority of children, dietary patterns continue as usual. However, whether there are changes in the quantity of foods consumed or shifts in nutrient intake cannot be determined in these data.

For some children a dietary shift occurs at some point during the episode. The shift may take the form of adding a helpful food item, such as fruits, bananas, or kichuri, or the reduction of a harmful food, such as chapati, vegetables, or milk. The role of appetite in this dietary shift is undoubtedly important. Mothers frequently voiced concern about the child refusing solid food, and the data on maternal perception of child appetite during diarrhea suggest that appetite is reduced in a substantial percentage of episodes.

The majority of mothers in the villages are worried about their children becoming weak when they have diarrhea, and many of them link their concerns about weakness to lack of food. Important dietary items, including chapati, may, therefore, not be withdrawn until the diarrhea goes on for more than a few days. This generalization needs to be tested further with additional data.

A number of previous studies have reported that mothers withdraw food during diarrhea. These findings are based mainly on informant testimony of what they would do in hypothetical episodes or did do in past episodes (Khan and Ahmad, 1986; Kendall et al., 1984; Kumar et al., 1985; Srinivasa and Afonso, 1983). There is no question that beliefs about the value or necessity of reducing food quantity (thereby reducing stool output) occurs in many cultures, but documentation of such beliefs should not be interpreted as an indication of widespread "starvation" of children suffering from diarrheal disease.

The results from this study in North India raise a number of cautions and a number of issues for future research. Clearly, it can be very misleading to accept reports from mothers about what they think they should do in the management of diarrheal disease as evidence of their behavior. In the matter of dietary practices the observational data indicate that most mothers do not, as a matter of course, immediately withdraw foods during a diarrheal episode. Many mothers do make alterations in the child's diet, adding foods they regard as helpful and withdrawing harmful foods, but it appears that the majority of mothers do not change their dietary patterns, for the majority of diarrhea episodes. Changes are more likely to occur if the episode continues beyond a few days.

Data generated from unstructured interviews, representing a wide variety of individuals, structures subsequent phases of research. For many settings, a good ethnographic investigation may be sufficient to design the local interventions. The use of "rapid anthropological" methods for public health and nutrition program interventions is becoming increasingly important (Scrimshaw and Hurtado, 1987; Bentley et al., 1988). However, even when conducting preliminary, qualitative research, care must be taken to select households and informants that represent the sociocultural and socioeconomic variability of the community.

The case following methodology is probably the best method for achieving an understanding of household and community diarrhea management. Observations within the household while the child is experiencing diarrhea will help to reconcile differences between reported and actual behavior.

It is important to note that these results were possible only by the use of complementary methods, drawn from both nutrition and anthropology. The methodological approach used in this study combined ethnographic, survey, and case following methodologies, and included both quantitative and qualitative data. In large part, both the fieldwork and data analysis involved a comparison of the findings from the different methods of inquiry.

5

Patients' Use of Freestanding Emergency Centers: A Multimethod Approach to Health Services Research

Barbara Rylko-Bauer

Since the early 1970s in the United States, a new set of alternative health care services has emerged that is part of the traditional biomedical system, yet challenging it, to some extent. This array of options includes surgicenters, birthing centers, various forms of health maintenance organizations (HMOs), retail dental centers, and freestanding emergency centers.[1] Their development has been influenced by converging trends within the health care delivery system, including cost concerns, technological advances, competition generated by a growing physician supply, and the development of corporate structures and capitalistic expansion into all areas of health care delivery (Brown, 1985; Emmons, 1988; Ermann and Gabel, 1985; Gray, 1986; Rylko-Bauer, 1988).

This chapter examines one of these recent innovations, the freestanding emergency center (FEC) from the perspective of how patients perceive and use such a clinic in relation to other options traditionally available for health care.[2] In the process of presenting the findings and analysis from a case study of FECs, several methodological issues are addressed concerning anthropological research on the use of health care services, in particular the value of a varied research methodology and integration of qualitative and quantitative data and analysis. This issue is not new to anthropology (see Pelto and Pelto, 1978), nor to the other social sciences (Cook and Reichardt, 1979; Smith and Louis, 1982), and continues to be of current interest (Bernard, 1988; Brewer and Hunter, 1989; Werner and Schoepfle, 1987a, 1987b; Yin, 1984).

History and Development of FECs

FECs are a noteworthy phenomenon in regard to the historical development of orthodox U.S. medicine. They reflect a number of changes that were occurring in the health care system in the 1980s, including increasing entrepreneurship and explicit commercialization of medicine, as well as the growth of ambulatory care.

FECs are basically walk-in clinics for the treatment of medical problems that do not need the resources of full-service hospital ER. They are not designed to treat life-threatening or serious emergencies, although most can stabilize patients who await an ambulance (Ling and Gold, 1986). Their focus on patient convenience is reflected in short waiting times with no appointment required, extended hours (often open during times when doctors' offices are traditionally closed), and visible locations (such as shopping centers or busy streetcorners). Most of these clinics can be characterized as "urgent care centers," since they treat minor and urgent problems (e.g., sprains, cuts, minor infections, etc.), perform routine services (such as school physicals and immunizations), and offer only limited follow-up care.

FECs were conceived in part to meet a documented need for a more efficient and less costly alternative to the hospital ER for care of nonemergency problems. Studies of ER use in the United States indicate that for the past two decades a large proportion of cases seen (from 33 percent to 85 percent, according to various studies) can be classified as nonurgent. Reasons suggested for this pattern of use include differences in how patients and physicians conceptualize the severity of specific medical problems, and a perceived unavailability of other sources of care at the time of need (Chyba, 1983; Gifford et al., 1980; Kleiman, 1981; Roth and Douglas, 1983; Weinerman et al., 1966).

The FEC industry has grown at a rapid rate. In 1978 fifty-five such facilities were identified in a survey of FECs (Orkand Corporation, 1979), whereas by 1990 the number was expected to grow to 5500 throughout the United States, with an estimated 100 million patient visits per year (National Association for Ambulatory Care, 1985). In the early 1980s FECs were considered quite controversial (American Medical Association, 1985a, 1985b; Burns and Ferber, 1981; Cohen, 1983; Hellstern, 1983; Katzman, 1985). They were established to provide short-term care with no expectation that such contacts would lead to long-term relationships between patient and practitioner. This led to a debate about whether FECs could deliver good patient care without providing continuity of care.

In addition, they were viewed as competing with more established providers such as the hospital ER and the doctor's office. Many of these clinics were set up by entrepreneurial physicians who did not hesitate to market the clinics aggressively through advertising, special discounts, and free services (e.g., blood pressure checks), with an emphasis on patient convenience. This led critics to compare FECs with the fast food industry, spawning epithets such as "Doc-in-the-box" and "7-Eleven Medicine" (Tanner, 1982). Physicians in more traditional practice settings, on the other hand, are still reluctant in many parts of the United States to market their services in this way, despite the lifting of restrictions against professional advertising (Folland, 1987; Rizzo, 1988).

Research Methodology

The research took place in a Midwestern city with a population of about 450,000 that had experienced rapid growth of FECs. Within three years, twelve FECs had opened and were functioning at the time of the study. The purpose of the case study was to examine how patients perceived and used the FEC in relation to the other two major alternatives of emergency and primary care that existed within the formal health care system: the doctor's office and the hospital ER. Was there competition and overlap in services, or were these clinics serving a separate population? Were patients using the FEC to supplement or substitute for other health care sources? What factors influenced patients' decisions to seek care at the FEC?

One of the advantages of the case study and a feature that distinguishes it from other research strategies is that it allows one to examine the social context of the phenomenon under study (Yin, 1984:24). In this instance, the research design included several stages that focused on this larger context.

Data Collection: The Broader Health Care Context

During the first year of the study, data were collected on the orthodox health care institutions already existing in this community, as well as the recently established FECs—their histories, structure and organization, the types of patients treated, and the community's response to the clinics. This provided a broad ethnographic context for the more focused part of the case study that was conducted from May 1983 to January 1984 at one FEC in this community, referred to here as the Prompt Care Clinic (a pseudonym).

Data Collection: The Specific FEC Context

This clinic was selected as the research setting on the basis of criteria such as length of existence, location, patient load, type of practice, stability and size of physician staff, and establishment of entree and rapport. The Prompt Care Clinic was comparable to most of the others in terms of equipment and services offered, and could be characterized as an urgent care center. It was one of the first FECs set up in this city, and had had a steady patient clientele for over two years. It was open twelve hours a day, seven days a week, and at the time of the case study, averaged fifty to sixty patients per day. It also had a small but stable staff of four physicians who rotated coverage, in contrast to some of the other FECs that were staffed from a large pool of physicians who worked part-time at these clinics.

To gain an understanding of how the FEC functioned, visits were made to the Prompt Care Clinic during the course of several months. Interviews were conducted with the staff, as well as the physician-owner of this clinic, who became a key informant. Time was also spent in the waiting room of the clinic, observing activities and collecting data on who came, when and with whom, the amount of time patients waited to be seen, and the nature of their health problems, as well as staff-patient interactions that occurred in this public area. Informal interviews were also conducted with patients while they waited.

This ethnographic approach (which was primarily qualitative, but included some quantification of patient flow, waiting times, etc.) provided insights into how the clinic was used and offered a context for analyzing the data collected from subsequent patient surveys. It was also valuable in designing a sampling strategy and refining subsequent data-gathering instruments.

Data Collection: Patient Survey at the Prompt Care Clinic

The third phase of the case study was a survey in which patients completed a questionnaire as they sat in the waiting room of the clinic. This instrument was administered by me during a two-week period.

Comparability of case study findings is enhanced if concepts, procedures, and variables are operationalized in ways similar to those of relevant past studies (Yin, 1984:33). Reliability has also been a problem for case study research, and can be addressed in part by making explicit as many steps of the research design as possible (Yin, 1984:40). These issues of comparability and reliability have also been problematic in anthropological research (Pelto and Pelto, 1978:43,77). For this reason, parts of the questionnaire were based on methods and concepts from other studies of health care use in the United States (e.g., Aday et al., 1980; Bohland, 1984; Bonham and Corder, 1981; Chyba, 1983; National Center for Health Statistics, 1982). For example, the variable "urgency of the medical problem" (see Table 1) was operationalized in the same way as found in past research on ER use (Gifford et al., 1980; Weinerman et al., 1966).

The sampling strategy was also based on methods previously developed in studies of ER use (Jonas et al., 1976; Roth and Douglas, 1983; Weinerman et al., 1966). It was not possible to draw a random sample of patients from a list of those who had attended the clinic, since the clinic owner felt that re-

TABLE 1

Urgency of Current Medical Problem as Perceived by FEC Patients
Who Used ER in the Past for Similar Problem[a]

Perception Of Need For Care		#	%
Within minutes		4	10.0
Within 1–2 hours		7	17.5
Within 2–12 hours	16 ⎫		
Within 12–24 hours	7 ⎬	29	72.5
Within days	6 ⎭		
Total		40	100.0
No response		4	

[a] This table presents data for the subsample of forty-four respondents who used the ER in the past for a similar problem.

leasing patients' addresses and phone numbers would breach confidentiality. Instead, patients were approached as they waited in the clinic.

An effort was made to get a relatively even distribution of time periods throughout the week, based on the assumption that different categories of people would frequent the clinic at different times (e.g., those employed during the day might come after work; parents who stayed at home with young children might come during the day, etc.). To take account of such varying demographic patterns of patient flow, two blocks of time (two hours each) were randomly selected for each day of the two-week survey period, and patients were sampled who came to the clinic during these times.[3]

An effort was also made to minimize selection bias by developing a set of rules for sampling patients that took into consideration constraints of the research setting. These rules are discussed in detail in note 4. Most significant was the fact that patient flow in a walk-in clinic tends to be irregular and unpredictable, which makes systematic sampling by volume (e.g., every fourth patient) difficult. There were times when the waiting room was empty for an hour, and other times when it was crowded with patients arriving in rapid succession. This problem was solved by choosing a patient every thirty minutes, or as close to this time interval as was possible. This allowed enough time for the study to be explained and for collection of additional data (from observations and discussions with patients) that served to supplement the survey findings.[5]

The acceptance rate was very high; of the 293 patients who came to the clinic during the sampling periods, ninety-nine were approached and ninety actually filled out the questionnaire. Data from this survey were analyzed using descriptive and correlational statistics.

Data Collection: Follow-up Interviews with Patients

Several months later, follow-up interviews were conducted with patients who had participated in the questionnaire survey. This was a self-
selected rather than random sample, since only those patients were contacted
who had initially agreed to such interviews, which took place at either the
respondent's home or place of work. The data were analyzed by content analysis as well as descriptive statistics.

The interview findings served to supplement the survey results, and
they demonstrate the value of combining qualitative and quantitative methods. For example, the questionnaire included a set of items asking patients to
compare coming to the Prompt Care Clinic with going to the hospital ER or
to the doctor's office. Three-point scales were used to tap seven dimensions.[6]
This provided a quantitative assessment of how patients compared the FEC to
other sources on features such as cost, waiting time, and others. During the
follow-up interviews, open-ended questions were asked about the FEC visits,
the illness episode, how FECs were similar to or differed from the ER and the
doctor's office, and about their decision to go to the FEC. The resulting descriptive data provided additional insights into patients' perceptions and
decision-making process, and were used in the analysis both to corroborate
and to elaborate the quantitative data, as will be demonstrated.

Case Study Results: Analysis of Patients' Use of the FEC

The FEC patients who participated in the questionnaire survey were
predominantly young, with a mean age of 26.9 years, and were equally divided among males and females. They were at a relatively high socioeconomic level, as evidenced by the fact that over half had at least some college
education, more than one-third had an annual family income (in 1983) of
$25,000 or more (with a sample median of $21,379). In addition, the most
common form of payment for care was private insurance (59.5 percent), followed by cash or credit card (45 percent). Medicare and Medicaid were used
in fewer than ten percent of the cases. These results are similar to findings of
nationwide FEC surveys, and reflect the preferred locations for such clinics
(e.g., in suburbs or neighborhoods with high employment rates, young families, etc.), and their payment policies (Orkand Corporation, 1979, 1983;
Stevenson, 1983).

Use of FECs in Relation to the Emergency Room

As was noted in the introduction to this chapter, FECs were conceived
in part as an alternative to the hospital ER for nonurgent care. The case study
results suggest that some patients are, in fact, shifting from the ER to use the
FEC for certain types of problems. Patients were asked what they did in the

TABLE 2

Summary of FEC Compared to Emergency Room:
Choice of Majority of Respondents (>50%) on Each
Measure of Perception

Dimensions	Perception	% Of Respondents
Cost	FEC less expensive	73.8
Hours		[a]
Location	FEC more convenient	63.5
Waiting time	Wait less time	81.9
Quality of care	Similar	62.7
Atmosphere of setting	FEC more pleasant	63.5
Courtesy of staff	FEC more courteous	52.4

[a] Responses were distributed over all three choices with no clear majority; the greatest number of these, 41.5%, viewed the FEC and ER as similar.

past for similar problems, before FECs were established, and 51.2 percent stated that they went to the hospital ER. Table 1 looks at how this subgroup of respondents assessed the urgency of their current medical problem. Only about one-fourth of these former ER users felt that they needed care either within minutes of coming to the FEC (10 percent) or within one to two hours (17.5 percent). The rest (72.5 percent) viewed their problem as not of immediate urgency, requiring attention either within two to twenty-four hours or within days. Thus, most of these patients came to the Prompt Care Clinic with a less urgent problem, which in the past they would have taken to the ER.

In an effort to identify factors that influenced this decision to come to the FEC, patients were asked to list why they decided to go there instead of to the ER or the doctor's office. Within this subgroup of former ER users the most frequently noted reasons were a shorter waiting time (mentioned by 43.1 percent), better or closer location (29.5 percent), and lower cost (15.9 percent).

Patients were also asked to compare the FEC to the emergency room on seven dimensions, using a three-point scale (see "Research Methodology" and note 6). Table 2 summarizes these data, by presenting the perception of the majority of respondents on each of these features. It is clear that more than half of the patients viewed the Prompt Care Clinic more favorably with respect to cost, location, waiting time, atmosphere, and courtesy. Similarity between the FEC and the ER was indicated only on quality of care. These access and convenience factors are likely to be important in the patient's decision about where to go for care.

In the follow-up interviews with twenty-two of the patients, many discussed their negative view of the ER as potentially exposing them to other patients who might be abusive or severely injured, or even dying. Another feature mentioned was the impersonal and hectic atmosphere of the ER, as indicated by the following quote:

> Have a more pleasant atmosphere [at the FEC]. Almost like sitting in your living room, with lots less trauma . . . In the ER [you] have many people moving around, a loudspeaker with the doctor being paged, a tense atmosphere.

Respondents were not asked specifically to identify the circumstances under which they would choose to go to the ER as compared to the FEC. However, in the course of the interviews, fourteen of the twenty-two respondents (64 percent) volunteered comments that pointed to severity of illness as the major determinant of where the patient would go for care. There seemed to be a clear choice between the emergency room for very serious or life-threatening problems (as defined by the patients), and the FEC for minor emergencies. Quite a few of the twenty-two patients (41 percent) also made comments suggesting that the ER was an inappropriate place for the treatment of minor or nonurgent problems. The following are examples of both types of comments.

> One patient felt "the ER is for accident victims, other serious things; for really hurt people. I feel guilty running to the hospital for small things. The Prompt Care Clinic is the place to go when you need such attention right away, or are sick and can't get in to see your doctor."
>
> Another patient saw the FEC as a variation on the ER "as an extension of the hospital to take care of the less seriously injured . . . They're there for taking the load off the ER with minor emergencies. However, things like convulsions, emergencies are not in their line . . . Severity of illness would determine if I would go to the emergency room or to the Prompt Care Clinic."

One interpretation of these data is that from the patients' perspective, the FEC fills a long-standing need within the existing health care system. Whereas other providers tended to view the FECs as competitors and perhaps even challengers of the status quo (American Medical Association, 1982; Burns and Ferber, 1981; Potter, 1982; Richards, 1984), patients did not seem to question the legitimacy of these clinics, and instead viewed them as logical and appropriate sources of after-hours care and for the treatment of minor problems.

Use of FECs in Relation to the Doctor's Office

Given the nature of FECs, with their walk-in policy and episodic care, it was hypothesized that a significant proportion of FEC users would not have a regular source of care, and might even be recent arrivals in this community. In cases where patients did have a family doctor, it was expected that they would be using the FEC primarily when they were unable to contact their doctor. This did not turn out to be the case.

Most of the patient sample (85.1 percent) did have some sort of regular source of care, and of these, 78.2 percent were either medical or osteopathic physicians. When asked what they did for their current problem prior to their FEC visit, over three-fourths of the respondents who had a regular doctor indicated that they actually used the FEC as their first point of medical contact; i.e., coming to the FEC was the first thing they did (see Figure 1). In addition, one-third of this subgroup of patients came during times when their own doctor's office was likely to be open (i.e., weekdays from 10:30 a.m. to 4:30 p.m.)[7] In only twelve cases (19.4 percent) did respondents with a personal physician actually try to contact him or her before deciding to come to the FEC. These findings serve as one indication that the FEC was competing

FIGURE 1

Respondents with a Physician as a Regular Source of Care: Categorized According to Behavior Prior to FEC Visit and Time of FEC Visit

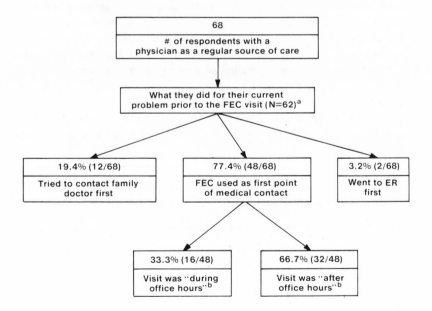

[a]There were six cases with no response for this variable.
[b]See note 7 for an explanation of these time periods.

with the doctor's office, since patients appeared to perceive the FEC as one of several alternatives to choose from, rather than as a point of second, third, or last resort.

In addition, FEC users appear to be long-term residents of the community. About three-quarters (74.4 percent) of the respondents reported living in this city for more than five years, and were probably aware of the various available alternatives for health care. Only 3.5 percent of the sample indicated that they had lived in the area for less than a year, and another 5.8 percent lived outside the area. In fact, this FEC was functioning as a neighborhood clinic to some extent, since slightly over half of the respondents (52.8 percent) lived within four miles of the Prompt Care Clinic.

Examining how patients perceived the FEC points to some of the factors that explain why patients were shifting at least part of their care from their regular doctor to the FEC. One set of items in the questionnaire asked patients to compare the FEC to the doctor's office on seven dimensions, using a three-point scale. As Table 3 indicates, the majority of respondents saw these two sources of care as similar in cost, quality of care, atmosphere of setting, and courtesy of staff. However, the FEC was viewed more positively in terms of convenient hours, location, and a shorter waiting time.

Patients do appear to spend a relatively short amount of time in the FEC waiting to be seen, since the average for the ninety respondents who participated in the survey was 15.6 minutes.[8] Other FEC studies have reported similar findings (Chesteen et al., 1986; Miller, 1983). These values can be contrasted with data from the National Health Care Expenditures Study, where respondents reported spending an average of 38.2 minutes waiting to be seen in the hospital ER, and 29.4 minutes in the doctor's office for a scheduled visit (Kasper and Berk, 1981).

During the follow-up interviews it was evident that this was an issue of special concern, and that waiting in the doctor's office was a fairly common

TABLE 3

Summary of FEC Compared to Doctor's Office: Choice of Majority
of Respondents (>50%) on Each Measure of Perception

Dimensions	Perception	% Of Respondents
Cost	Similar	63
Hours	FEC more convenient	94.1
Location	FEC more convenient	62.5
Waiting time	Wait less time	59.3
Quality of care	Similar	81.9
Atmosphere of setting	Similar	73.6
Courtesy of staff	Similar	80.7

experience. Such delays often result from overscheduling that is done to maximize the doctor's productive time. This implies, of course, that the doctor's time is considered more valuable than that of the patient (Schwartz, 1975:7). Patients also interpreted their experience in this way, as the following quote demonstrates:

> If they [FECs] force the physicians to be more bending to the general public, then good. People don't get sick from nine to five . . . Doctors expect people to adjust. No matter when you have an appointment, you have to wait. I'm professional in my job. My time is valuable. Why should I be expected to wait an hour? If the doctor had an appointment with me, I certainly wouldn't expect him to wait for me.

Such comments of frustration for having to wait in the doctor's office, despite having an appointment, were spontaneously expressed by nine out of twenty-two patients who were interviewed. This type of problem is less likely to occur at the FEC (unless it is understaffed), because patients may walk in at any time and the clinics are geared toward an efficient processing of patients. In fact, under these circumstances it is the physician who may have to wait, if the clinic is not busy.

The follow-up interviews also suggest that patients tend to use the FEC situationally to supplement rather than substitute for their family doctor, based on two factors: perceived availability of the doctor, and nature of the problem (its severity and whether it was episodic, chronic, or routine in nature).

Almost a third of these respondents made comments, such as the following, indicating that they would go to the FEC if the family doctor was not available.

> If this problem had occurred during regular office hours, I would have called my family doctor to see what to do. Might go [to FEC] in the future under certain circumstances if my regular doctor is not in his office, and if it's not serious enough to go to the hospital.

Of course, availability as defined by patients may be based on an actual attempt at contact, on knowledge that the office is closed, or a perception that it would be difficult to get an appointment on short notice, based on past experience.

Others mentioned the nature of the problem as a factor in deciding if they would go to the FEC. During the interviews over a third (36.4 percent) made a distinction between "regular care" and "emergency situations," as demonstrated in the following comments:

One patient stated that she would not go to the doctor's office for emergencies, in most cases. "The Prompt Care Clinic deals with [minor] emergencies, whereas the doctor's office is more for regular problems."

Another respondent indicated that if the FEC had not existed, she would probably go to the ER for minor things such as a sprain or break. It was not worth bothering her doctor because he'd send her there anyway. She uses her family doctor more for checkups and prescriptions. "Doctors now don't like to deal with minor emergencies; they tend to send patients on to the ER."

These comments suggest that there are some problems, defined as "minor emergencies," that patients feel more comfortable taking to the FEC, and there is another set of "regular problems" that patients might choose to take to either the doctor's office or the FEC, depending in part on their perception of the relative availability of these sources of care.

The situational nature of the decision to use the FEC is also reflected in the large number (42.7 percent) of survey respondents who reported that their visit to the Prompt Care Clinic was a spur-of-the-moment decision made while they were out taking care of other business.[9] These unplanned visits tended to be within a few hours of onset of the health problem, were almost entirely for injury or illness, and respondents were more likely to live relatively close to the FEC.[10] Interestingly enough, there was no significant relationship between unplanned versus planned visits, and the respondent's perceived urgency of the problem ($\chi^2 = .08$, 2df). In other words, features of convenience rather than a perceived need to receive care immediately seemed to be the salient factors in this decision for many of the respondents.

Relative Importance of Factors in Deciding Where to Seek Care

The survey data suggest that factors of convenience and access are important in the decision to seek care at the FEC. Another feature that distinguishes the FEC from the doctor's office is continuity of care, which stresses the importance of an ongoing, continuous relationship between the patient and the doctor. FECs, on the other hand, tend to provide episodic care, and in the early 1980s were criticized on this point by other primary care providers (American Medical Association, 1982).

It is not clear whether continuity of care is more of an ideological construct or if it truly guides primary care practice today. There is some disagreement in the literature about the meaning of continuity, its relationship to quality of care, and its relative importance vis-a-vis other factors (Rogers and

Curtis, 1980; Wall, 1981). Some studies indicate that patients differ from physicians in their perception of its meaning and importance (Chatterton et al., 1982; Parker et al., 1976). In fact, the rapid growth of FECs raises the question of the extent to which patients value continuity and consider it an important factor in deciding where to seek care.

During the follow-up interviews, the twenty-two respondents were asked to rank eight features (derived from the earlier stages of research) as factors that might be considered in deciding where to go for routine health care or for a minor emergency. They were asked to think of general rather than specific situations, and to focus on problems that potentially could be taken to the family doctor, the ER, or the FEC.[11]

Table 4 lists the eight factors, which represent four general concepts; quality, access, continuity of care, and cost. For each participant, the most important factor was assigned eight points, down to the least important, which was given one point. The values for each factor were then added up to get a total number of points, and divided by the number of respondents who completed this task. The resulting mean ranks have a descriptive rather than statistical meaning, since this is ordinal and not interval level data. The higher the mean value for a factor, the greater the number of respondents who assigned it a relatively high ranking.

As is evident from Table 4, a large number of respondents considered quality of care most important in deciding where to go for medical attention. It is also clear from this table that access was generally assigned a higher priority than continuity of care. Two of the access factors, waiting time and hours, formed a cluster with mean rank values of 5.6 and 5.2 respectively. The next cluster of values (ranging from 4.3 to 4.0) was made up of the continuity of care factors, as well as another access factor, travel time. Least important were the cost factors, which probably reflected the high proportion of respondents who had some form of insurance coverage.

The fact that patients generally ranked access above continuity does not necessarily mean that they did not value the latter. Their approach, however, was pragmatic. It is evident from the comments accompanying the ranking task that many patients distinguished between regular and emergency situations. The ability to see the same doctor, for example, was considered by one respondent as

> important in general or if you have a chronic disease, but I don't think it's important for an emergency situation.

Analysis of interview data indicates that many patients also differentiated between the FEC and the family doctor as far as the nature of the relationship and interaction were concerned. Some patients characterized the FEC as

TABLE 4

Ranking of Factors Related to the Decision of Where to Seek Health Care

Factors As Presented To Respondents[a]	Concept	Total # Points	Mean Rank (N = 21)
Quality of the medical care	Quality of care	148	7.0
Amount of time you have to wait before the doctor can see you	Access	118	5.6
Convenience of hours of the doctor or the clinic	Access	110	5.2
Ability to see the same doctor each time	Continuity of care	91	4.3
Travel time needed to get to the doctor	Access	87	4.1
Availability of my past medical records to the doctor	Continuity of care	85	4.0
Cost of the medical care	Cost	64	3.0
Methods of payment that are accepted	Cost	53	2.5

Note: These factors are separated into clusters, based on total number of rank points.

[a] There was a fair degree of agreement among the respondents as to how they ranked these various factors, measured by W, the coefficient of concordance (Kerlinger, 1973:292–95). W = .394; significant at α = .005, with F = 10.72. The average rank order correlation among interviewees = .32 (see note 7).

"anonymous or quickie medicine." The family doctor, on the other hand, was seen as offering personalized care. One respondent summed up this distinction very well when he remarked that "the doctor treats the person, the Prompt Care Clinic treats the problem."

Nevertheless, many patients appeared to have a different set of priorities and needs when it came to emergency situations, and as the following quote suggests, getting the problem treated was at the top of the list.

> You do get a secure feeling knowing your doctor, knowing the face that will be coming through the door. In choosing and in going to him you get to know his basic philosophy and approach to health care. But if it's an emergency you don't really care about all that, [you] just want it taken care of.

Conclusions

Implications for the Study of Health Services Delivery

This case study of how patients perceived and used the FEC suggests a situationally oriented health care-seeking process. It appears that the FEC was being used primarily by patients who already had a regular provider, and that in many cases the FEC was their first choice of care, rather than a point of last resort. Patients tended to perceive the FEC as being more similar to the doctor's office than to the hospital ER; nevertheless, this clinic was competing with both types of providers, as evidenced by the use of the FEC for the treatment of problems that patients would have taken elsewhere in the past.

The severity and the nature of the problem (whether an emergency or routine case) appeared to be key determinants in choosing between the ER, the doctor's office, and the FEC. Once patients decided that a problem or health care need was appropriate for treatment at the FEC, then perceived availability of the family doctor, as well as other factors related to convenience and access played a role in the decision of where to seek care. Which factors had the greatest relevance depended on the nature of the health problem, the time of day, where it occurred, and other aspects of the social context, as well as what resources the patient saw as available to him or her at the moment. This is, in fact, a very adaptive approach to health care-seeking.

Much of the literature on use of health care services in the U.S. has dealt with the decision *to* seek care, rather than looking at *how* patients choose among various health care alternatives. This, to some extent, reflects the assumption by researchers of a fairly uniform, biomedically dominated health care system in the United States (Zola, 1972). In anthropology, the focus has been more on the differential use of health care alternatives, primarily in non-Western settings. There has been a recognition of the multiple factors (cultural, social, economic, etc.) that influence such choices, and more recently, the importance of the context within which such decisions are made, since this can vary with each illness episode (Kroeger, 1983; Stoner, 1985). The recent growth of alternatives within the U.S. biomedical system (Gesler, 1988; Goldstein et al., 1988; Levin and Coreil, 1986), underscores the importance of recognizing that this decision-making process is a dynamic one, and that salient factors affecting individual treatment choices will vary depending on the person's assessment of the particular situation (Mechanic, 1979).

FECs also raise questions about the nature of the doctor-patient relationship, since by definition the encounters are relatively short, episodic, and there is no guarantee that the patient will see the same doctor on subsequent visits. It appears that patients come to the FEC because of the services offered, and may even view the doctors as basically interchangeable. This is similar to the situation in the hospital ER (where the patient comes for reasons other than that a particular doctor is on duty), but differs from the way in which a doctor's office functions. In fact, organized medicine has been very protective of the "right" of patients to choose their physician (American Medical Association, 1988:12–13), based partly on the assumption that it is the particular physician and his or her skills or reputation that form the basis of a patient's choice. FECs, as a new mode of health care delivery, provide an opportunity to examine such past assumptions and current changes that may be occurring in how patients seek care and how they view the providers of that care.

Policy Relevance of the Case Study

This study was not commissioned by a client group to address a problem or set of issues. However, it did have policy relevance, because it was found by the National Center for Health Services Research (recently renamed the Agency for Health Care Policy and Research) to provide descriptive data on a relatively new and controversial innovation in health care delivery.[12]

At the time of the case study, there were a number of public policy-related issues being raised concerning FECs (see Rylko-Bauer, 1988 for a discussion of issues and impact of FECs nationwide). Some critics charged that these clinics, through their payment policies and emphasis on nonurgent care, drew healthier, paying patients from the ER, leaving the hospital to subsidize the twenty-four-hour emergency room.

A related question was whether FECs were primarily serving the more prosperous segment of the population, thereby supporting the continuation of a class-segregated health care system. Findings from several FEC studies, including this one, suggest that this may be the case to some extent, since patients tend to be from a relatively high socioeconomic level. There was also concern about the potential overlap of services with both the ER and the private practitioner, and the competition rather than integration of these clinics with the rest of the health care system. Although the case study could not address this question of integration, the findings did suggest that even though FECs were competing with other providers, they were also filling a long-standing need for nonurgent, after-hours care.

Methodological Implications

This study used a variety of data-gathering techniques, as well as adaptations of a sampling strategy and concepts from other studies of health care services in the United States. Ethnographic techniques such as observation of daily behavior in the clinics, informal discussions, and key informant interviews were combined with examination of documents and archival records, a questionnaire survey, and both open-ended and focused interviews. The use of multiple sources of data is a key element in conducting effective case studies (Yin, 1984:89–91), and in this case it provided a means of addressing the problems and complexities of doing research on the use of FECs in the United States.

The value of such an approach is well recognized within applied anthropology (van Willigen and DeWalt, 1985:3). There have been a number of studies demonstrating the utility of an integrated methodology that includes both qualitative and quantitative data and analysis (e.g., Barger and Reza, 1989; Boone, 1989; Gilbert, 1989; Reeves et al., 1987; Trotter, 1987). Such a strategy provides opportunities for developing innovative ways of studying complex social phenomena, and it increases research reliability and validity by allowing for corroboration of evidence, elaboration of specific findings within a broader sociocultural context, and fleshing out of abstract numbers (i.e., demonstrating that the findings are about real people and real problems) (Pelto and Pelto, 1978; Rossman and Wilson, 1985; Yin, 1984). This not only makes sense in terms of research quality, but also increases the potential for impacting policy and practice.

It has been suggested that anthropology's limited success as a policy science is due in part to the relative lack of methodological rigor and sophistication in the use of quantitative techniques (Weaver, 1985). The inclusion of quantitative data and statistical analysis may well increase credibility of the research findings with decision makers. This can be particularly important in situations of political debate, where data have to be convincing and the policymaker cannot afford to have the research discounted because of uncertain methodology (Weiss and Bucuvalas, 1980).

On the other hand, there is also evidence that qualitative research is valued by policymakers because it is seen as relevant, concrete, and more likely to be usable (Beyer and Trice, 1982; van de Vall et al., 1976). Thus, a strategy

that creatively combines qualitative and quantitative methods and analysis
may well increase the potential for utilization of anthropological research
findings in both the development of public policy and its implementation
(Beyer and Trice, 1982; Gilbert, 1989; Rylko-Bauer et al., 1989; Schensul,
1987).

6

The Sociocultural Environment in the Genesis and Amelioration of Opium Dependence

Joseph Westermeyer

As an anthropology student and physician in the early 1960s, I wanted to work as a physician while also undertaking a field study. An opportunity arose to work with a refugee relief program in Laos. My original plan was to study psychosomatic disorders among refugees. After unsuccessfully pursuing this plan for a half-year in Laos, a new study was adopted midstream: the study of opium, its agroeconomics, uses, advantages, and disadvantages. This new study was formulated with methodologic principles in mind as outlined by Pelto (1970). These principles were as follows: (1) Listen, observe, ask, learn, seek many teachers (the qualitative task); this step informs step 2. (2) Whenever possible, count, measure, compare, analyze statistically (the quantitative task); step 1 plus step 2 facilitate step 3. (3) Examine the topic under consideration from several points of view, i.e., separate samples, methods, cultures, topics (the "many observations" task); this may eventually lead to step 4. (4) Careful descriptive work in steps 1 to 3 by individual researchers should permit at least microtheory building, and possibly contribute to macrotheory building through subsequent work by other researchers.

Using this strategy, I began a series of projects that were to continue over the 1965–75 decade in Laos. Over the subsequent decade, 1975–85, efforts continued with indigenous collaborators in several countries of Asia. As the third decade began in 1985, refugee opium addicts from Asia were being studied here in the U.S. These activities are described in the next section.

Methods of Study

Chronology

These studies on opium began in Xieng Khouang province, northern Laos, in 1965 and continued up to 1989 in Minnesota (where opium smoking persists among refugees from Laos). During the interim, a total of four years were spent in Asia on the "opium trail." The first two years (1965–67) were in Laos, primarily involved in the qualitative task (Pelto's step 1), with some early quantitative work (Westermeyer, 1971). Over the subsequent several years (1967–75), six additional trips—each about two months in duration—were made to collect further data in Laos and to consult with the Ministries of Public Health and Social Welfare in Laos regarding the large number of refugee opium addicts in the country. At this point there was considerable expansion of the quantitative task (step 2), with studies in several community and clinical settings using various sampling approaches (step three). In 1977 several weeks were also spent at addiction treatment facilities in Hong Kong, the Philippines, Singapore, Kuala Lampur, Penang, Djakarta, Bangkok, and Rangoon under the aegis of the Public Health Division/USAID and the Special Office on Drug Abuse Prevention (White House). This 1977 work entailed interviews with opium users, their families, and various local people whose work involved opium addicts (e.g., social and psychological scientists, physicians, nurses, social workers, police). It was the beginning of efforts to facilitate step four, the involvement of numerous researchers on the topic with many sources of data.

In 1977 the World Health Organization (WHO), goaded by its parent agency, the United Nations, initiated the study of opium use and dependence in several countries of Southeast Asia, the Middle East, and Africa. This provided further opportunity to work with colleagues from about twenty countries, some of whom replicated the earlier Laotian studies in other samples. From 1977 to 1990 I spent approximately one year (over some twenty trips) in Thailand (Westermeyer, 1980a, 1980b), Hong Kong, Malaysia, and India, with several meetings in Geneva (WHO headquarters). During this extended project, in which I served as a consultant to WHO, collaboration was established with colleagues in Hong Kong, the Philippines, Malaysia, Thailand, Nigeria, Egypt, Pakistan, Afghanistan, Bangladesh, Burma, Vietnam, Indonesia, and Singapore.

From 1985 to 1991, a new opium project appeared serendipitously. I had established a psychiatric clinic for Indochinese refugees in 1977. Beginning in 1985, a number of refugee opium addicts sought treatment at that clinic. This has provided yet another opportunity to study opium use, as well as opium dependence and its treatment.

Topics Under Study

Initially the agroeconomics and sociocultural aspects of poppy culture and opium commerce were studied in Laos. The great diversity of cultural groups and ecological niches throughout Laos provided many "experiments in nature" vis-a-vis opium. The peripatetic nature of my public health work at certain times of the year allowed me to visit many areas of the country, staying in the homes of village chiefs, health workers, and farmers (Westermeyer, 1971, 1982).

Once the social, economic, and cultural context of poppy and opium were appreciated, the next step was to study opium users and opium dependent persons. The prevalence rate of users (number of people in a population at any one time who were users, but not addicted) was small, and such subjects were difficult to obtain. In contrast, certain ethnic groups had a high prevalence rate of opium-dependent persons, or addicts, and they could be readily obtained as subjects. Subsequent work by myself in Laos and by colleagues in Thailand (Poshyachinda et al., 1978; Suwanwela et al., 1977) indicated that addicted persons usually remained secretive about their addiction during the first few to several months, but very few could maintain the fiction that they were not addicted beyond the first year. Addicts were studied in various contexts: several relatively undisturbed villages, a few refugee sites, opium dens, and a general hospital. Studies included both individual case studies (Westermeyer, 1974a, 1974b, 1977a) and prevalence rates in various communities (Westermeyer, 1979, 1981a).

Next, an opportunity arose to study addicts seeking treatment. The Buddhist Women's Auxiliary, in cooperation with the Ministry of Social Welfare in Laos, made arrangements to send several hundred refugee addicts to treatment at a temple in Thailand. Unexpectedly, several thousand addicts—refugees and nonrefugees—from diverse ethnic groups around the country appeared for treatment. I was invited to visit the temple and to study the addicts there. Data were obtained on over a thousand addicted people, mostly villagers. In view of the unexpectedly large number of addicts wanting treatment, a decision was made by the Laotian Ministry of Health to establish a medically oriented treatment program for addicts. I was invited to develop, consult, and evaluate this effort during five trips to Laos over the period 1972–75. These efforts provided an opportunity to make several comparisons as follows:

- Addicts *in situ* in their home villages vs. addicts seeking treatment (Westermeyer, 1981b);
- Addicts from various ethnic groups in Laos, including tourists and other foreign visitors (Westermeyer, 1971, 1977a, 1978a; Westermeyer and Berger, 1977; Berger and Westermeyer, 1977);
- Addicts choosing treatment in the Buddhist temple vs. addicts choosing treatment in the medical setting (Westermeyer and Bourne, 1978; Westermeyer 1980a, 1980b);
- Treatment outcome in the Buddhist temple vs. treatment outcome in the medical program (Westermeyer, 1979; Westermeyer et al., 1978);

- The effect of community factors on treatment outcome (Westermeyer and Bourne, 1978).

In the course of these studies, heroin addiction appeared in certain areas of Laos for the first time; this was also studied and described (Westermeyer, 1976; Westermeyer and Bourne, 1977; Westermeyer and Peng, 1977a, 1977b). Efforts at self-help among refugee opium addicts were also described (Westermeyer, 1973). In 1982 a book was prepared to review this work over the decade 1965–75 (Westermeyer, 1983).

The work of colleagues in other countries is not addressed in this paper. However, a book in progress does cover these efforts, most of which remain unpublished. Currently, refugee opium smokers from Laos are being studied in Minnesota. Up to this time, the study of these expatriate addicts has been primarily descriptive (Westermeyer et al., 1989).

Samples

As already suggested, numerous samples have been studied over time. They include the following:

- Poppy farmers, both addicted and nonaddicted, and opium merchants;
- Opium addicts in villages, refugee relocation sites, opium dens, hospitals in Laos and the U.S., a Buddhist temple, and a medical treatment facility for addicts;
- Opium addicts from several indigenous Asian ethnic groups in Laos (i.e., Lao, Hmong, several tribal groups) (Westermeyer, 1980c);
- Expatriate Asians and Caucasians in Laos addicted to opium and heroin (e.g., Chinese, Thai, Vietnamese, Europeans, Australians, North Americans).

Data collection methods varied with the research topic under consideration. They included field observation, interviewing, questionnaires, clinical observations, and clinical rating scales.

Variables

The following topics were studied:

- When, where, why, and how poppy was grown, and by whom (with observation, interviewing);
- Modes of opium commerce (observation, interviews);
- Mode and duration of opium use in addicts (observation, interviews, questionnaires) (Westermeyer and Neider, 1982);

- Attitudes, norms, and practices with regard to opium in several ethnic groups (observations, interviews);
- Demographic and clinical characteristics of opium users and addicts (interviews, questionnaires, clinical rating scales);
- Prevalence rates of opium addicts in various communities and ethnic groups (interviews);
- Demographic and clinical characteristics of addicts seeking treatment (interviews, clinical observations) (Westermeyer and Peng, 1978);
- Dosage levels and durations of medication needed to abate withdrawal symptoms in opium addicts (clinical observations) (Westermeyer, 1983);
- Posttreatment course, e.g., abstinence, craving, social affiliations (interviews, informants, questionnaires) (Westermeyer and Soudaly, 1984);
- Acculturation of refugee opium addicts in the U.S. (observation, interviews, questionnaires);
- Comparison of Hmong addicts in the U.S. with Hmong addicts in Asia (interview, questionnaires, clinical observations).

A summary of results obtained in these various investigations is presented in the next section.

Findings

Agroeconomics of Poppy

Poppy is a labor-intensive cash crop, requiring careful preparation of the field, weeding, thinning, and well-timed, high-effort harvesting. Despite these disadvantages, poppy offers numerous advantages as a cash crop in the Golden Triangle, as follows:

1. It is grown at a time when cereal food crops (e.g., rice, corn) are not grown.
2. Poppy takes a small amount of nutrients out of the soil, so that plots can be used for years and even decades (unlike soils farmed with upland rice that can be used only for a few years, followed by dormant periods of a few decades or longer).
3. The climate, soil, and topography in the region yields a high-potency product (i.e., 10 percent morphine or above).
4. Although the total poppy production effort is lengthy, intensive, and laborious, parts of it are light enough to be performed by older children, women, and the elderly.
5. The numerous ridges and heavy monsoon rainfall in the Annamite Chain make roads difficult to build and maintain. Thus, a cash crop must be compact in order to be transported by human backpack,

mountain pony, or mule. Potatoes, fruits, or coffee can be grown, but are too bulky to transport economically out of the area. One family's annual opium production amounts to several kilograms of smoking opium.

6. Insecurity, climate, topography, and remoteness preclude rapid shipment. Opium has a long "shelf life" and actually gains in percentage morphine content over a period of months.

7. Due to its long storage time and high value per unit weight, it can be used like money, as a standard item of barter. That is, it possesses the elements of currency in parts of Southeast Asia.

8. Opium can be used as an effective, or at least symptomatic medicament for local diseases (diarrhea, dysentery, bronchitis, pneumonia, tuberculosis, malaria).

9. As a cash crop, opium permits the upland farmer to enter the international economy and purchase trade items (cloth, blankets, umbrellas, shoes, iron bars, pots, salt, canned fish, paper, pencils, radio, flashlight, kerosene lanterns and stoves, aspirin).

10. In areas of population concentration (e.g., refugee relocation sites in the foothill areas), poppy can be grown on small plots. Opium may then be used in trade to purchase rice from nearby lowland paddy rice farmers.

11. The range of land that can still be converted to poppy culture is virtually limitless; number of skilled farmers, extent of demand, and controls over production and commerce are the limiting factors.

12. Most opium produced in Southeast Asia is consumed illicitly by addicts, rather than used for medical purposes. These addicts compose a group with high brand loyalty—i.e., most will consume opium daily in large doses for the rest of their lives.

13. The large profits to be made by commerce in opium ensure a steady supply of opium to markets.

14. Bribes lead to the corruption of local officials, who might otherwise attempt to stifle the opium trade because of its untoward effects on individuals and families.

15. Remoteness, difficult terrain, and a tradition of armed hunter-warriors among poppy-producing tribal peoples pose a serious threat to police or others trying to stifle production (Westermeyer, 1971, 1982).

These powerful economic and political forces have consequences in the cultural arena, from norms, to mores, to interethnic and social class relationships.

Sociocultural Aspects of Opium and Its Use

Norms and mores vis-a-vis opium varied with the ethnic group. This in turn was related to access, availability, and familiarity with opium. Three groups could be discerned vis-a-vis access: poppy farmers, opium merchants, and others.

Poppy farmers (Hmong, lu Mien, some Khamu, some Tai Dam, some Lu) viewed poppy and opium much as a Carolina farmer might view tobacco: as basically a neutral substance with good (i.e., financial) uses and bad (i.e., addictive) uses. Some mountain people always kept at least a small supply of opium available for use as medication or to offer guests (along with tea or rice whiskey). Others might grow poppy and sell their opium, but would not consume it as medicine or offer it to visitors. Addiction alone was not an acceptable rationale for a wife to leave a husband, but a husband might divorce a wife immediately if she were addicted. Opium was consumed primarily in the home. Social or recreational use usually involved smoking; consumption for cough, pain, or diarrhea might be by eating or smoking. Virtually all men and women in poppy-producing villages handled opium and had it in their homes for various lengths of time.

Shopkeepers and itinerant merchants, importer-exporters, creditors, truck drivers, boatmen, and similar persons had commercial access to opium by virtue of moving trade goods up to the mountains and moving opium back down to the Mekong River and to other countries of Southeast Asia. Police, military, and political leaders were sometimes involved in larger shipments. These opium mercantile occupations occurred among ethnic Lao, Chinese, Vietnamese, and Cambodians in Laos. They lived in various-sized market towns located in valleys of the Annamite chain, lowland towns between the mountains and the Mekong River, and along the Mekong River. Relatively few people among these ethnic groups had personal access to opium unless involved in opium commerce, or through opium-using friends. Other townspeople had access to opium through opium dens, of which there were hundreds in larger towns. Opium dens were semiprivate places with a stable clientele, including government functionaries, laborers, technicians, artisans, teachers, foreign workers, and others. Although many of this group of opium den addicts were Lao, they also included expatriate Thai, Chinese, Indians, Pakistanis, French, indigenous refugees, and disabled veterans, as well as tourists from Europe, Australia, and North America. Norms and mores vis-a-vis opium possession or use were more negative in these commercial centers than in poppy-producing villages. Use was rarely open. Many addicts did not smoke at home because of hostile attitudes among family members. For research purposes, it was more time-consuming to obtain town-dwelling subjects, who were more secretive about their addition. Prior to 1972 opium could be purchased openly in the valley market towns of the north (usually in the same stalls that sold tobacco, betel-areca supplies, cannabis, and cooking herbals). After 1972, outside of the mountains, opium was not sold openly; however, bulk supplies of opium could be purchased at dens. Travelers and

guests were not offered opium as a matter of course in towns, as often occurred in villages of poppy-producing regions.

A third group consisted of villages and ethnic groups involved neither in
poppy culture nor in opium commerce. Villagers and townspeople near these
routes usually knew about opium, although they may have never seen it or
observed its use. Their attitudes towards opium were strongly negative, and
they were against its introduction into their homes and communities. Some
remote villagers and tribespeople (especially in southern Laos, where poppy
was not grown) had never heard of opium. If its properties were described to
remote villagers, they would respond that no such agent existed or they would
name another substance such as alcohol (Westermeyer, 1971, 1982).

Next, the social stereotype of addicts as being mostly male and elderly,
with a predominance of Chinese, was pursued.

The "Elderly Chinese Male Addict" Stereotype

In addition to interviewing poppy farmers and addicts, I interviewed
numerous other informants in 1965–67. This was at a time well before large
numbers of refugee addicts had become a social problem in Laos. Those
interviewed included local and foreign health care workers, village chiefs,
government officials, rural development workers, and foreign missionaries.
These people reported the same notions: i.e., that only elderly, retired, often
sick and dying persons smoked opium; that virtually all were men; and that
opium use produced no personal, family, or social ills. Lao officials noted that
most addicts were Chinese, adding some statement to the effect that "the Lao
do not like opium."

Data collection on opium addicts revealed most of these stereotypes to
be untrue. The age distribution at which opium use first began is shown in
Table 1 for several samples of addicts from Laos. Most addiction began during late adolescence and early adulthood (twenties and thirties). A large minority among some groups began in middle age (forties and fifties). Few
addicts ever began opium use after the age of sixty. Addiction usually ensued
within a few months to a few years of the first opium use. Tribal poppy farmers started opium use at an earlier age and had a shorter preaddictive opium
use period, as compared to the others. Table 2 shows the current age of opium
addicts when interviewed in their villages, in opium dens, or when seeking
treatment at a temple, medical facility in Laos, or medical facility in the U.S.
In most samples, the predominat age groups were in the thirties, forties, and
fifties. A prevalence study among the Hmong demonstrated that fewer elderly
people were addicted as compared to younger adults. This finding is probably
due to two facts: (1) few addicts began use late in life and (2) few addicts sur-
vived two or three decades of opium addiction, dying in the meantime of in-
tercurrent pulmonary infections, emphysema, secondary heart complications

TABLE 1

Age at Initiating Opium Use

Source of Sample

Age	Hmong, village survey		Hmong, medical treatment		Hmong, Buddhist therapy		Hmong, Univ. Minn. Hospital*		Expatriate Asians, medical treatment		Lao, medical treatment		Caucasians, medical treatment	
< 20 yrs.	3	(11%)	14	(17%)	8	(7%)	3	(5%)	7	(9%)	23	(7%)	8	(14%)
20–29 yrs.	11	(39%)	32	(40%)	48	(41%)	21	(38%)	15	(20%)	77	(24%)	41	(73%)
30–39 yrs.	12	(43%)	28	(35%)	47	(40%)	17	(31%)	28	(37%)	112	(35%)	6	(11%)
40–49 yrs.	2	(7%)	5	(6%)	11	(9%)	11	(20%)	20	(26%)	74	(23%)	1	(2%)
> 49 yrs.	0	(0%)	2	(2%)	4	(3%)	3	(5%)	6	(8%)	34	(11%)	0	(0%)
	28	(100%)	81	(100%)	118	(100%)	55	(99%)	76	(99%)	320	(100%)	76	(99%)

*This sample was obtained in the U.S.; other samples were obtained in Laos.

TABLE 2

Current Age of Addicts

Age
Source of Sample

Age	Hmong, village survey	Hmong, medical treatment	Hmong Buddhist therapy	Hmong Univ. Minn. Hospital*	Expatriate Asians, medical treatment	Lao, medical treatment	Caucasians, medical treatment
< 20 yrs.	0 (0%)	2 (2%)	0 (0%)	0 (0%)	1 (1%)	1 (0%)	1 (2%)
20–29 yrs.	2 (7%)	6 (7%)	6 (5%)	6 (11%)	4 (5%)	11 (3%)	45 (80%)
30–39 yrs.	7 (25%)	33 (41%)	45 (38%)	16 (28%)	15 (20%)	45 (14%)	7 (13%)
40–49 yrs.	9 (32%)	26 (32%)	32 (27%)	8 (14%)	23 (30%)	96 (30%)	2 (4%)
50–59 yrs.	8 (29%)	11 (14%)	27 (23%)	19 (33%)	17 (22%)	84 (26%)	1 (2%)
> 59 yrs.	2 (7%)	3 (4%)	8 (7%)	8 (14%)	16 (21%)	84 (26%)	0 (0%)
	28 (100%)	81 (100%)	118 (100%)	57 (100%)	76 (99%)	321 (99%)	56 (101%)

*This sample was obtained in the U.S.; other samples were obtained in Laos.

TABLE 3

Ethnic Distribution of Addicts

Ethnicity	Sample			
	Medical Treatment		Buddhist Therapy	
Lao	321	(60%)	1029	(86%)
Hmong	81	(15%)	119	(10%)
Other tribal Laotians*	25	(5%)	32	(3%)
Expatriate Asians**	76	(14%)	12	(1%)
Caucasians***	29	(5%)	0	(0%)
	532	(99%)	1192	(100%)

*Khamu, Mien, Tai Dam, Akha
**Thai, Vietnamese, Chinese, Indian, Pakistani
***Europeans, Australians, North Americans

from lung disease (cor pulmonale), and lung cancer (Westermeyer, 1971, 1974a, 1974b, 1977a, 1982).

Table 3 shows the ethnic distribution of opium addicts seeking treatment for addiction in two settings: a Buddhist temple and a medical facility in Laos. Ethnic Chinese composed a small percentage of addicts in both of these samples (Westermeyer, 1977a, 1978a). Ethnic Lao were by far the most numerous.

The male dimension of the stereotype had validity in some groups. As shown in Table 4, the ethnic groups who did commerce in opium had relatively few female addicts. Among the poppy-growing Hmong, the proportion of women is high: about one woman to every two to three men. Even in this group, however, the stereotype was that men smoked opium but women did not (Westermeyer and Peng, 1978; Westermeyer, 1988).

As data accumulated in subsequent years, possessors of these stereotypes were able to surrender their old ideas—albeit reluctantly and painfully. Why were these convictions so powerful, even when people had knowledge of individuals who did not fit the stereotype? I believe the following attitudes and ideal norms drove people's perceptions (creating misperceptions):

1. People in poppy-producing areas could accept the notion of an elderly, ill, failing person becoming addicted. This is not so different from the accepted American concept of a terminal cancer patient becoming addicted to morphine or another opioid drug.
2. Elderly, retired persons no longer in life's mainstream could be tolerated as addicts. Parents, teachers, and productive community members were not socially acceptable as addicts.

TABLE 4

Sex Ratio Among Opium Addicts

Sample	Number of Subjects		Number of Males to One Female
	Male	Female	
Hmong, village survey 1	21	11	1.9
Hmong, village survey 2	19	9	2.1
Hmong, Univ. Minn. Hosp.	40	17	2.4
Hmong, medical treatment	59	22	2.7
Hmong, Buddhist therapy	93	25	3.7
Caucasians, medical treatment	45	11	4.1
Lao, medical treatment	302	19	15.9
Expatriate Asians, medical treatment	73	3	24.3

3. It was more permissible for men to be addicted than for women to be addicted. This may be in part related to women's childbearing responsibilities (addicted women became amenorrheic and were usually barren), in part to child raising tasks (addicted mothers neglected their children), and in part to the higher moral code that both men and women expected of women (as exemplified by the double standard regarding other deviant behaviors, such as alcohol intoxication and premarital and extramarital sexuality).

4. The Chinese stereotype could have several origins. Numerous Chinese merchants were involved with the opium trade (trading in opium themselves, providing credit for opium purchase by others, lending mules to traders for opium transport). Chinese proprietors owned many (but not all) opium dens. They were thus closely associated with opium commerce. Those few Chinese who became addicted were widely visible through their commercial roles in the trade. In addition, the Chinese were admired for their industriousness, sophistication, and ambitiousness, although also envied for their wealth and despised for their clannishness and profit-taking at the expense of local people. In association with these ambivalent attitudes, the Chinese were assigned numerous other negative stereotypes as well (e.g., fat, ugly, loud, lacking in decorum and "face," inconsiderate, materialistic, aggressive).

Epidemiological Distribution of Opium Addicts

It was next of interest to discern whether cultural and environmental factors were associated with the prevalence of opium addiction (i.e., to search for possible etiological or predisposing ecocultural factors). These data are summarized in Table 5. First, the size of the community was studied. This

TABLE 5
Prevalence Rates of Opium Addiction
in Various Communities

Location	Population	Number Of Addicts	Crude Prevalence Of Addiction Per 100
1. Poppy producing communities			
Yao villages	400	39	9.8
Hmong villages	175	16	9.1
2. Opium commercial communities			
Yao town	2,740	150	5.5
Lao town	1,000	53	5.3
Cambodian district*	123	6	4.9
Chinese district	5,916	245	4.1
3. Consuming communities without production or commerce			
Vietnamese district*	9,710	209	2.3
Lao villages	4,000	72	1.8
Tai Dam district*	4,955	89	1.8

*All districts were located in Vientiane town; population figures are from census data.

failed to show a consistent trend: crude rates in villages (i.e., number of addicts in the total population) could vary from 0 to 9.8 per 100; rates in towns could vary from 0 to 5.5 per 100. Next, the ethnic group was studied. Although those groups who raised poppy had higher rates, one commercial Mien town had a rate comparable with those of other towns dealing in opium: 5.5 addicts per 100 in the Mien market town of Houei Aw (population 2740) vs. 5.3 addicts per 100 in the northern ethnic Lao market town of Mouang Xieng Khouang (population about 1000). Finally, the community role in relation to opium was studied. Those villages engaged in poppy culture had crude prevalence rates (i.e., rates per total population, including men and women, children and adults) of 7.0 to 9.8 addicts per 100 people. Communities engaged in opium commerce had lower crude prevalence rates, ranging from 4.1 to 5.5 per 100. Other communities had low rates, ranging from under 3 down to 0 per 100.

These prevalence rates suggested that the strongest etiological factor was the degree of access to opium (highest in the communities of poppy growers, intermediate in the towns of opium commercial centers, and lowest where inhabitants had to travel to obtain opium). Other data bolstered this hypothesis. One was the high rate of addiction among poppy-growing Hmong women, who were exposed to opium through their own harvesting of opium and through the prevalence of opium in the home, and the low rate among

Asian women in the other settings where their access was low. Expatriate Caucasian tourists likewise had similar access to opiates, whether they were male or female, so that more women were addicted in this group. Among the Asian groups not growing poppy, it was men who were exposed to opium in their mercantile occupations; women in these groups were exposed mostly through their addicted husbands.

Other data supported the pathogenicity of ready access to opium. One of these was the younger age at onset of addiction among poppy farmers as opposed to others. Another was the more rapid progression from use to addiction among poppy farmers (Westermeyer, 1982).

Factors Affecting Treatment Outcome

A follow-up study six to eighteen months following treatment provided an opportunity to develop hypotheses regarding factors affecting treatment efficacy (Westermeyer and Bourne, 1978; Westermeyer, 1982). Factors that were studied included the following: age, sex, and ethnicity of addicts; size of community; type of community (poppy-producing, opium commerce, neither of these); type of treatment (Buddhist temple vs. medical facility); severity of addiction (i.e., doses per day, opium cost or value per day, initial methadone dose needed to relieve withdrawal) and duration of addiction; effect of having an addicted spouse; effect of having a supportive person committed to the addict's abstinence from opium; and percentage of addicts in the community seeking treatment at the same time or within the previous year. Only one factor showed a consistent relationship to abstinence: the percentage of addicts in the community entering treatment around the same time (see Table 6). Fur-

TABLE 6

Percentage of Addicts Seeking Treatment and Treatment Outcome

Location	Total Number Of Addicts	Addicts Treated		Treated Addicts Abstinent (%)	
High success					
1. Khamu village	3	3	(100%)	3	(100%)
2. Lao town	53	45	(85%)	40	(89%)
3. Hmong village	16	13	(81%)	11	(85%)
4. Lao town	72	62	(86%)	43	(69%)
Low success					
5. Yao villages	39	4	(10%)	1	(25%)
6. Yao town	180	58	(32%)	10	(17%)
7. Yao villages	100 +	9	(<10%)	0	(0%)
8. Akha villages	100 +	3	(<5%)	0	(0%)

ther study of communities sending a high percentage of addicts to treatment showed that they shared the following characteristics:

1. Refugee moves had driven up the price of opium in central and northeastern Laos, where most "high percentage" communities were located. "Low percentage" communities were mostly in northwestern Laos near the Burmese border, where the price of opium was lower.
2. In high percentage communities, the local chief and elders had organized the sending of addicts to treatment. Typically they were sent in two or three groups over a six-month period. While they were gone, fellow villagers looked after their homes, families, animals, gardens, and fields.
3. Upon returning home, ex-addicts in the high percentage communities formed spontaneously into a subgroup that socialized together, accompanied each other to local rituals and ceremonies (which they had largely abandoned while addicted), supported each other's abstinence from opium, and often intervened actively in the event that one of their number resumed opium use.

The follow-up data also indicated that treated women living with opium-smoking husbands had a high rate of relapse, regardless of community factors. In some cases the husband had refused treatment, and in other cases the husband had relapsed to addiction. The numbers of such cases were small and the statistical analyses borderline, so that subsequent studies of this group are needed.

Larger towns did not fall into either the high percentage or the low percentage category, but rather fell in between. This was probably due to the fact that large communities could not organize to send addicts off to treatment, although public announcements regarding treatment were intense. In these intermediate percentage communities, access to a nonfamily support person regularly predicted subsequent abstinence. Such helpers included health workers, employers, elected community leaders, Buddhist monks, and foreign missionaries.

Discussion

Methodological Issues

Research on deviant, problematic, stigmatized, or psychopathological behaviors presents several inherent difficulties not encountered when conducting research on such topics as kinship terminology or housing styles. Since these conditions are stigmatizing not only for the individual but for the family and the community, access to subjects and to valid data is difficult and requires special approaches. These conditions can at times be more readily studied as they are dealt with by the local political, religious, social, legal, or health care systems. At the point of social recognition these conditions have usually been present over a long period of time and are modified by the crisis atmosphere of the situation. In order to obtain the assistance desired, the individual or family may modify the facts of the situation, or selectively choose certain facts while deleting others. Total reliance on clinical data is guaranteed to present only part of the story, or to be misleading. The early beneficial, enjoyable, or life-enhancing aspect of psychoactive substance use is usually glossed over.

The advantages and disadvantages of three methods that can be used to study drug use (ethnographic, epidemiological, and clinical) are presented here in light of these efforts to understand opium use and addiction in Asia.

1. Ethnographic study of poppy culture in Laos and northwest Thailand during the 1960s and 1970s could be undertaken once rapport with informants was established. Poppy farmers had to trust the investigator before such research could begin. They wanted to know the purpose of the research, the kind of information to be collected, and the purposes to which it would be put. An intermediary person, or entree, greatly facilitated this process. Ideally, the entree should know well both the investigator and the local people being studied. Trust both between the local people and the entree and between the entree and the researcher is crucial. In order for such trust to develop, the researchers must be in the area long enough to develop mutually trusting relationships with one or more entrees. Entree persons must be carefully chosen, since an entree person not trusted by the local people will lead to either no data or to erroneous data. Once these conditions of trust and rapport are satisfied, one may study poppy agriculture. As Geddes (1976) and Miles (1979) have demonstrated in Thailand, extremely detailed data on opium production can be collected over prolonged periods. Commerce in opium presents somewhat greater obstacles for the ethnographer. Farmers have ambivalent motives regarding public awareness of their cash crop revenues. On the one hand, they want others to believe that they are skilled farmers who can raise a successful crop. On the other hand, they do not want to appear too wealthy, since that may put them at a disadvantage in bartering, extended family dealings, and village reciprocity. In Laos, and to some extent in Thailand, it was also possible to interview mountain traders and foothill merchants who bartered opium for various trade goods. At this level, rapport was more difficult to establish and precise information was less available than at the agricultural production level. The best informants were elderly merchants who traded in their youth, but no longer did so. Obstacles at this level were related to the more stigmatized, risky, and dangerous aspects of the opium trade. Data collection on the lowland opium trade and international opium trade through direct interviewing cannot be readily accomplished in a standard, reliable, valid, or even safe manner. Traders at this level maintain strict secrecy regarding their identity, activities, and profits. Often they have other legitimate identities in business, government, the police, or the military. Still, it was possible to glean some information from former traders (retired or disavowing their former activities), from their families (seeking to rid the family of the opium-trading stigma), or from hired help previously engaged in the trade (especially addicts in treatment). So long as the researcher holds identifying information in confidence and does not attempt to interfere with or report the trade to officials, acquisition of such knowledge is not dangerous. Local authorities might need to approve confidential collection of such data, since some national laws may require reporting.

2. *Epidemiolocial surveys have several advantages over clinical studies.* Field studies give access to early cases before serious crises develop. The benefits of opium use for the individual can be discerned (e.g., relaxation with friends, relief of chronic symptoms such as cough, headache, or insomnia). However, opium users and addicts are not readily identified and studied during the period between regular, heavy use and early addiction. This is a time when they are engaged in the struggle to control their usage and avoid both the social identity and the self-labeling as an addicted person. Serious personal and family crises may not be encountered during brief periods of field observation. On the basis of field data alone, opium addiction might be viewed as a relatively benign habit with minimal personal or social consequences.

3. *Clinical facilities are excellent sites to study opium addicts in later stages of use.* Such facilities do encounter the problems that eventually afflict many, if not most addicts. The researcher can appreciate the hold that opium possesses on it users and the great personal struggle required to cease its use. Early cases are seen only infrequently, and the period of nonaddictive use is not usually encountered in the clinical setting. Persistent opium use in the face of repeated adverse experiences may appear irrational if the observer has never seen the early phases of use, when opium users obtain much gratification from their use without the problems that ensue with time.

Combined Qualitative-Quantitative Approaches

In the study of these stigmatized conditions via different methods, the data sometimes conflict with each other. This result, if not anticipated, can produce confusion and discord among researchers wedded to diverse methods of study. If such data conflicts can be perceived as a natural state of affairs, disagreements in the data can lead to new hypotheses and better understanding of stigmatized conditions. A more holistic picture evolves, which can in turn lead to a more enlightened social policy, more preventive approaches, and more humane clinical strategies. These latter goals are well served by diverse and careful sampling, collection of quantitative as well as qualitative data, statistical analyses and comparisons among diverse samples, and replication of studies in several cultures and countries.

The integration of qualitative and quantitative measures (as advocated by Pelto 1970) is a particularly potent method available to researchers. Conflict at the level of the individual qualitative-quantitative researcher is a critical element in this approach. So long as conflict occurs between or among separate qualitative researchers and quantitative researchers, theoretical advances are often obstructed, since each researcher may demean and discard the findings of the other researchers employing different methods. Individual qualitative-quantitative researchers do not have the luxury of disregarding their own findings. Instead, they must seek means to resolve the cognitive dissonance induced by their own conflicting findings. This personal conflict can lead to new hypotheses and to new studies designed to resolve the dissonance. Out of these personal resolutions, our science grows.

IV

Microlevel/Macrolevel

Introduction to Part Four

Since the time of Franz Boas, who stressed the importance of collecting primary data on the world's peoples, the strength of anthropological research has been the richness of its descriptions and analyses of people in relatively small communities and groups. This kind of microlevel research may have been appropriate during an era in which it was important to document the disappearing range of variation of cultural traits and forms of organization among the peoples of the globe. In the present age of rapidly expanding communication and incorporation of people into the world system, work that treats small communities and groups as isolates is increasingly inappropriate. Anthropologists and other social scientists have become much more concerned with how the people they study are affected by and affect the dynamics of larger regions, nations, and global systems. Although the focus on small populations may remain, we see increasingly sophisticated studies that situate peoples in space and time, as well as within the larger processes of which they are a part (see Poggie and Lynch, 1974; DeWalt and Pelto, 1985).

Demonstrating the linkages between micro- and macrolevels creates new methodological challenges for anthroplogists. Participant observation and key informant interviews must be used in conjunction with other techniques suited for making microlevel/macrolevel linkages more apparent. Often anthropological work, of necessity, becomes more multidisciplinary, incorporating types of data or analysis from other social or even natural science disciplines. This is especially true in research that addresses issues of contemporary policy importance.

The chapters in this section provide excellent examples of some of these trends. Stonich blends economic, ecological, and anthropological data on communities, the region, and the country to demonstrate linkages between agricultural development and environmental deterioration in southern Honduras. DeWalt and DeWalt write about a project in Mexico to investigate how larger trends in Mexico's agricultural and food systems have affected people at the microlevel. Their work on four communities, widely separated from one another in very different regions of Mexico, is a good example of team research because the project included professionals and student assistants from a large number of disciplines. These two papers demonstrate how local level processes are partially determined by events occurring at the regional, national, and international level. At the same time, however, they show how individuals and communities respond to, modify, and adapt (and ultimately have an effect on) these events and influences.

Both the Stonich and DeWalt and DeWalt contributions deal with issues of resource use and abuse in developing countries. This is an important area in which microlevel and macrolevel variables and influences must be utilized. Resource-poor farmers are increasingly attempting to compete in a global marketplace. Their ability to gain access to the resources that will enable them to effectively contend with the national and global market will be important for their, and their local environment's, survival.

Kilbride deals with another aspect of the increasing incorporation of individuals and communities into the world system. His contribution focuses on how "delocalization" has affected patterns of child abuse and neglect in Kenya. Because this phenomenon is difficult or impossible to study using survey methods, Kilbride used an interesting mix of methods. At the village level, he sought out cases that he could intensively follow up. On the national level, he used newspaper accounts of child abuse and neglect. Using these, he has been able to come to some interesting conclusions and recommendations concerning the etiology of child abuse.

7

Society and Land Degradation in Central America: Issues in Theory, Method, and Practice[1]

Susan C. Stonich

This paper is an outcome of the converging and potentially complementary trends that took place during the 1980s in research on the relationship between development efforts and the state of the environment; in theoretical perspectives within anthropology; and in methodological advancements related to those theoretical reformations. The period was distinguished by a growing global understanding that the process of development and the condition of the biophysical environment are closely connected. The conclusions and the recommendations of international councils such as the United Nations World Commission on Environment and Development, published in its influential volume *Our Common Future* (1987), as well as recent environmental initiatives on the part of funding institutions such as the National Science Foundation, the Social Science Research Council, and the MacArthur Foundation, attest to the widespread acceptance of the interrelationship among social, economic, and environmental processes. These initiatives have emphasized the need for interdisciplinary research efforts aimed at halting escalating environmental and human impoverishment in the Third World. In addition, they have opened the door to enhanced social science participation in research related to global environmental change.

Concomitant with the shifting attentions of policymakers and the public regarding the connection between development and the environment were changes within the discipline of anthropology. In response to criticisms that community-focused anthropological studies did not adequately consider the relationships between such communities and the larger political and economic systems of which they are a part, many anthropologists expanded their research focus to examine how relatively small groups are integrated into larger regional, national, and international systems (Ortner, 1984). By restoring human agency to a central place in social scientific investigation and by demonstrating that individuals and institutions in the Third World have a substantial impact on modifying international pressures, these efforts also helped correct the excesses of dependency and world system theory that were in vogue during the 1960s and the 1970s (Ortner, 1984). In their worst presentations, these paradigms proposed an all-powerful metropolitan capitalism as the explanation for underdevelopment in the periphery—in effect denying that local initiative and local response had any significant role in the making of history (Mintz, 1977).

These changes within anthropology have raised a number of theoretical concerns related to the general processes involved in sociocultural change and in the nature of integration of systems, as well as more specific methodological issues regarding appropriate levels and units of analysis. In the book *Micro and Macro Levels of Analysis in Anthropology*, DeWalt and Pelto stress that social scientists have augmented their efforts to understand the relationships between relatively small-scale and larger-scale processes (i.e., between micro- and macrolevel phenomena) and that this escalating concern has brought about the need to develop appropriate methodologies to guide research (1985:187). The two most important methodological tasks that are demanded are the clear depiction of conceptual models and of systems of postulated relationships among levels and precise definitions of the relevant factors (i.e., sets of variables) that are used as the specific linkages that articulate levels of analysis (DeWalt and Pelto, 1985:187).

This paper combines these diverse trends to examine significant social and environmental processes associated with natural resource-based development in southern Honduras (Figure 1); demonstrates the linkages between development processes and environmental degradation in the region; and shows how the patterns that emerge apply to wider areas of Central America. The paper begins with a discussion of how environmental questions were incorporated into a political-economic analysis of agricultural development in southern Honduras. This integrated historical and political economy approach shows the close connections among the dynamics of agricultural development, the associated patterns of capital accumulation, and the serious problems of environmental degradation. In sum, this paper is an explicit illustration of how larger international and national forces evolved and affected people and natural resources and how, in turn, local level enterprise and response affected these larger systems.

Political Economy

This research integrates environmental concerns into political-economic analysis (see de Janvry, 1975; Crouch and de Janvry, 1980) that shows the close linkages between social processes and environmental deterioration in

FIGURE 1

INTSORMIL Research Sites in Southern Honduras

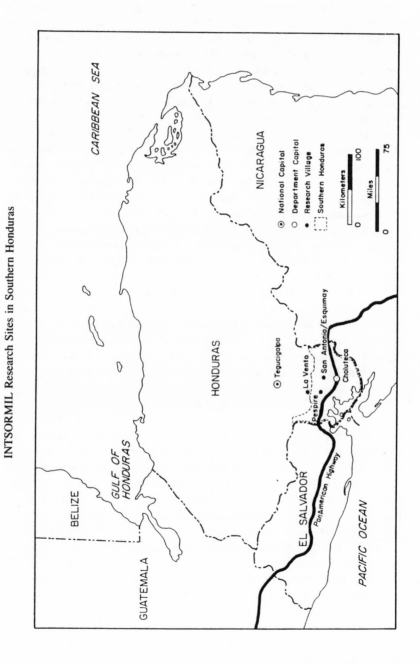

the region.[2] This is accomplished by scrutinizing the important multilevel and intersystem processes involved in the expansion of capitalist agricultural production, their connections to changes in the allocation and use of land, and their impact on the regional ecology. Using this framework, the uneven growth of agriculture in southern Honduras is demonstrated; i.e., as commercial agriculture expands, certain commodities become preferentially produced by large capitalist farmers who are more efficient and who also control the available resources. Simultaneously, the small farmers' range of alternatives is reduced as their control of resources diminishes. The results are that an increasing proportion of total agricultural output comes from the capitalist sector, while a growing number of resource-poor farm households are pressed to intensify their own agricultural production. The environmental outcomes of these processes have included extensive forest conversion, having as secondary costs both land degradation and watershed deterioration.

The expansion of capitalist agriculture in southern Honduras is shown to be a multilevel process that includes the reorganization of local, regional, national, and international systems of production, distribution, and consumption in order to facilitate the process of capital accumulation. Previous forms of social and economic reproduction are altered as the process and logic of capitalist accumulation spreads. The outcome is that producers at all levels— Honduran small farmers, medium farmers, large farmers, and transnational corporations—often find it in their best interests to move toward the most modern and productive methods of cultivation, management, and marketing, and to turn to the most profitable commodities.

Research Methodology

The goal of the methodology was to provide a systemic framework in which to articulate the relevant factors and levels of analysis involved in the social and ecological processes related to the expansion of capitalist agriculture (Figure 2). The ultimate objective was to integrate a representative sample of microlevel studies (of individuals and of communities) into a hierarchical structure composed of multiple, relevant, and increasingly macrolevels of analysis. A further aim was to add a historic dimension by positioning the traditional microlevel foci of anthropology—individuals and the community—at the convergence of local and world history. The underlying assumption that variability existed in terms of all factors and at all levels required that sampling strategies be designed so as to be capable of collecting data representative of that heterogeneity.

Here, it is possible only to sketch the research methodology designed to accomplish these numerous objectives.[3] The fundamental task was to identify the factors (defined and operationalized in terms of sets of variables) that

FIGURE 2

Contributions of Data Sources on Land Utilization to Levels of Analysis

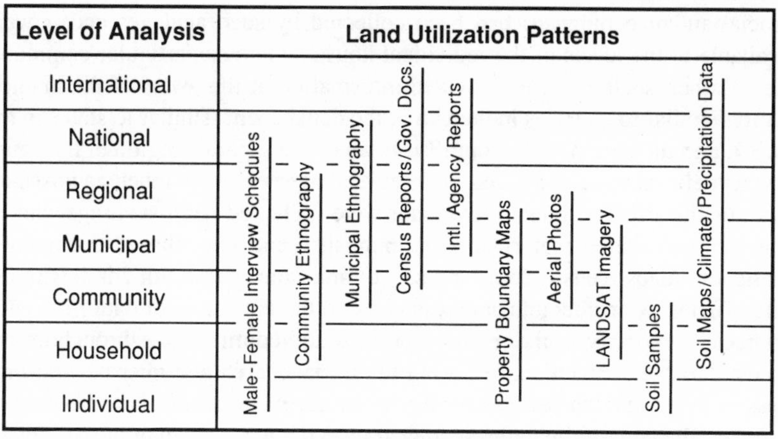

Level of Analysis	Land Utilization Patterns
International	
National	
Regional	
Municipal	
Community	
Household	
Individual	

Data sources (columns): Male-Female Interview Schedules, Community Ethnography, Municipal Ethnography, Census Reports/Gov. Docs., Intl. Agency Reports, Property Boundary Maps, Aerial Photos, LANDSAT Imagery, Soil Samples, Soil Maps/Climate/Precipitation Data

Source: Adopted from Susan C. Stonich, Development and Destruction: Interrelated Socioeconomic, Ecological, and Nutritional Change in Southern Honduras, (1986), p. 32.

could be used to link the relevant social and ecological processes through the appropriate levels of analysis. Of the several factors that could have been chosen, patterns in land use appeared the most germane, and an analysis of changes in land utilization patterns emerged as the most promising means of synthesizing the social and ecological processes occurring in the region. Employing land utilization patterns as a window for integrating these processes was particularly useful for a number of reasons. First, the spread of commercial agriculture in such contexts fundamentally alters the ecology in areas in which it occurs. An examination of changes in land utilization patterns—the changes in the ways in which human populations exploit land resources—specifically focuses on these ecological transformations, highlighting the interaction of biophysical and social processes. Second, land use changes could be examined at many levels, from the study of the land use decisions of one farmer, to superhousehold and community patterns of land use, and from those to regional, national, and ultimately worldwide configurations. Finally, such an analysis could aid in the evaluation of determinants influencing the evolution of land utilization patterns through identifying the producers, the beneficiaries, and the losers of a given pattern of production, and the changes in consumption patterns that accompany such transformations.

The choice of specific levels of analysis from which data were gathered was based on theoretical considerations, but also influenced by the conceptualization and construction of levels of analysis reflected in the data available from national and international sources. For example, little relevant data (social and/or ecological) had been collected by such agencies and/or were available at the levels of the individual householders or particular communities. Rather, such agencies provided information at the levels of the municipality (similar to counties in the U.S.), the department (similar to states in the U.S.), and the region ("the south" is treated as a separate region of the country, as defined by national and international agencies). As much as possible, both qualitative and quantitative data were collected from such agencies in the form of written materials (e.g., published and unpublished documents, statistics, maps, census data, and so on) and interviews with administrators and officials. Considerable care was given to the collection of data from such sources, both early in the research process and continuously throughout the study, and the contacts made during the initial search and interviewing process proved invaluable. Given the macrolevel focus of data from such sources, the core of the anthropological research was the study of individuals and communities—the traditional loci of anthropological research. The objective was to obtain data from a sample of communities that were representative of the variation in social/environmental interactions that existed in the region. After a preliminary study of written documents, numerous interviews with officials, and a short period of initial field research throughout the south, a sample of research communities was chosen to represent the agro-ecological variation present within the region. Using a combination of ethnographic (including both qualitative and quantitative observations) and survey research methods, primary data were collected from samples of male and female householders in these communities. Variables were defined and operationalized so as to be analogous to the more macrolevel data available from the published and unpublished reports of national and international agencies. In summary, the research methodology involved the integration of data on land utilization patterns from the level of the male or female householder, through the community, municipality, region, and nation. Minimally, for each level, data were obtained on: (1) the ways land was classified (in terms of biophysical characteristics, quality, use, and so on; (2) the relative allocation of land (e.g., crop land versus pasture); (3) the agricultural and other practices that involved the use of land (e.g., farming and cropping systems and fuelwood collection); and (4) land tenure (the distribution, size, and ownership/rentership of land).

Because research goals included understanding trends over time, an attempt was made to collect data that spanned a number of years. At the levels of the nation, region, department, and municipality, government publications were most useful. Agricultural censuses from 1952, 1965, and 1974 were consulted (DGECH, 1954, 1968, 1976) and then supplemented by data from more recent regional development, natural resource, and agricultural reports, as well as by data from remote sensing devices (aerial photos and satellite imagery). At the local level, additional interviews designed to measure changing use of land resources over the same thirty-year period were administered to farmers. These were augmented by monitoring selected parcels of land for a period of one year.

Documented changes in land utilization patterns were tied to social factors influencing the evolution of such patterns and to their ecological outcomes through an integrated master data base. This data base was used first as input to the geographic and agroeconomic information system developed by the Comprehensive Resource Inventory Evaluation System Project at Michigan State University (CRIES, 1984) and later disaggregated into files managed by dBASE—although other data base managers could have been used. The master data base consisted of physical, ecological, and agricultural information contained in digitized land use, topographic, soil, and land parcel maps; tabular ecological data collected from parcel monitoring; and primary data collected through various agricultural, socioeconomic, and nutritional household surveys. The result was a geographically referenced data base keyed to the level of the household, but capable of being disaggregated to the levels of the male and female householder or concatenated to the levels of the community, municipality, or region. In addition, the identification variables (of individuals, households, communities, etc.) in the master data base were keyed to those in the computer-coded ethnographic field notes, making it possible to coordinate searches of field notes with analyses of the more "quantified" information included in the master data base.

Altogether the research methodology facilitated overall analysis capable of integrating qualitative and quantitative sources of data. It resulted in a regional land use study that linked social and ecological processes through different levels. The dynamic data base was not only able to answer descriptive questions, such as "To what extent has pasture expanded into highland areas?" or "Where and to what degree does burning take place?", but also questions aimed at understanding processes, such as "Why do farmers continue to burn fields even though they are aware of the negative environmental consequences?" and "How does the allocation of household labor influence land use decisions?"

Agricultural Development in Southern Honduras

The transformation of southern Honduran agriculture is understood best in the context of the global capitalist expansion that occurred after World War

II, during which time the U.S. and other industrialized countries attempted to extend capitalist enterprises through increased foreign investment (see White, 1977; Boyer, 1983; and Stonich, 1986 for more complete discussions of the history of the growth of capitalist agriculture in southern Honduras). The world depression and World War II led industrialized countries to create new institutions designed to regulate the international economy, while simultaneously national security considerations stimulated the U.S. government to increase significantly programs of economic and military assistance. Throughout Central America, the cumulative effects of these interrelated processes were economic growth, alterations in dependency relationships, and "apparent prosperity" (Perez Brignoli, 1982). Economic growth, based on the extremely favorable external conditions that characterized the 1950s, was sustained during the 1960s through industrialization and the process of Central American economic integration (the Central American Common Market—CACM). By the 1970s this pattern was reversed, and the region fell into economic crisis and related social conflict.

In Honduras, the interaction of these international and national forces resulted in a new role for the Honduran state—as an active agent of development. A variety of state institutions and agencies were formed to expand government services, modernize the country's financial system, and undertake infrastructural projects (White, 1977). As part of the government's efforts to stimulate national economic growth, southern Honduras for the first time was drawn intimately into national, Central American, and foreign (especially U.S.) markets. During the 1950s and early 1960s, the U.S., the World Bank, and the Inter-American Development Bank helped fund a variety of projects in the region. Port facilities at Amapala and San Lorenzo were improved; the Pan American highway linking Nicaragua and El Salvador with a section connecting it to Tegucigalpa was completed; a system of penetration roads linking the hinterlands to municipal centers and to the Pan American Highway was built; and government supervised bus lines were established (Boyer, 1983). This period of intensified public sector investment coincided with temporary high prices for primary commodities on the world market. Large landowners in the south historically had been unable to respond to favorable economic conditions due to the lack of necessary infrastructure such as transportation, markets, and credit. With the infrastructure now in place, these owners found it profitable to expand production for the global market. The terms of trade later became unfavorable, but by that time much of the southern agrarian economy had been transformed.

A domestic capitalist agricultural sector emerged in the south in the 1950s, and by the mid-1970s large foreign agricultural enterprises began investing in the area, competing with regional capitalists for land and labor. From midcentury to the 1980s, diversification and growth of agricultural production for export characterized the southern Honduran economy. Cotton, then livestock and sugar, were the primary commodities involved in the conversion of the south. By the mid-1970s, these commodities were supplemented by sesame and melons, and later by a wider variety of nontraditional exports (CSPE/OEA, 1982).

The production of basic grains took place largely on small farms and did not expand sufficiently to keep pace with foreign and domestic demand brought about by population growth and by the growth of urban centers within and outside the south. The result was a reduced grain supply in the rural areas by the early 1960s (O'Brien Fonck, 1972:92). Most of the market expansion was associated with export growth, and favored large farmers. With the exception of coffee, export crops were (and still are) primarily produced on large farms, whereas traditional basic grains, the major human food crops, were produced on small units of less than twenty hectares (Stonich, 1989). Since 1950 there has been a marked decline in the production of basic grains, whereas the production of export crops has increased significantly. By 1982, the amount of land planted in maize had increased only 1 percent over its 1952 level, sorghum increased 15 percent, and beans decreased to 85 percent of the area planted in 1952. Only the amount of land planted in such export crops as sugar, melons, and cotton increased significantly (Stonich, 1989).

The Honduran government has contributed to the stagnation of basic grain crops by placing price ceilings on basic staples as a way of maintaining cheap food for the growing urban population. Between 1970 and 1981, real farm prices for maize, beans, rice, sorghum, eggs, milk, chicken, pork, and a variety of other crops declined in spite of stagnating production (Larson, 1982). Between 1980 and 1986, real farm prices for corn, sorghum, and beans remained the same or declined (IHMA, 1987). On the other hand, the government continued to provide subsidies to encourage export agriculture for foreign exchange. To give just one example of these subsidies, consider the disbursement of loan funds allocated by the central bank (BANTRAL) and by the national agricultural development bank (BANADESA). Overall, between 1980 and 1986 the major proportion of central bank funds were apportioned to the industrial, commercial, and service sectors (>70 percent), whereas the agricultural sector was allocated approximately 21 percent of funds (BANTRAL, 1987). Of the agricultural loans disseminated, only 1.6 percent to 2.2 percent were allocated to basic grains (corn, beans, sorghum, rice); the rest was allotted to export commodities (BANTRAL, 1987). A similar pattern of capital disbursement is evident in the loans provided by the national agricultural development bank: between 1980 and 1982 only 5 percent of the loan funds went to the production of corn, beans, and sorghum, with the rest going to livestock, cotton, and sugar—commodities produced by large farmers primarily for export (Stonich, 1986:124–27). Since then, the distribution of funds has changed somewhat, reflecting government policies established in the early 1980s aimed at making Honduras more self-sufficient in the production of basic food grains. As shown in Table 1, in 1986 the percentage of agricultural loans apportioned to basic food crops was 25 percent of all agricultural loans, with most of the remaining funds allocated to livestock, cotton, sugar, and various fruits and vegetables produced mainly for foreign markets (BANADESA, 1987). However, during the 1982 to 1986 period the amount of loan funds allotted to basic grains actually declined 12 percent, whereas livestock loans increased by 216 percent (BANADESA, 1987).

The combination of price ceilings and limited credit contributed to the stagnation of small farm food production, the major supplier for the national market. Nationally, per capita production of basic grains declined 31 percent between 1950 and 1985 (USDA, 1985). As a result, Honduras has become a net importer of such basic staples as maize, beans, and sorghum (see Stonich, 1986:124–26). Between 1974 and 1985 cereal imports grew 90 percent and food aid in cereals multiplied 280 percent (World Bank, 1987:212). Albeit

TABLE 1

Crop Loans and Livestock Loans Made by the National Agricultural
Development Bank of Honduras and Percent Change in
Loan Disbursements, 1982–86

Commodity	Lempiras[a] (Millions)	Percent Of Crop Loans	Percent Of Agricultural Loans	Percent Change In Lempiras Disbursed 1982–86
Maize	20.7	30.0	19.0	−12.7
Beans	2.5	3.6	2.3	.9
Rice	3.9	5.6	3.6	−31.6
Coffee	12.6	18.3	11.6	−39.0
Tobacco	.4	.6	.4	−33.0
Cotton	7.3	10.6	6.7	16.0
Sugar	8.2	11.9	7.5	−58.4
Other*	13.4	19.4	12.3	74.0
Total Crop Loans	69.0	100.0	(63.4)	−20.0
Livestock	39.9		36.6	216.0
Total Loans	108.9		100.0	10.0

* Primarily fruits and vegetables, such as melons.
[a] US $ 1.00 = L 2.00 (Lempiras).

Source: Computed from data contained in BANADESA, 1987.

between 1981 and 1986 the amount of corn imported into the country declined 17 percent (from 18,100 tons to 15,100 tons), this decrease was outstripped by a 73 percent boost in the amount of imported wheat flour and processed bread products (from 75,000 tons in 1981 to 130,000 tons in 1986), a shift that is influencing dietary patterns within the country (Stonich, 1991b).

Macroeconomic Factors Affecting Agricultural Development

Government efforts aimed at expanding export agriculture in order to generate foreign exchange are more understandable, given Honduras' current fiscal condition. Although the Gross National Product grew from 2 percent to 3 percent annually between 1983 and 1987, *per capita* growth actually declined, with concomitant drops in wages, in living conditions, and in the quality of life (ADAI, 1987). The outcome has included a drop in the demand for food, services, and semidurable goods, which in turn has reduced tax revenues. In addition, between 1979 and 1986 Honduras' balance of payments deficit fluctuated between $100 million to $300 million annually, jeopardizing the country's international foreign currency reserve. During the same period, external debt rose 169 percent (to 73 percent of the GNP in 1986); the percentage of external debt payments swelled from 19 percent to 27 percent of state revenues; and the percentage of earnings from exports that went toward servicing the external debt expanded from 10 percent to 20 percent (ADAI, 1987). Given such macroeconomic conditions, it is unlikely that the national government will reorient significantly its agricultural policies away from attempting to expand export production.

Ecological and Human Consequences of Development

The expansion of capitalist agriculture affected the allocation of land and, in the context of regional population growth, exacerbated the concentration of landholdings (Stonich, 1986:139–43). At first, capitalist expansion was concentrated on large holdings located in the coastal lowlands, but subsequently extended to include smaller holdings in foothill and highland areas (Boyer, 1983, 1984; Stonich, 1986). Regionally, the result was a reallocation of land from forest, fallow, or growing food crops to the production of export crops and livestock (Stonich, 1986:129–39). The change in land use patterns was striking (Figure 3): between 1952 and 1974 the amount of land in forest dropped 44 percent and the area in fallow plunged 58 percent, while simultaneously the area in pasture rose 53 percent. By 1974, deciduous and pine forests covered only 13 percent of the region, whereas pasture extended over 60 percent of the total land area. A more recent land use classification of the Department of Choluteca (CRIES, 1984), based on remote sensing data and field reconnaissance, confirmed that pine and deciduous forests extended

FIGURE 3

Changes in Land Use in Southern Honduras: 1952–1974

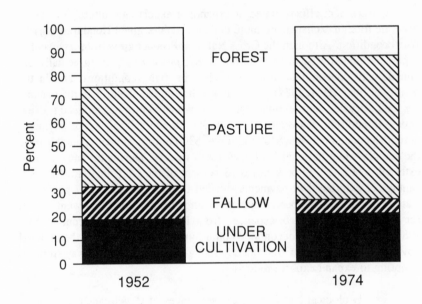

Sources: DGECH, *Censos Nacional Agropecuaria 1952 and 1974*, (1954, 1976).

over 13 percent of the department in the early 1980s. A vivid display of the results of these land use changes is presented in Figure 4; since 1952 the number of farms, the areas in production, and the total production of corn, beans, and sorghum (the basic food crops) have stagnated or declined, whereas the area in pasture and the production of cattle has risen dramatically. At the same time, the number of farms raising cattle has increased only 5 percent—implying increased concentration of production in the hands of fewer farmers.

Augmenting holdings for expanded commercial production, population growth, and in-migration to the region all contributed to the further concentration of landholdings—especially in the exclusion of small farmers for

FIGURE 4

Percentage Changes in the Number of Farms, Area in Production, and Total
Production of Corn, Beans, Sorghum, and Cattle in Southern Honduras: 1952–1974

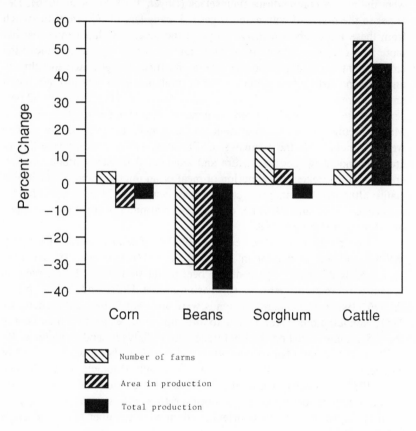

Sources: DGECH, *Censos Nacional Agropecuaria 1952 and 1974*, (1954, 1976).

whom land became increasingly scarce. In general, greatest population den-
sities and smallest landholdings were located in the highlands, the areas with
least agricultural potential (Stonich, 1986:155–56). Nevertheless, farmers
strove to enlarge production in these marginal areas by more intensively farming land already in cultivation and/or by farming previously uncultivated,
steeper, and even more marginal areas (Stonich 1986:Chapter VI). Despite
these efforts, per capita production of food crops in the region dropped dras-
tically between midcentury and the 1980s; corn production fell 71 percent,
sorghum 73 percent, and beans 81 percent (Stonich, 1986:137).

Although the regional expansion of export-oriented, capitalist agriculture initially resulted in the growth of wage labor opportunities, these jobs were limited in number and subject to the same "boom and bust" cycles as were the export commodities themselves (Boyer, 1983; Stonich, 1986). Declines in the prices of cotton and sugar led many large landowners to switch from these more labor-intensive crops to the much less labor-intensive but more land-extensive alternative—cattle raising. These decisions reduced the employment opportunities in the region and further aggravated the already unequal land distribution pattern. Overall rural unemployment in 1980, based on the corresponding monthly supply and demand of labor, averaged 62 percent for the year, ranging from 16 percent in September to 95 percent in March. Actually, the unemployment rate was much higher, because women were not included in the estimates (CSPE/OEA, 1982). Neither were the increased amount of land in pasture and augmented livestock production accompanied by greater consumption of meat or an improvement of nutritional status: although the total production of beef increased 231 percent in Honduras between 1960 and 1980, per capita consumption of beef actually declined by 20 percent (DeWalt, 1985).

After rising over 500 percent after 1950, beef exports reached their peak in 1981, and beef production in 1982 (USDA, 1987). Between 1982 and 1986 beef exports declined 50 percent and beef production dropped 30 percent in response to reduced demand (primarily in the U.S.) and falling prices (USDA, 1987). These national trends were apparent in the south where, by 1981, Honduran producers, unable to force up the prices paid for their beef in the U.S., reintroduced on-the-hoof trade with El Salvador and Guatemala. By 1982, meat packing plants frequently were shut down because of the lack of an adequate volume of cattle to operate efficiently (Stonich, 1986:117–18). Since 1982, national agricultural policy has been directed at diversifying agricultural production in the region; however, these efforts remain directed toward the expansion of export-oriented commodities, rather than food crops (ADAI, 1987).

The transformation of the agrarian structure in the south that included significant changes in land use, the radical fall in per capita production of basic grains, and restricted employment opportunities with which to earn cash to buy food aggravated widespread regional undernutrition. In 1979 the national planning agency concluded that 41 percent of all southern families did not meet subsistence levels (SAPLAN, 1981). Analysis of the household/community level data collected between 1981 and 1984 as part of this study showed that approximately 37 percent of households in rural communities were unable to meet energy needs (Stonich, 1986: Chapter VII) and 65 percent of the children under sixty months of age were stunted (i.e., under 95 percent of the standard height-for-age ratio recommended by the World Health Organization) (DeWalt and DeWalt, 1987:39). My regional breakdown of the results of the national nutritional study conducted in 1986 by SAEH/INCAP (SAEH/INCAP, 1987) indicated that 36 percent of all first graders in the south were more than two standard deviations below the height-for-age ratio of the WHO reference population—indicating widespread, moderate to severe degrees of undernutrition.

Local Level Responses to Capitalist Expansion

A number of studies have examined the expansion of capitalist agriculture into hinterland highland areas and the associated effects of this penetration on rural households and communities (Stares, 1972; White, 1977; Durham, 1979; Boyer, 1983, 1984; DeWalt and DeWalt, 1982; Stonich, 1986). The development of capitalist agriculture provided the means for the socioeconomic differentiation of households and the subsequent requirement for many households to engage in a variety of off-farm activities in order to survive. This process of differentiation was dependent on a number of inter-related factors, including differential access to land, limited growth in wage labor positions, and expanding opportunities for the investment of capital (Stonich, 1986:254–56). Diminished access to land made most farm households increasingly dependent on wage labor, migration, and remittances that came predominantly from family members living outside the household (Stonich, 1991a). Simultaneously, the evolution of a class of "rich" peasants depended on opportunities for realizing capital—particularly through cattle raising and through mercantile activities. As wage labor, cash-earning activities, and short/long term migration became increasingly essential, the number of social and economic ties outside communities expanded and became more complex (Stonich, 1991a). Agricultural cooperatives, truckers acting as marketing middlemen, and community members who traveled outside the community to take advantage of regional and national markets through the sale of their own produce, dairy products, and meat, all functioned as links in growing regional and national networks (see Stonich, 1986: Chapter VI). Land-poor and landless peasants unable to produce enough for their own needs became integrated into the capitalist agricultural sector. Farmers with medium holdings who were able to produce enough for their families had little incentive to produce a surplus of basic grains. Instead, they and the large landholders continued to accumulate land, mechanized that part of their operations that they could, and turned more and more to export-oriented cattle production.[4]

The Ecological Consequences of Local Responses

The short, steep slopes, highly erosive soils, and concentrated, irregular precipitation patterns that characterize southern Honduras leave the region highly vulnerable to environmental deterioration (see USAID, 1981, 1982; CRIES, 1984; Stonich, 1986:Chapter II for more thorough discussions of the environmental context and the natural resource/agricultural potential of the region). Agricultural practices having deleterious effects on the environment were associated with the agricultural systems of each socioeconomically differentiated subgroup—"rich" farmers, medium farmers, small farmers, and renters. Table 2 summarizes data collected from highland communities and relates a number of such practices to land tenure.[5] It shows that renters used their land more intensively than any other group, planting 95 percent of the land that they rented in annual food crops. It clearly reveals that truly intensive use of land was confined to small farms, especially to those of under one hectare. At the same time, the percentage of land in pasture and the mean number of cattle owned was significantly related to the size of landholdings (the Pearson Correlation Coefficient between the size of landholdings and the number of cattle that were owned was .915).[6] These same relationships among size of landholdings, the percentage of land in cultivation of annual food crops, and the percentage of land in pasture were repeated at the municipal and regional levels (Stonich, 1986:137–38).

The implications of such intensive use of land by small farmers are considerable. In the shifting cultivation system of the highlands, such farmers are faced with the choice of reducing fallow periods or forgoing fallow cycles altogether; renting land from others if they choose to allow their own land to return to fallow; or substituting wage labor to earn cash to buy food. In highland communities all these options were being exercised. Table 2 shows that the number of years that farmers allowed land to return to fallow increased as the size of landholdings rose, ranging from a mean of 2.7 years for farmers with access to less than one hectare of land to six years for the largest farmer, with access to seventy-five hectares. Farmers also chose to shorten fallow periods; within the memory of the active farmers, fallow periods had decreased from an average of fifteen to twenty years to an average of zero to seven years. Finally, more than 50 percent of farmers who owned less than one hectare of land rented land to supplement their own inadequate holdings (Stonich, 1986:Chapter VI).

Renters had little motivation to practice conservation measures. The land that they rented was generally the worst, the steepest, and the most degraded. Landowners feared that if renters had the use of the same parcel for any length of time it would be difficult to make them leave. Consequently, renters generally had access to the same parcel of land for a maximum of three years, and had insufficient incentive to implement and maintain mechanical soil conservation measures. In addition, after the three-year period, renters were often required by the landowners to sow pasture grass along with the last year's food crops, thus making renters a vital link in the forest-to-pasture

TABLE 2

Agricultural Practices by Land Tenure Arrangements, Highland Village Data, Southern Honduras, 1983

Type Of Tenancy	(N)	Percent Of Land In Food Crops[a]	Percent Of Land In Pasture	Mean Number Of Cattle Owned (Range)		Length Of Fallow (Years)
Renters[b]	(74)	95	–	.17	(0–4)	2.7
Owners less than 1 ha[c]	(23)	80	–	.22	(0–3)	2.7
1–5 ha	(87)	51	4	.22	(0–3)	3.2
5–20 ha	(15)	23	21	2.5	(0–13)	3.8
20–50 ha	(5)	6	48	8.0	(7–9)	5.0
more than 50 ha	(1)	6	20[d]	50.0	(50)	6.0

[a] Maize, sorghum, and beans.
[b] Mean area of rented land, 1.4 ha.
[c] 51% of such owners also rent land.
[d] Largest landowner rents additional grazing land in lowlands.

Source: Author's calculations based on an unpublished sample survey conducted by author. Details on survey data, methodology, and results available from author.

conversion process (DeWalt, 1983). In addition, rents were high, ranging from one-third to one-half of shared crops, leaving renters unable to afford other inputs. Finally, renters were more likely than any other subgroup of farmers to continually burn their parcels, a practice most continued because of the labor demands imposed by the hand removal of thorny regrowth (Hawkins, 1984; Stonich, 1986:219). In summary, the agricultural practices of renters (including the most intensive cultivation of the most marginal land; the clearing of all trees and saplings; the repeated burning; and the lack of mechanical soil conservation methods and fertilizers) constituted an agricultural system that was extremely destructive to the environment. To a lesser degree, these same deleterious procedures were found in the agricultural systems of the small, resource-poor, owner farmers (those with access to less than five hectares of land). These farmers were more prone to preserve saplings and useful trees and to construct rock-wall barriers and other soil conservation measures. In contrast to landless and land-poor farmers, medium and large farmers maintained longer periods of fallow, were most likely to sustain soil conservation measures, and were least apt to burn their fields. However, erosion caused by overgrazing, especially during the dry season, and by cattle browsing saplings and trees in fallow fields, was widespread.[7] In addition, it was these medium and large landholding farmers who were actively engaging limited-resource farmers in the process of forest-to-pasture transformation.

In summary, major causes of highland deforestation have involved the intensification of agricultural production and the expansion of agricultural and pasture lands into steeper, more marginal areas.[8] The shortening of fallow periods, the continuous burning, the prevailing lack of conservation measures, and the overgrazing that have accompanied forest depletion have led to extensive land degradation (i.e., loss of soil fertility, erosion, and landslides). The effects of the destruction of highland environments, however, has not been limited to the highlands. Widespread watershed deterioration has escalated siltation of rivers and of the mangrove areas along the coast of the Gulf of Fonseca. Increased sediment loads caused by degeneration of highland environments have combined with agricultural runoff contaminated with pesticide residues from large-scale, export-oriented, lowland farms. Along with the considerable harvesting of mangroves for use as fuelwood in the Pacific coastal salt extraction industry, these multiple factors have contributed to the ongoing, substantial destruction of the mangrove forests, thereby also threatening the rich shrimp and fishing grounds these areas nourish.

Conclusions

Since midcentury, southern Honduras has been characterized by expanding capitalist social relations that have transformed the agrarian structure. Consequently, the ways in which natural resources have been exploited have been greatly decided by the dictates of capitalist accumulation. The agrarian structure that now exists includes an intricate network of classes and interest groups, each controlling differing proportions of social power. Those groups that possess positions of wealth and privilege also tend to have a greater say in the domain of public policy. As a result, the agencies of the state are inclined to satisfy the requirements of the dominant classes. International and national forces have combined to influence the adaptive responses of highland farmers in the south. These adaptive responses have necessitated agricultural strategies that have accelerated ecological decline. The major conclusion of this paper is that environmental degradation in southern Honduras arises from the fundamental structure of society. Small-scale, resource-poor farmers often directly cause environmental deterioration because they are forced to do so by existing social relationships. They are under such pressure to secure a livelihood that the short-term costs of conservation efforts are prohibitive.

The effects of environmental deterioration are gradual, difficult to measure, and vary from place to place. It is the more powerful groups that are best able to adjust to these effects and who also are least likely to experience these consequences on a day-to-day basis, thereby making it more difficult to mobilize them around issues of environmental destruction. It is necessary, however, to understand the systemic interrelationships among different power-holding groups before determining the causes, directions, and solutions to environmental problems. It is simplistic to point to the agricultural practices of one or the other group when determining blame. For example, the practices of renters and the smallest landholders in southern Honduras appear to be the most destructive; however, given their environmental, economic, and demographic limitations, such farmers have little alternative and in fact frequently act as agents of the more powerful, larger landholders in the forest-to-pasture conversion process. In southern Honduras, environmental degradation is intricately connected to problems of land tenure, unemployment, demography, and poverty.

Theoretical Conclusions

These results have a number of general implications for directing efforts in theory building in anthropology, as well as more specific implications for explaining environmental deterioration. First, understanding the relationships among social processes and environmental decline in southern Honduras depends on comprehending the multifarious interrelationships among complex biophysical environments and social hierarchies. A focus constricted to demographic, social, or biophysical factors or limited to a single level of analysis (from the most microlevel to the most macrolevel) would have resulted in a far less comprehensive, and likely erroneous explanation. In addition, the research results demonstrated that causality was not unidirectional but rather multidirectional (and multidimensional), involving dynamic, interactive mechanisms that linked human goals with material constraints and were mediated through social institutions. Together, this research supports the need to expand more narrowly focused anthropological research concerned with explaining the complex, worldwide, social and ecological processes involved in what Bennett (1976) has called the "ecological transition." In this paper, I have used political economy in order to emphasize the roles that macrolevel social institutions play in providing constraints and possibilities that affect the human decisions that, in turn, affect the biophysical environment. This political-economic analysis, however, was embedded within a systems perspective (Stonich, 1986) that integrated social and ecological factors and that corresponds closely to "socionatural systems" (Bennett, 1976) and "human systems ecology" (Smith and Reeves, 1989) frameworks. Together, these perspectives share a systems orientation that is multidimensional and multifaceted, and provide a framework in which to articulate human adaptation into institutional and biophysical hierarchies.

Methodological Conclusions

The most important methodological consequence of this study is that it highlights the need for genuine interdisciplinary efforts to deal with the vital social and environmental issues emanating from the world transformation. The traditional holistic orientation of anthropology, combined with a systems approach that allows the operationalization of that holism, furnish anthropologists with the means of providing an essential role in such interdisciplinary endeavors. However, although anthropologists control special and significant knowledge, they must rely on other disciplines for critical information. In order for anthropologists to be able to interact effectively in interdisciplinary research contexts with other professionals, such as natural resource specialists, agronomists, soil scientists, plant breeders, and others who could provide such information, anthropology training must be more interdisciplinary than it usually is now. The anthropologist member of a research team composed primarily of members from other disciplines will not be accepted as a fully participating scientist unless he or she understands other techniques and can make useful suggestions about research design and analysis.

Policy Conclusions

The results presented in this paper are germane to understanding human and environmental impoverishment in other parts of Central America. There is overwhelming evidence from throughout the region that because of economic and population pressures, economic actors at all levels, from governments to individuals, are overexploiting the natural resources that they control in order to generate income to satisfy immediate needs—whether those requirements are to generate foreign exchange at the national level, or to increase current income at the level of the household. The costs of these short-sighted strategies are already apparent in accelerated deterioration of forests, soils, fisheries, and other crucial resources, and in probable longer-term declines in food security, in economic growth, and in well-being. The continued destruction of Central American natural resource systems will doubtless exacerbate the existing widespread problems of economic stagnation, rural impoverishment, and social instability (Leonard, 1987; USAID, 1989).

Recommendations directed at allaying the environmental and social problems in southern Honduras are pertinent to a larger region because the patterns in social trends, in resource exploitation, and in consequent environmental deterioration that have been identified in this paper are widespread in Central America (Williams, 1986; Leonard, 1987). Throughout the region, environmental and resource management policies that attempt to conserve or restore long-term ecological sustainability often contradict the logic of capitalist accumulation and, as a result, the concerns of the more powerful social actors. Therefore, any efforts to amend the patterns of exploitation of the natural environment in ways that involve the redistribution of costs and benefits, such as access to resources or transformations in the forms of production, must ultimately cope with a broad realm of contending social, economic, political, and ideological factors. It would seem that the likelihood of effective interventions would be heightened if these competing forces were candidly faced and addressed during the processes of environmental policy design and implementation.

8

Agrarian Reform and the Food Crisis in Mexico: Microlevel and Macrolevel Processes[1]

Kathleen M. DeWalt and Billie R. DeWalt

During the twentieth century Mexico experienced a political revolution that resulted in the first comprehensive land reform in Latin America and two green revolutions that substantially modernized its agricultural sector. Despite these revolutions, the agricultural and food systems of Mexico have been in a severe crisis since the early 1980s. For these reasons, Mexico provides an extremely important case study in the impact of food and agricultural policy on issues of health and nutrition.

As anthropologists, we tend to focus on the microlevel—that is, on communities and the households in them—in our studies of economic and nutritional systems. However, to address policy issues we need to approach the identification of research questions, data collection and analysis in ways that allow for the inclusion of the policy climate in our community level analyses. The purpose of this paper is to use both macrolevel data on the Mexican food system and microlevel data on four agrarian reform communities to determine the dimensions of the current crisis. We will show how our anthropological research in these four communities was structured in such a way as to allow us to demonstrate linkages between microlevel and macrolevel processes (see DeWalt and Pelto, 1985).

The research to be presented here is drawn from several years of study of the effects of increasing sorghum production on Mexican agriculture and food security. In a series of publications, we have documented national level trends in the Mexican food system and agricultural policy since 1940 (B. DeWalt, 1985a; Barkin and B. DeWalt, 1985, 1988; B. DeWalt and Barkin, 1987; B. DeWalt et al., 1987). In this paper, we focus much more on how these larger trends in Mexico's agricultural and food systems have affected people at the microlevel. In other words, we want to explore what microlevel data can tell us about macrolevel processes in Mexican food and agricultural systems.

An evaluation of the effects of agrarian reform and Mexican food and agricultural policy on rural communities during the past half-century is important for several reasons. The first is that, after a bloody civil war during the decade between 1910 and 1920, eventually about half of the arable land in the country was put into the hands of small farmers. Mexico is the Latin American country with the longest experience with agrarian reform. It has served as both a model for other agrarian reforms and a model case in the debate concerning the success or failure of agrarian reform. The effects of land reform on food security can be evaluated on several levels, including effects on the household, specifically the small farm household; effects on rural communities; and effects on regions and the nation.

A second important reason for focusing on Mexico is that the country was the birthplace of the green revolution. With initial funding from the Rockefeller Foundation in the early 1940s, the country undertook a major effort to apply modern technology to its agricultural production over the next several decades. Work on high-yielding varieties of wheat in Mexico earned Norman Borlaug the Nobel Peace Prize in 1970, and the institution with which he was associated eventually became the International Center for Maize and Wheat Improvement (CIMMYT), one of the models for the thirteen international agricultural research centers that are now part of the Consultative Group for International Agricultural Research (CGIAR) system.

Third, Mexican policymakers and researchers have been involved in an ongoing debate concerning the issue of food self-sufficiency. For much of the last half-decade, the debate has centered on whether Mexico needs to strive for food self-sufficiency or whether the country should rely on agricultural trade to meet its needs. This debate became especially salient during the late 1970s, when there was talk in the United States of using food as a political weapon—especially using food to trade for oil—at approximately the same time that the country had to begin importing significant quantities of food from the United States. Estimates in the late 1970s and early 1980s indicated that, if current trends continued, by 1990 Mexico would be using most of its oil revenues to import food. As a result, the Sistema Alimentario Mexicano (SAM)—Mexico's well-publicized plan to return to food self-sufficiency—was created (see Austin and Esteva, 1987).

Finally, and perhaps most important, as we and others (Dewalt and Barkin, 1987; Rama and Rello, 1982; Hewitt, 1976) have shown, Mexico's agricultural and food policies since the 1940s have created what is now widely referred to as a crisis (Yates, 1981; Barkin and Suárez, 1986; Austin and Esteva, 1987). Technological success in modernizing agriculture has not been accompanied by the anticipated social, nutritional, and economic successes.

Agrarian Reform and Food Policy in Mexico—The Macro Dimension

Agrarian reform, especially during the 1930s, led to a situation in which the beneficiaries of the land redistribution, the *ejidatarios*, came to control about 50 percent of the arable land in Mexico. Although much of the land received by small farmers was of poor quality, they did make better use of it than the former owners of haciendas, and agricultural production rose substantially. In 1940, ejidatarios were producing about 51 percent of the total value of Mexican agricultural production on the 47 percent of the land that they held (see de Janvry, 1981:127).

Since then, however, the Mexican government has provided little support to the small farm sector (see Sanderson, 1984). Instead, it has chosen to invest in large irrigation districts whose lands are generally controlled by large landholders, rather than small. Little agricultural credit is provided to the small farmers, with the result that a "bimodal agriculture" has been created in the country. A segment of the agrarian sector (the large farmers) use technology as modern as any in the world and get very high yields. The small farm sector makes do with only some elements of improved technology, resulting in yields that are quite low. As a consequence, the value of agricultural products from the ejidal sector has dropped substantially.

Over the years, the crop choices of larger farmers have shifted significantly as well. Because of government attempts to keep the prices of basic staples low for urban consumers, commercial farmers do not find these to be profitable crops. Increasingly they have switched to higher-value crops for more affluent consumers or for export. The result has been a rapid increase in the production of fruits and vegetables (Rama and Vigorito, 1977), and a boom in the production of livestock products (see Barkin, 1982).

During the 1950s and 1960s, these trends seemed to be quite positive. There was a substantial expansion of the amount of land under cultivation, heavy government investments led to an increasing percentage of irrigated land, and there was an increasing use of fertilizers. These were all factors that led to the intensification in the use of land resources. Yates estimated that the Mexican agricultural sector grew at the phenomenal rate of 5.7 percent per year from 1940 to 1965 (1981:15). Because of this growth, there were many in the 1960s who referred to Mexico as having experienced an "agricultural miracle" (Yates, 1981). The more intensive use of land also led to the creation of much-needed employment in the rural areas, where population was growing rapidly. Employment in modern agriculture in Mexico grew at a cumulative annual rate of 2.3 percent between 1950 and 1980. At the same time, in Latin America as a whole, the growth rate was only 0.5 percent (Couriel, 1984:55).

However, some warning signs tempering this generally positive picture were emerging. Hewitt (1976) and others pointed out that most of the modernization in Mexican agriculture was occurring among larger farmers; the many small farmers to whom land had been redistributed after the revolution were not sharing in the "miracle." Indeed, the employment figures show that whereas employment in the modern rural sector (i.e., commercial agriculture) expanded from 31.7 percent of the total employed in agriculture in 1950 to 51 percent in 1980, there was an absolute reduction in the number of self-employed agricultural workers (Couriel 1984:56). In other words, fewer farmers were working their own land and were becoming agricultural workers for larger operations.

At the same time, the kinds of crops that were being grown changed substantially. Basic grain production has been displaced by soy, alfalfa, sorghum, oats, and other cultivars oriented toward livestock production. These trends have been encouraged by government credits and subsidies for these products (see Barkin and B. DeWalt, 1988; B. DeWalt, 1988; B. DeWalt, K. DeWalt, Barkin, and Escudero, 1987). Since the late 1970s, the amount of land planted in maize and beans has decreased or remained steady. The amount of land planted in wheat, the first green revolution crop in Mexico, stagnated as well. On the other hand, sorghum production has continued to rise, going from an insignificant crop in the 1950s to Mexico's second largest crop in the 1970s. This trend has been called Mexico's second green revolution (B. DeWalt, 1985a).

The result was that the proportion of cropland devoted to animal production increased from about 5 percent in 1960 to over 23 percent in 1980 (Barkin, 1982:66–67) and the proportion of grains fed to animals increased from 6 percent of total apparent consumption in 1960 (Meissner, 1981) to 32 percent in 1980 (B. DeWalt, 1985a), to over 48 percent by 1985 (reported in the Mexican newspaper *UnoMásUno* January 10, 1985:1).

The country, which was largely self-sufficient in food during the 1950s and 1960s, has become a major importer of food. By 1984 the country imported 53 percent of its basic grain needs in wheat and maize and 43 percent of its needs in sorghum (Adelski, 1987:26). Between 1981 and 1985, the country was spending an average of 842 million dollars a year to import cereal grains, and its average food import bill was 862 million dollars a year (IDB 1987:49). In 1983 agricultural imports comprised 17 percent of all Mexican imports, and in 1984 Mexico was importing 25 percent of the total of all the agricultural products imported by Latin America (IDB, 1986:82).

Large and small farmers have in recent years been trying to boost the profitability of their operations by becoming more capital-intensive and more land-extensive. That is, farmers have increasingly turned to mechanization and chemical pest control (especially use of herbicides) and to alternative crops as ways of eliminating the need for labor. Significant changes in the use of labor have occurred; permanent employees were replaced by machinery and by temporary and migratory laborers, causing substantial increases in the numbers of unemployed and underemployed individuals. The percentage of the labor force involved in agriculture had fallen from 60.4 percent in 1950 to 36.6 percent in 1980 (IDB, 1987:105). Many of these people, formerly employed in agriculture, have migrated to cities. About 70 percent of the population is now urban and, although Mexico had an official urban unemployment rate of only 4.8 percent in 1986 (IDB, 1987:120), it has been estimated that about 42 percent of those "employed" in the urban areas of Mexico City, Monterrey and Guadalajara are in the informal sector (Sethuraman 1981; quoted in IDB, 1987:126).

In terms of income, Mexico is classified as an upper middle-income country by the World Bank, having a GNP per capita of $2040 in 1984 (World Bank, 1986:181). These average figures, however, mask one of the most unequal income distributions in the world. Data from 1977, for example, show that the percentage share of household income of the poorest 20 percent of the population is only 2.9 percent (in the U.S. it is 5.3 percent), whereas the percentage share of the wealthiest 10 percent is 40.6 percent (in the U.S. it is 23.3 percent). In the agricultural sector, 61 percent of those employed have a monthly income of less than $47 dollars a month (IDB, 1987:197).

The inequalities in the distribution of income in Mexico are mirrored in the health and nutritional situation. The Mexican food system provides an affluent diet for wealthy and middle-class Mexicans whose relative participation in national income increased substantially during the 1970s (see Hardy, 1982), increasing their demand for sources of animal protein. Gonzalez Casanova estimated that the 15 percent of Mexicans with the most purchasing power consume 50 percent of the food, whereas the bottom 30 percent consume only 10 percent (1980:202). The government itself reported in 1980 that twenty-five million Mexicans (over 35 percent of the population) *never* eat meat (see Redclift, 1981:13–14). Government data from surveys by the National Nutrition Institute indicated that severe malnutrition is common in many rural areas and that nineteen million Mexicans (over 27 percent of the population) have a daily calorie and protein intake below the minimum required for physical well-being (summarized in Redclift, 1981:13–14).

Health indicators in Mexico also lag far behind those of other less affluent countries. The infant mortality rate of 51 per thousand in 1984 (World Bank, 1986:233) was far worse than that of many other countries at similar levels of development, and life expectancy had only increased to 66 years (IDB, 1987:342). Despite the country's heavy investment in medical services, many Mexicans continued to be plagued by gastrointestinal illnesses and to succumb to infections. These problems were worst in rural areas where poverty, poor nutrition, and poor health were common.

Thus, to sum up the macrolevel data, Mexico did not follow up agrarian reform with programs designed to help improve the productivity of small farms. Instead, agricultural development in Mexico has been characterized by the development of a bimodal pattern in which the large farmers grow export crops and livestock products to sell to affluent parts of the population. Small farmers continue to grow the basic staples, but with little support for improving their productivity and without price incentives to produce surpluses. The result is that Mexico has moved from being a major exporter to a major importer of agricultural products. Employment in the agricultural sector has been declining, and the rural population is migrating to cities or the United States. Mexico is characterized by an extremely unequal distribution of income and the consequence is widespread malnutrition and poor health.

Because of the food and agricultural crisis in Mexico, a substantial debate has arisen concerning the viability of agrarian reform communities and their role in the national economy. There are those who argue that the *ejido*-based production is inefficient, and that ejidos should become absorbed into partnerships with the private sector (see Solis, 1973; Yates, 1981) or be substantially restructured (Escárcega López and Botey Estapé, 1990; Secretaría de Agricultura y Recursos Hidráulicos, 1990). They argue that the agrarian reform did not benefit either rural communities or the nation as a whole, and that Mexico should more profitably invest its land and capital resources in the commercial agricultural sector.

It was one objective of our research to address this issue through an evaluation of the effects of agrarian reform on the economy and the health and nutrition situation of rural communities. For theoretical as well as practical reasons we chose to examine the economic, social, and health processes surrounding the adoption of a particular commodity—sorghum—in rural agrarian reform communities in Mexico. The cultivation of sorghum can be viewed as a case illustrating the transformation of Mexican agriculture in the decades since land reform. Grain sorghum is grown as a feed crop in Mexico and is representative of the shift from basic grain production to the production of higher value foods to meet middle- and upper-class demand for animal products. The cultivation of sorghum has increased over the last thirty years to become Mexico's second most important agricultural product in terms of area planted, and has displaced the production of food grains, principally maize. Increases in sorghum production have been encouraged by national agricultural policies favoring cash crop production, mechanization of production, and irrigation, as well as the development and diffusion of hybrid seed from the southern United States. Although sorghum production was adopted first by private, commercial farmers, the small farm, ejidal sector has increasingly adopted sorghum as a cash crop, replacing semisubsistence maize production (DeWalt and Barkin, 1987). In the small farm sector, sorghum production represents the adoption of a technological package that includes the use of agrochemicals, mechanical harvesting and, in some instances, land preparation, agricultural credit, and more formal marketing arrangements.

The Community Studies—Methodology

The research strategy adopted for the community studies was drawn from several approaches. Following Pelto and Pelto's (1978) admonitions, it was based on a mix of qualitative and quantitative data-gathering techniques and organized into three phases in the field: an ethnographic phase, punctuated with a preliminary report based on qualitative research, a quantitative phase, using structured interviews based on forms developed and refined on the basis of ethnographic information, and a final phase, in which a second preliminary report was prepared in the field.

Strategies adopted from Farming Systems Research (FSR) approaches to diagnostic surveys (CIMMYT, 1980; Shaner et al., 1982; B. DeWalt, 1985b) were incorporated in the design of the research and the selection of fieldworkers. Field teams were recruited from among graduates of the Universidad Autónoma Metropolitana (UAM) who had to complete a required year of public service before receiving their degree. Each team contained at least one agronomist, one social scientist (anthropologist or economist) and one woman. Following assumptions inherent in FSR, members of different disciplines were expected to attend to different aspects of the production process and its socioeconomic impact. The community studies were carried out by field teams of three or four people with supervision by the principal investigators.

Selection of Study Communities

Several criteria were used in selecting study communities. Because we were primarily interested in small farmers and landless workers, who represent the segments of the rural population thought to be at greatest nutritional risk, and were interested in assessing the role of the agrarian reform and agricultural policies directed towards this sector, we focused on ejido communities. We wished to include communities that varied with respect to ecological conditions, date of land grant, average size of land holdings, access to irrigation, access to technical assistance and credit, and proximity to markets and migration routes. Finally, we wanted to avoid regions such as the Mexican central highlands, where a substantial amount of social science research has already occurred. For the same reason we eliminated indigenous communities from consideration. We wished to choose regions that were more typical of the sorghum-producing areas of Mexico, and representative of the largest number of small farmers and the agrarian reform sector in general.

Our research, however, is not generalizable to those parts of the ejidal sector located in highland areas or indigenous communities.

Production figures for sorghum and other grains were collected by state and municipality (where available). Regions were identified in which increases in sorghum production in recent years were coupled with decreases in production of subsistence crops, most notably maize. An attempt was then made to identify variation among sorghum-producing regions with respect to climate and rainfall; the availability of important aspects of infrastructure, most importantly irrigation; how long ago land was granted to the ejido; access to marketing centers; and the presence or absence of large-scale development projects.

Sorghum-producing regions of four states were identified: the *municipios* (counties or municipalities) of Apatzingan, Michoacán; Quebrantadero, Morelos; Abasolo, Tamaulipas; and Cerritos, San Luis Potosí. Visits were made to each region. Local extension agents, other development personnel, community leaders and ejidal presidents were interviewed. We then chose ejidos that varied along the dimensions mentioned above.

The Research Process

Teams spent a total of five months between July and December 1984 in the communities selected. In the first predominantly ethnographic phase of research, team members engaged in participant observation and conducted informal interviews concerning agricultural practices, cycles of production, constraints to production, community history, patterns of food use, and general health. Field teams followed a research guide that included a wide range of data categories, including production practices, production costs, adoption of technology, alternative economic strategies, local and ejidal history, attitudes concerning different crops, methods of production, credit, perceptions of health and nutritional status, food preferences, and infant and child feeding practices. Interviews on these topics were conducted with key informants from the community, health professionals in the region, bank officials, and staff of the regional offices of the ministry of agriculture and natural resources. The first preliminary report identified groups with differing access to resources and production strategies in order to guide sampling for the survey phase of research.

In the second phase of research, a sample of families was selected from among the identified groups within the community. Research teams did a map of all households in each community. Our goal was to randomly select a percentage of households in each community, but, because of logistical problems and the size and nature of each community, the sampling design was somewhat different in each. In Michoacán, there were two communities, seven kilometers apart, which were part of a single ejido. The study team lived in one of the two communities. All households (N = 49) from that community were included in the sample. Because of the difficulties of travelling to the other community during the rainy season, a ¼ sample of the 120 households of that community was interviewed. In San Luis Potosí, the research team sought to interview a 50 percent random sample of the 159 households in the community. Only seventy-six interviews were completed, because five households refused to participate. The community in Morelos was by far the largest studied. The research team established a goal of doing 100 interviews. Numbers of the 436 houses mapped were put into a hat and the first 100 drawn were included in the sample. In Tamaulipas, 70 percent of the 107 households in the community were sampled. In all communities (except that in San Luis Potosí) if members of a household refused to participate, a replacement household was randomly selected.

Male and female household heads were interviewed using four separate interview schedules—one focused on agricultural production, one on household socioeconomic conditions, one on reproductive and health histories, and one on household food resources, including a one-week market basket interview. In addition, height and weight for children five years of age and younger in sample households were measured to assess nutritional status.

The Community Studies—Microlevel Data

The total population of the communities ranged from a low of 610 in the community in Tamaulipas to over 2800 in the community in Morelos. The ejidos connected to these communities received their land at different periods of time; the communities in San Luis Potosí and Morelos received their land in the late 1920s, whereas ejidos were not formed in Michoacán and Tamaulipas until the 1960s. Extensive cultivation of sorghum in these communities dates from the late 1960s or early 1970s. Agricultural mechanization also dates from about this same time. Tractors are now available in all four communities to carry out some of the agricultural labor.

The ecological and infrastructural conditions of these communities are quite different. Land grants in Tamaulipas, although much larger than the other communities', were initially (before irrigation) almost useless for crop production. Many ejidatarios abandoned their land to work as migrant laborers. With the extension of irrigation to this area in 1972, ejidatarios returned to work land of good quality and in quantities far larger than the average ejido holding. The resources available to these farmers are more like those of private landowners in Mexico. The situation of farmers in Michoacán and San Luis Potosí is more typical of ejidos in Mexico; they have relatively small, rainfed landholdings that make agriculture extremely precarious. In Morelos, the quality of some of the land has improved significantly because of the wells drilled for irrigation, but access to the irrigated land is very unequal. Morelos also has the advantage of being close to the major urban markets of central Mexico.

Economic Comparisons

The first objective of our research was to determine the access to economic resources of the people in the four communities. We were especially interested in (1) access to land; (2) access to other employment opportunities; (3) the cash income resulting from these activities; and (4) migration patterns, which would serve as an indicator of whether community members perceived these communities as economically viable.

All of these communities were beneficiaries of the agrarian reform that resulted from the Mexican Revolution, so that many people have access to land. There is a little private land in and around some of the communities, and we also tried to determine how much renting and sharecropping of land was occurring.[2] A composite score of land access was created that summed the total of all ejido, private, rented land, and half of all the land sharecropped, then subtracted any land rented to others by the household.

Figure 1 compares land access among the households sampled in our research. Despite the agrarian reform, in all of the communities, between 20 percent and 30 percent of households do not have access to land. Landholdings are most scarce in the community in Morelos, where about 36 percent of households have access to fewer than three hectares of land. In Tamaulipas, in contrast, the 69 percent of families with access to ejido land each have about twenty hectares, fifteen of which are irrigated. Thus, although many households do have access to land, there is substantial inequality of land distribution within and among these different communities.

As we have noted earlier, access to land is only one element in the ability to use agricultural resources to provide for one's family. Mexican agrarian history since 1940 has been characterized by a relative lack of support for the ejido and small farm sector, in terms of credit, technical assistance, infrastructure, and research.

One indicator of whether these communities are successful in terms of their agricultural systems is the portion of income that is derived from agricultural pursuits. Table 1 summarizes the proportion of income derived from various sources for the households sampled in the four communities. This table indicates that households depend on a wide range of sources in order to satisfy their economic needs. Grain crops such as sorghum and maize that are extensively grown in each of the communities provide the major part of the reported income only in the community in Tamaulipas. The community in Morelos is least dependent on selling grain crops; sales of livestock provide the most income, with substantial contributions also coming from sales of

FIGURE 1

Distribution of Land Among Farmers in the Four Communities

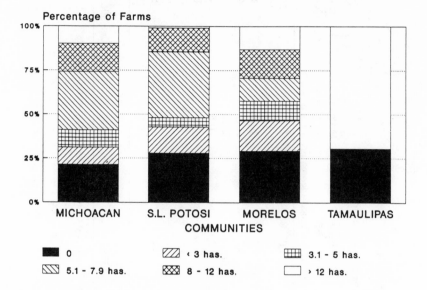

Percentage of Farms

■ 0	▨ ‹ 3 has.	▦ 3.1 - 5 has.
▧ 5.1 - 7.9 has.	▩ 8 - 12 has.	☐ › 12 has.

MICHOACAN   S.L. POTOSI   MORELOS   TAMAULIPAS
COMMUNITIES

fruits and vegetables and from wage labor. Wage labor is least important in San Luis Potosí; here remittances from people working legally and illegally in the United States are quite important in maintaining the community economically.

Mean cash income for the households indicates that the communities in San Luis Potosí and Michoacán are quite poor and had an estimated household annual income of only $1358 and $1858 in 1984. In contrast, in both Morelos and Tamaulipas the households have a mean cash income of well over $2500 per year (Figure 2). These are average figures, and it should be emphasized that they mask considerable variation; many households have cash incomes much smaller than the average figure. A few households have cash incomes substantially higher than the average.

Because estimates of income are relatively unreliable, we also constructed a material style of life (MSL) scale to measure the relative wealth of the household. MSL is based on the number of consumer items that are owned by the household.[3] The MSL scale scores demonstrate somewhat different patterns than income. The households in the community in Morelos have the most material goods; those in Michoacán have the least (see Figure 2).

TABLE 1

Sources of Income for the Four Communities—1984

	Michoacan (N = 79)	S.L. Potosi (N = 70)	Morelos (N = 85)	Tamaulipas (N = 73)
		Percentages of Total Income From Each Source		
Sorghum	20.2	10.0	14.7	27.7
Other grains	5.4	3.7	1.4	31.9
Fruit and vegs.	4.4	0.0	10.9	4.6
Livestock*	24.7	3.6	30.9	4.3
Wage labor	21.4	15.4	28.8	15.4
Equipment rental	9.2	0.2	0.5	4.2
Remittances	3.6	8.5	3.0	1.4
Other	4.1	5.9	8.1	6.4
Value of subsistence crops**	2.8	10.1	1.6	1.6
U.S. income	4.1	42.6	0.0	2.4
Mean total income in U.S. Dollars	1859	1358	2748	3066

*This category includes income from sales of animals, as well as livestock products such as milk, cheese, and eggs.
**Market value of agricultural products consumed in the home.

FIGURE 2

Comparison of Economic Indicators in the Four Communities

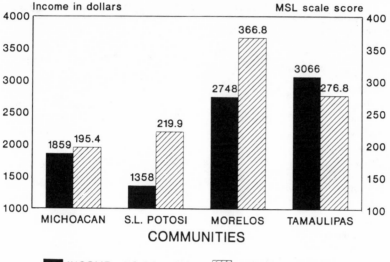

Other indicators of the relative success of agriculture in these communities are provided in Table 2. In a direct question about whether the household head earned the greater part of his or her income from agriculture, only in Michoacán and Tamaulipas did more than 50 percent indicate that they did. In San Luis Potosí and Morelos, less than 20 percent of the household heads indicated that they earned a major part of their income from agriculture. In all the communities over 60 percent of the household heads indicated that they had at some point worked outside the community; more than 95 percent in San Luis Potosí had temporarily migrated from the community to work. Over 80 percent of the household heads in this community had at one time worked in the United States. A smaller percentage of the household heads in the other communities had also worked in the United States.

The relative success of the agricultural economy may also be gauged by comparing the residences of the children older than fifteen years of the households in these communities. That is, the agrarian reform may have benefitted the older generation by providing access to land, but what has happened to the children and grandchildren of these individuals? A substantial percentage (ranging from 37 percent to 56 percent) of these younger people have found it necessary to leave their community. Tamaulipas, the community in which ejidatarios have access to the largest amount of land, has been able to retain

TABLE 2

Migration Reported for the Communities in Complete Household Censuses

	Michoacan	S.L. Potosi	Morelos	Tamaulipas
Earn majority of income from agriculture	53%	10%	20%	73%
HH heads who have worked outside community	66%	95%	61%	68%
HH heads who have worked in the U.S.	25%	80%	15%	23%
Children over 15 still residing in the community	51%	44%	55%	63%
HH with child in U.S. at time of the interview	23%	43%	15%	5%
Children over 15 who reside in the U.S.	19%	32%	12%	6%

the largest percentage of its children. In San Luis Potosí not only have a majority of these children left the community, but at the time of the interview almost one-third of the children over fifteen were living in the United States, most as illegal aliens. A smaller percentage of children from the other communities were in the United States. The attractiveness of the United States as a way of deriving income is indicated by the fact that 43 percent of households in San Luis Potosí and 23 percent in Michoacán had children in the United States. More children from these four communities had migrated to the United States in search of work than had gone to any Mexican city.

Thus, in terms of the economic welfare of these communities, the picture is somewhat mixed. The agrarian reform provided access to land—but this has not led to economic security. Only in Tamaulipas and in Michoacán does agriculture provide households with a major part of their income. But even here the picture is mixed. Tamaulipas seems to be a thriving agricultural community, but Michoacán is very poor. Although agriculture is important in Michoacán, it seems that this is the case only because people have not found better alternative employment opportunities.

The communities in Michoacán and San Luis Potosí are especially poor, with cash incomes and material goods scores substantially less than those in Morelos and Tamaulipas. The poverty in the former communities has led many of these individuals—both in the older generation and the younger generation—to migrate temporarily or permanently in search of better opportunities. The favorite destination of these individuals is the United States.

Economic Characteristics and Land Access

The data on differences within the communities confirm many of the patterns noted in the comparisons of communities. We were interested in comparing the economic characteristics of households with access to land to those of households without access to land.

Comparing total cash income for families with access to land to those without access to land we see that, in general, those with land have substantially higher total incomes (see Table 3).[4] Families with access to land have a higher total income in all communities except for that in Morelos. This difference is significantly different in San Luis Potosí and Tamaulipas. In Morelos, there are only small differences in income between the landless and those with land.

Table 3 also shows that in most communities there is a somewhat greater amount of money earned in nonagricultural pursuits by those who do not have access to land, although this difference is not statistically significant. The relative lack of importance of agricultural land in Michoacán is indicated by the finding that even those with access to land earn more money in non-agricultural pursuits.

We might expect that land access would lead to differences in the number of children in the United States. There are, however, no statistically significant differences in the number of children in the U.S. between the two groups. In three of the communities, those families with land actually have a larger percentage of their children who are over fifteen years of age in the United States. This indicates that access to land does not necessarily mean there are greater opportunities in the local community for the children of these families.

A summary measure of the relationship between land access and economic status within the communities can be seen in a comparison of the material style of life (MSL) of households in the two groups. Table 3 indicates that having access to land does not mean that families will be any better off in terms of their material possessions. The quantity of land clearly makes a difference. In Tamaulipas, the community in which some people have access to the largest amount of land, those with access to land have significantly more material goods than the landless. In Morelos, however, just the opposite pattern is true. Those without land have higher MSL scores. In the other two

TABLE 3
Mean Values of Economic Variables for Households with Land
Compared with Landless Households

	Total Income	MSL	Income from Non-Agriculture Activities	# Of Children In U.S.
Michoacan				
with land	321,277	203.1	61,814*	.25
	N = 63	N = 61	N = 65	N = 61
landless	215,383	151.1	22,363	.13
	N = 12	N = 25	N = 27	N = 23
S.L. Potosi				
with land	258,335**	208.7	12,612	.49
	N = 54	N = 49	N = 54	N = 53
landless	71,314	241.4	41,495	.29
	N = 13	N = 20	N = 21	N = 21
Morelos				
with land	426,699	353.8*	109,857	.20
	N = 66	N = 72	N = 74	N = 70
landless	436,778	415.0	182,900	.08
	N = 18	N = 25	N = 25	N = 25
Tamaulipas				
with land	582,835**	307.2*	51,868	.04
	N = 48	N = 46	N = 50	N = 49
landless	275,459	221.0	57,773	.05
	N = 22	N = 26	N = 27	N = 22

*p < .05 (T-test based on separate variance estimate, two-tailed probability)
**p < .01

communities, the differences are not meaningful. This indicates that agriculture is just one way of making a living and that (on the average) those without access to land in these four communities have found other means of surviving that bring them a level of living roughly commensurate with that of their neighbors with access to land.

Community Comparisons of Nutrition and Infant Mortality Rates

We used several different measures of health status in this research, including the nutritional status of children. These data were designed to give us some indication of the current situation with regard to the nutritional adequacy of households in the different communities.

Estimates of nutritional status were based on anthropometric measurements of children sixty months of age and under. Length was measured in centimeters, using an infantometer for children unable to stand unaided. Height was measured for children able to stand using a measuring board in which a metal meter tape had been imbedded. A sliding head board was used to read the height. Weight was measured to the nearest 100 gms. using a dial-faced spring scale (ITAC). Children's weight for age, height for age, and weight for height were calculated as a percentage of standard using the NCHS median values.

Figure 3 shows a comparison of the children under five years of age in the communities in terms of average nutritional indicators. These averages demonstrate that, as a group, these children are fairly well-nourished. One-way analyses of variance on these data showed that, on the average, children from the community in Morelos are significantly heavier for their age than children from Michoacán and San Luis Potosí.[5] The children in Morelos also are significantly taller for their age than children from the communities in Michoacán and Tamaulipas. The average weight for height of children does not differ significantly among the four communities.

Despite the generally good average nutritional level of children in the communities, there are problems of undernutrition. The children whose

FIGURE 3

Average Nutritional Status: A Comparison of the Communities

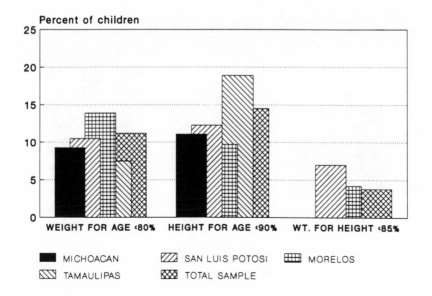

Based on NCHS Standards

weight was less than 80 percent of standard weight for their age, suggesting undernutrition at some point in their lives, ranged from a low of 7.5 percent in Tamaulipas to almost 14 percent in Morelos.[6] Stunting (height for age less than 90 percent of standard: WHO/NCHS), an indicator of chronic undernutrition, characterized only 9.7 percent of children in Morelos and nearly 19 percent in Tamaulipas. The percentage of children whose current weight for height was under 85 percent of standard (wasting) was a problem only in San Luis Potosí and Morelos; no children in Michoacán or Tamaulipas were found to suffer from wasting (Figure 4).[7]

The problems of undernutrition are quite different in the various communities. The most severe problem is stunting; that is, a fairly large proportion of the children in these communities are shorter than the norms for their age. This problem that indicates chronic undernutrition was very prevalent in Tamaulipas and affected the lowest percentage of children in Morelos. In contrast, a deficit in weight for age (indicating current nutritional status) was most significant in Morelos, and least affected children in Tamaulipas. Our interpretation of this is that some children in Morelos are underweight be-

FIGURE 4

Rates of Undernutrition: A Comparison of the Communities
(Children Under 6 Years of Age)

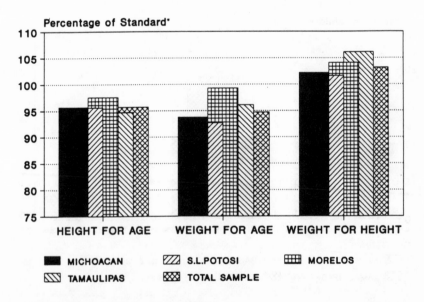

Percentages compared with NCHS median values

cause they have been affected by diarrheal disease, dengue, or other illnesses. In Tamaulipas, on the other hand, we suspect that some families became used to low levels of nutrition during the lean years before irrigation was introduced. Their chronic undernutrition is reflected in nearly one-fifth of their children's stature being below the norm. Wasting affected a very small portion of the sampled children and was most significant in Morelos and San Luis Potosí. This indicates that in these communities, although children may be short for their age, their body weight is sufficient for their height.

A recent historical review of food consumption between 1950 and 1984 indicated that undernutrition has remained one of Mexico's gravest public health problems. In 1984 it was estimated that between 40 percent and 50 percent of the population experienced hunger or malnutrition (Reig, 1985:43). The data in the communities we studied are substantially better than the national level data. The fact that many people do have access to land on which to produce food seems to have resulted in a diet that is adequate for normal growth of most children. On the other hand, in spite of the agrarian reform and the agricultural modernization of recent years, nutritional problems continue to exist.

As another indicator of the health conditions of these communities, an estimate of infant mortality was drawn from reproductive histories from all women in the sample households. Infant mortality was estimated from reports of women about the number of children born, the number surviving, and at what age and in what year children died. By aggregating responses on number of births, children still living and the number of children who had died, we were able to assemble a historical pattern concerning infant and child mortality rates in the communities in terms of infant and child mortality per thousand births by decade. These data should be viewed as tentative. As retrospective data they include recall problems, especially for earlier decades. Perhaps more important, as with any retrospective analysis it is impossible to account for information from respondents who have disappeared from the sample.

Figure 5 shows the number of mothers and the number of children that they report as having died. In terms of all children born, women in San Luis Potosí reported the smallest proportion of children having died, women in Michoacán the largest proportion.

Figure 6 shows the infant mortality (i.e., deaths of children under one year of age) and child mortality rates for children in the four communities and compares these rates with those for Mexico as a whole. As is indicated there, the infant mortality rates for these communities were all substantially above 100 per thousand live births during the 1940s and 1950s. During that time period, only in the community in Morelos was the infant mortality rate below that for Mexico as a whole.

FIGURE 5

Proportion of Children Born Who Have Died

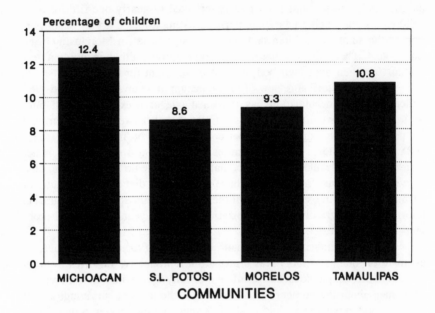

The infant mortality rate dropped substantially in the community in Michoacán during the 1960s. It is not unreasonable to suggest that this came about as a result of the improved economic circumstances that would have accompanied the creation of the ejido in 1962. Many of the individuals who received land were actually poor landless individuals who had been living around Lake Chapala. They were given land and resettled in the Apatzingan region in 1962. Although it is somewhat speculative to draw such a conclusion on the basis of small samples, the infant mortality rate since the 1960s appears to have increased in the community in Michoacán. The ejido grants of three hectares may have been an improvement in these individuals' life circumstances, but it has not been a sufficient amount of land to lead to long-term economic improvement, especially with the population growth occurring. Infant mortality rates, which had dropped below the average for Mexico as a whole in the 1960s, were higher than those for the country in the 1970s and 1980s.

Further support for the beneficial effects of land redistribution on small farmer welfare comes from an examination of the data on infant mortality for the community in Tamaulipas. Although the ejido was created in 1964, the

FIGURE 6

Infant Mortality by Community for Decades 1940–1980

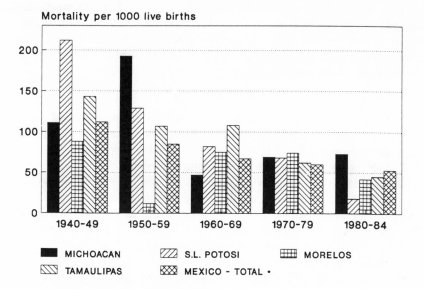

* Data for 1940–1979 adapted form UN Demographic Yearbook, 1980. Data for 1982 from World Bank, 1984.

land could not profitably be cultivated until the opening of the irrigation system in 1972. The marked decline in infant mortality rates in the 1970s and 1980s roughly coincides with this period of time. Many of the people who received land in Tamaulipas migrated to the area from the state of San Luis Potosí during the late 1950s and early 1960s.

The community in Morelos began with lower infant mortality rates than the other communities—probably due to its larger size and closer proximity to Mexico City. Its health care system has been more developed for these reasons. Rates were quite low in the 1950s, though we are inclined to believe that they were probably not as low as the twelve per thousand indicated by our data. But during the 1960s and 1970s they were a bit above the national average. In 1978, wells were drilled that provided irrigation to the land of many of these ejidatarios in Morelos. Infant mortality rates did drop, though again we cannot be sure of the linkage.

Perhaps the most surprising result concerning infant mortality rates was the very low rate in recent years for the community in San Luis Potosí. This cannot be related to any improvement in access to land or to irrigation. We are more inclined to believe that this decline relates to an improvement in the medical services and transportation system in the region. During the last several years, nurses visit the community once a week to attend to those needing medical attention. In addition, this community is located approximately ten miles from a relatively large town in which there are several medical doctors and government clinics. Transportation into town is readily available. This increase in access to health services seems to have resulted in a dramatic improvement in infant mortality rates.

Intracommunity Patterns of Health and Nutrition

Some of the patterns noted in the community comparison hold in the data comparing families within communities. There are other important exceptions to the general pattern.

Table 4 compares the health and nutritional status of households with access to land to those families without access to land.[8] The table shows that, in three of the four communities, those who have land on the average have children with better nutritional status measurements. In San Luis Potosí, on the other hand, the children of households with access to land have slightly poorer average weight for age and poorer height for age. None of the comparisons of the anthropometrics, however, is statistically significant. The same holds true when all of the communities are aggregated; there is no difference between the nutritional status of children whose families have access to land and those children whose families do not have access to land (K. DeWalt, B. DeWalt, Escudero, and Barkin, 1990:402). On the basis of these data, we must conclude that there is little or no relationship between access to land and an improvement in nutritional status.

Other health data also indicate this mixed picture. In three of the communities, the proportion of household members reported as having some sort of illness at the time of the interview is lower in households with access to land. This difference is statistically significant for the community in Michoacán. Having access to land does seem to be associated with members of the household having better health, probably because these individuals have somewhat better living conditions in terms of housing and diet. On the other hand, those in Morelos with access to land have a slightly greater percentage of household members sick (see Table 4).

In contrast, the proportion of children who have died in the families in all four communities is *higher* in those households with access to land. This finding is statistically significant in both Morelos and San Luis Potosí. We must admit that this is a curious finding that runs counter to most of the other data that we have presented. We suspect that what we may be seeing in this finding is the effect of the age of the individuals in the families studied. Many of those individuals with access to land are older individuals who raised their

TABLE 4

Comparison of Measures of Nutrition and Health Status for Households with and without Land

	Weight For Age[1]	Weight/ Height	Height For Age	Prop. HH Members Sick	Prop. Children Dead
Michoacan					
with land	91.9	101.6	95.0	.27*	.13
	N = 57	N = 57	N = 57	N = 61	N = 58
landless	88.9	101.0	94.2	.50	.10
	N = 21	N = 21	N = 21	N = 23	N = 21
S.L. Potosi					
with land	92.5	102.0	95.1	.21	.12**
	N = 42	N = 42	N = 42	N = 53	N = 52
landless	93.3	100.4	96.8	.24	.01
N = 15	N = 15	N = 15	N = 15	N = 21	N = 21

continued

TABLE 4 (*Cont.*)

Comparison of Measures of Nutrition and Health Status for Households with and without Land

	Weight For Age[1]	Weight/ Height	Height For Age	Prop. HH Members Sick	Prop. Children Dead
Morelos					
with land	100.0 N = 49	104.8 N = 48	97.5 N = 48	.20 N = 70	.10 N = 66
landless	98.7 N = 21	102.7 N = 22	97.8 N = 22	.17 N = 25	.05 N = 24
Tamaulipas					
with land	97.1 N = 37	106.2 N = 37	95.1 N = 37	.14 N = 49	.10 N = 46
landless	93.8 n = 16	105.8 N = 16	93.8 N = 16	.23 N = 22	.09 N = 17

*p < .05 (T-test based on separate variance estimate, two-tailed probability)
**p < .01
[1]Percent of NCHS standards.

families in decades when they had poorer access to health care facilities. Younger families, many of whom do not yet have access to land, have had their children more recently when the overall health care situation has substantially improved.

Policy-Relevant Conclusions

The data presented here can be related to current debates in Mexico regarding the potential of ejidal agriculture to provide a viable living in rural areas. As we noted in the introduction, there is much discussion about whether the ejido system is an institution that has outlived its usefulness. Others point out that since the 1940s the ejido system has systematically been discriminated against in Mexico's agricultural development. They argue that the ejidos are productive, and socially and economically efficient, given the infrastructural support, agricultural research, access to credit, and other resources to which they have access (see Barchfield, 1979).

What our data indicate is that access to land—especially good quality irrigated land—and other resources necessary for agriculture has some association with a general improvement in the economic, nutritional, and health situation of rural communities. Among the four communities studied here, the community with the best access to land and resources (in amounts usually only available to commercial farmers) had the best overall economic situation. Farmers were productive and were making good use of their resources. The amount of outmigration was the lowest of any of the communities, and nutritional status and infant mortality rates seemed to be improving. This was also the case in the community in Morelos, where access to land and other employment opportunities was quite good.

The communities in Michoacán and in San Luis Potosí, on the other hand, are much like many other Mexican villages and towns that are in crisis. The several hectares of rainfed land available to ejidatarios there do not provide a decent living. Land resources are poor; economic access is poor; and the people are poor. Infant mortality rates are high, especially in Michoacán. Access to land does seem to provide these families with sufficient food, so the nutritional status of children in both communities is not as poor as in many other villages and regions of Mexico. In these communities in Michoacán and San Luis Potosí, outmigration has been a solution for many individuals. This is especially the case for the children. Illegal migration to the United States is a major factor in allowing these communities to continue to exist, albeit in marginal circumstances (see also Camara and Kemper, 1979; Cornelius, 1976).

The data from within communities suggests that it is not only those who gain access to land through the agrarian reform who benefit. Instead, the level of living in more prosperous agricultural communities seems to improve the level of living and health and nutrition indicators of all people. This is undoubtedly due to the creation of wage employment opportunities, both within agriculture and in sectors providing ancillary goods and services. The small quantities of irrigated land in Morelos, combined with a generally more favorable environment for finding wage work, and the large quantities of irrigated land in Tamaulipas have made families in these communities wealthier and healthier than in the land-poor communities of San Luis Potosí and Michoacán. Families in Morelos and Tamaulipas have average cash incomes higher from both agricultural and nonagricultural pursuits.

We think that the implications for agrarian reform policy are plain. Critics of agrarian reform can point to communities such as those we studied in Michoacán and San Luis Potosí as failures—but these failures are understandable, given the ecological, technological, and economic circumstances within which these farmers operate. Farmers there are not succeeding in agriculture, and the results are poor health and nutrition, and considerable outmigration. In contrast, families in Morelos and Tamaulipas are succeeding, and the benefits of their success are reaching their landless neighbors. In these latter two communities, levels of economic well-being are better, a higher percentage of children are remaining in the community, and their nutritional and health status are far better. We conclude that agrarian reform can be an effective means of improving rural welfare if the amount of land redistributed is in sufficient quantity and quality. In addition, agricultural policies must follow up the distribution of land with programs designed to provide access to the technology, infrastructure, research, and credit resources generally available to larger farmers.

Theoretical Conclusions

We have been able to address these issues because of our early emphasis on understanding the role of agricultural and agrarian policies on the national level and on identifying a policy context for community studies. Our emphasis on both community contrasts and intracommunity variations allowed for the identification of community level effects as compared with household variation. Finally, an emphasis on a mix of qualitative and quantitative research methods allowed for the collection of a large amount of data in a relatively short period of time. The linkages that we were able to establish between the microlevel and macrolevel data enabled us to make much more informed judgments concerning the issues that we raised in the introduction.

9

Unwanted Children as a Consequence of Delocalization in Modern Kenya[1]

Philip L. Kilbride

One of the most striking current social problems in the United States is a perceived high rate of child abuse. Behaviors that are harmful or injurious to a child, such as battering, burning, or starving have become common enough to be of concern to a wide lay and professional public. This is so even though disagreement exists about whether the present rate of child abuse is increasing in the United States (Segal, 1979). The prevailing view of a growing rate of abuse is supported by Demos (1987), who shows that child abuse was minimal in Colonial America, as compared to the present.

In the social sciences, it is sometimes argued that psychopathological or other causes at the individual level are most important in understanding the etiology of child abuse. For example, the abuser is frequently seen as having a personal history of being abused, inaccurate knowledge of child capability, poor impulse control, and/or alcohol or drug problems. Other researchers advocate a social systems position, with such factors as unemployment or isolation from potentially supportive kin or neighbor networks as constituting significant antecedents to child abuse. Another emphasis on etiology concerns findings that the victim of child abuse is often exceptional, such as being born premature, or handicapped (for a theoretical overview, see Garbarino, 1977; Korbin, 1981; Gelles and Cornell, 1985).

Theoretically, anthropological research on child abuse emphasizes the need to define child abuse for cross-cultural comparison (Korbin, 1981; Scheper-Hughes, 1987). Should culturally appropriate but painful initiation ceremonies in New Guinea be called child abuse (cf. Langness, 1981)? Although it is often socially approved, is joint parent-child suicide in Japan abusive (Wagatsuma, 1981)? A sociobiological perspective highlights the "rational" context in which for some cultures instances of infanticide may contribute to the overall adaptive potential for the group (Gelles and Lancaster, 1987). Infanticide thus viewed is seen as "benign neglect" in South America, where stronger infants are fed at the expense of weaker ones (Johnson, 1981). On the whole, anthropological work would seem to support relativistically inclined child abuse theorists who define child abuse, for example, as "when the child suffers nonaccidental physical injury as a result of acts—or omissions—on the part of his [or her] parents or guardians that violate the community standards concerning the treatment of children" (Segal, 1979:580). We shall follow this definition in the present paper.

We will see that in Kenya the macro-micro interaction of traditional with modern gender role expectations has proven unfavorable for women, and consequently for children too. The latter nowadays suffer from child abuse, argued herein theoretically to be a contemporary consequence of economic and moral delocalization.

To date, cross-cultural research does suggest that in societies where collective social institutions such as family or neighborhood are emphasized, that child abuse is not common. Korbin (1981:208) writes concerning "embeddedness" of child rearing in kin and community networks that, "A network of concerned individuals beyond the biological parents is a powerful deterrent to child abuse and neglect. This shared responsibility for child rearing acts in many ways to reduce the likelihood of child maltreatment . . . an extended network further helps to guarantee that someone will intervene when standards of child care are violated." Thus, for example, child abuse is rare in "traditional" Africa (LeVine and LeVine, 1981) and in rural Kenya, in particular, where the extended family or clan is important (Fraser and Kilbride, 1981; Kilbride, 1986). Even research in the United States, where kin or neighborhood bonds are comparatively weak, has found that "Families isolated from relatives and friends show higher rates of violence than do other families, probably because people with relatives and friends can turn to them for help and also because relations and friends can intervene if the situation deteriorates too far" (Strauss and Gelles, 1970).

Of particular concern to this study is the work of the LeVines. In their view, traditional African society offers a contrast with the contemporary Western world, where child abuse and neglect are seemingly endemic. The LeVines, for example, state: "Our experience in East and West Africa suggests that corporal punishment occurred everywhere, was more talked about than practiced, and was reserved by most parents for serious infractions of family rules. We have not seen cases of children injured by parental punishment" (1981:38). On the other hand, the LeVines point out that, "It is our impression, moreover, that both battering and sexual molestation are more common where the impact of social change is conspicuous" (1981:38).

The present paper will argue that materials collected by the author in Kenya in 1984–85 provide strong theoretical support for those theorists who claim that the etiology of child abuse is best understood from a social systems or ecological perspective (see also Bronfenbrenner, 1974; Garbarino, 1977; Kent, 1979). Kenya, as we show, is now experiencing child abuse as it is understood in the West. At the same time, the extended family, although threatened by modern economic conditions, is a powerful social support network which, among other things, functions to protect abused children. Ethnographic cases provided here are therefore to be construed as providing cross-cultural support for the social systems theoretical perspective. In our interpretations we will also extend our social analysis to account for the appearance in modern times of social-economic conditions particularly unfavorable to women and children; many of the latter are consequently unwanted.

In Kenya during the precolonial agrarian past, procreation, marriage, and economic success were interrelated for both men and women. Children were highly valued, as were women, who enjoyed social power particularly for their childbearing capacity. The moral order contained clear notions of right and wrong in matters concerning sexuality, marriage, and procreation. These ideas were not particularly unfavorable for men, women, or children, at least as perceived by the people themselves. On the other hand, the contemporary moral order, itself a delocalized product of colonial and postcolonial economic change, is ambiguous. In Kenya formerly, for example, kinship was everywhere the essential idiom of social relations, in what was a subsistence mode of production. Today both kinship and the capitalistic element of money relations are each salient, but often contradictory, idioms of social interaction. Specifically, modern Kenyans still care and provide for children, since they are highly valued as formerly, but nowadays they are costly in terms of clothing and schooling; although their labor is important, it is less significant than in the past. We argue here that one of the consequences of such a contradiction is modern child abuse, observed by the LeVines (1981) and the author previously and to be further substantiated (cf. Fraser and Kilbride, 1981). Later we discuss the micro-macro dynamic of moral delocalization, to be here argued as an institutional antecedent to child abuse.

Economic Delocalization

P. Pelto (1973) and Poggie and Lynch (1974) believe that economic delocalization is a useful construct for comparative analysis in modernization research. The latter writers describe economic delocalization as a chain of complex events that results when food, energy resources, and services which had formerly been provided within the local setting are transferred into market exchange commodities, most of which originate from sources outside the local area. See Pelto (1973) for an ethnographic study of delocalization resulting from the decline of reindeer technology as one result of the impact of the snowmobile on the Lapps of Finland.

Economic delocalization is derived from a colonial heritage throughout East Africa. In the colonial era, land began to become scarce due in large part to the usurpation of land by Europeans. Africans in colonial Kenya became essentially squatters living on European farms, many of which were as large as hundreds of thousands of acres. The colonial legacy introduced such devices as the deed and private ownership, with land usually registered by the male head of the household, who becomes the owner.

The colonial era also saw the Hut Tax (1901 in Kenya), an obligation that prompted men to migrate from rural areas to towns in search of monetary employment. The city of Nairobi, numbering now over a million people, did not even exist less than a century ago! This outmigration has had drastic effects on rural social life, particularly its economic structure.

Kayere (1980) reports that fifty percent of the jobs in the modern economic sector are in the cities of Nairobi or Mombasa. She continues, "The migrants are predominantly young adult males with some form of education; conversely, those who are left behind are predominantly females, children, and old people with hardly any formal education or skills. Thus an estimated ⅓ (or 400,000) of all rural households in Kenya are headed by females" (1980:2). One of the consequences of male migration is the fact that women are now the primary source of rural labor in food production, encompassing work done previously by men. Women now do, for example, preplanting land preparation, ploughing, planting, and other tasks for both subsistence and commercial crops. Kayere (1980:4) writes: "Though the current participation covers a wider sphere, there are some pitfalls relating to its efficiency. These are mostly noted through the decreasing agricultural productivity in rural areas, explained by the ever-growing urban centers and the accompanying drain on rural labor (particularly male labor)."

Residents in our research area were surveyed to ascertain what economic problems they perceived to be troublesome in their lives. In general, their problems can be attributed directly to economic delocalization, as we have reported elsewhere. The Kilbrides write, "The small-farm (sisal) community members are overall much more preoccupied with fundamental subsistence issues such as water problems, insufficient land, and money for school fees and other needs. The large-farm group (schemes) . . . more frequently expressed desires for services needed for success in large-scale farming such as transportation, roads, farming specialists, etc. Such concerns, while not absent among small-scale farmers, are voiced to a lesser degree" (Kilbride and Kilbride, 1990:154).

Methodology

In my most recent East African fieldwork (1984–85) residence with my wife and infant was established in a rural community in western Kenya. With the assistance of local secondary school-educated residents, a census was undertaken, along with other survey projects pertaining primarily to children and normative problems of child rearing. Our theoretical interest focused also on a form of deviant behavior, child abuse and neglect. Our objective, following Pelto and Pelto (1978), was to consider intracultural variation as a means for testing theoretical ideas. That is, we assume variation. This assumption compelled us to consider the variable of gender as we found a women's world and a men's world, particularly as differentially structured by power (cf. Kilbride and Kilbride, 1990).

Child abuse, as is also true for most other forms of "deviant" behavior, is difficult to research through direct observation or survey methodology. I necessarily relied on the informed judgment of his local nurse assistants to discover past or ongoing episodes of child abuse. Over a period of about eight months, only two cases of past child abuse, and no present cases of such behavior, were discovered through these assistants. Extensive household visiting and daily participant observation revealed only one current instance of child abuse in a geographical area containing several thousand residents.

Two Kenyan community nurses assisted me in his ongoing search for cases of child abuse. Each nurse lived in the village and, as a specialist on child health, was expertly familiar with the local status of children. Since only two cases were discovered it seems reasonable to assume that child abuse is not common, a finding similar to another location in Western Province reported earlier (Fraser and Kilbride, 1981). Nevertheless, child abuse is present, a situation in marked contrast to precolonial times, as we show later from ethnographic sources. Our own case materials were obtained through direct interview, sometimes with assistant collaboration, by me in English or *Ki Swahili*. Repeated visits were made to selected homes as a resident anthropologist consistently in search of informed encounters.

During fieldwork (and before and after, while in Nairobi), a regular perusal of the English language daily newspapers was undertaken. The *Daily Nation*, the *Standard* and *Kenya Times* were read over a nineteen-month period from January 23, 1984 until August 7, 1985. The newspapers constituted one source of information on cases of child abuse in the nation at large. Unfortunately, there were no formal statistics available, given the likely recency of child abuse in Kenya. Moreover, measurement is difficult, given the attempts to mask episodes of abuse, itself a highly stigmatized behavior. In fact, my nurse assistants felt that a few cases of burns on children were probably intentional, but they could not be sure. Our mass media perusal, although obviously to be construed only as preliminary data, did nevertheless reveal some patterns that are not inconsistent with our impressions gained through discussions with informants. The reader is referred to Wagatsuma (1981), who used newspaper reports in his research on child abuse in Japan, also a case where government statistics were not available. Finally we were able to locate one published source in Kenya that contains some information on types of child abuse cases seen at Kenyatta National Hospital in Nairobi.

My overall research strategy was ideally intended to conform to what the Peltos (1978) refer to as a "quantitative-qualitative mix." Concerning child abuse per se, circumstances dictated that most of our time be invested in work on a few available cases. Repeated informal interviews with a small number of families was, however, very productive of contextual materials. In two families, for example, the veracity of their collective remarks concerning abuse in their family, a subject of public shame, was reaffirmed to me over time and across occasions in a cross-checking fashion. Simultaneously, our communitywide survey work provided results on standard, approved child-rearing values, which became, in turn, a conversational source for focused elaborated discussions (Kilbride and Kilbride, 1990). Such work also provided "normative" (nonideologically deviant) cases for comparison with abusive practices under study in those two families where abuse had been discovered.

By far the most significant event in my research happened as a by-product of participatory "hanging out," being always in search of case material. Being constantly on the scene provided an opportunity not only to interview about past child abuse but also to observe it while in process.

One day in May 1985, while visiting informants, my wife and I observed a large crowd gathering at the local secondary school. Joining the crowd, we arrived just in time to see a newborn infant being lifted out of one of the school's pit latrines. The infant's mother, Sarah (a pseudonym), who had attempted the infanticide, was being hustled into her dormitory for interrogation by local officials and nurses while we observed the proceedings and the crowd continued to gather outside. Through observation and interviews, this incident and its aftermath were followed for several weeks, sometimes with the collaboration of my nurse assistants. Settings included school, hospital, jail, and home situations. Discussions were conducted with the girl herself, various members of her family, police, school officials, and many other members of the general public.

It became clear through personal involvement with Sarah and her family that our bridgehead into their social field was one of mutual self-interest. Financial assistance for the infant's needs was offered and eagerly accepted in exchange for the chance to acquire data by involving ourselves in their present misfortune. Throughout our encounter with them we all cooperated as agreed, although we resisted continuous attempts to persuade us to take on added economic responsibility for the mother. It was indeed apparent that she was suffering from economic deprivation and related powerlessness to control her own fate. She seemed a passive depository for decisions concerning her but made by others such as relatives, the police, school officials, and so on. Her male relatives were also feeling monetary obligations, not in terms of their own personal needs, but in relation to stresses associated with extended family responsibility for helping Sarah and her infant. Their social power potential and responsibility were greater than Sarah's (and her mother's), and probably for this reason they appeared to be under almost as much personal stress as Sarah herself concerning their extended family tragedy.

In conclusion, we believe that our case material provided ethnographic evidence for the role of the extended family as a social support network for abused children. Moreover, a commonly repeated pattern of child abuse reported in the press, infanticide, was experientially contextualized such that modern female powerlessness emerged as a potentially insightful theoretical perspective for emphasis in future empirical research and interpretation.

Family, Women, and Children: Ethnographic Context

My previous fieldwork has been among Abaluyia communities in western Kenya, where modern, rural life still retains many of the social features prevalent in the precolonial era of about a century ago (Kilbride, 1980, 1986; Wagner, 1949, 1956). The majority of people continue to be oriented to an agrarian lifestyle and depend on their own labor for subsistence foods and cash crops. This includes women and chidren who are, as in the past, the most important source of farm labor. For this reason large families are still desired by both men and women, and polygamy is seen as a means of increasing family size and thus providing additional "free" labor. In our research, for example, when asked, "What do you like most about your child?" most of the twenty-five mothers interviewed mentioned work activities, although "obedience" and "respect for elders" were not uncommon responses. For example, one mother said of her nine-year-old daughter, "She is very much willing to help me. She does not feel comfortable when she sees me working when she is playing; she has to come and help me." Another mother noted admiringly about her nine-year-old son that "He helps in planting and weeding flowers and vegetables; he can also wash things and sweep the home."

Rural family life is still very much a collective enterprise, constituting an interpersonal, *interdependent* system where kinship, age, and gender roles are clearly utilitarian and reciprocal (Kilbride, 1986). It is probably for this reason that only a small number of present or previous cases of child abuse—three—were directly observed or came to the attention of the author during a lengthy project devoted to the subject of child abuse and neglect. There were, however, many cases of neglect occurring through omissions in valued standards of child care, particularly nutritional (cf. Kilbride, 1986). Nevertheless, child abuse, although now infrequent in rural areas, is already becoming a national problem, particularly in Nairobi. Social and economic forces are likely to produce more child abuse in the future unless policy steps are taken. We return to the issue of public policy in the conclusion.

In general, rural children are still highly valued, serve important economic roles in family life, and are the responsibility of extended family members in situations where parents are unable to provide care. That most mothers are conscientious in their child care responsibilities was revealed in the study just mentioned. All twenty-five mothers interviewed reported accurately where their children were and what they were doing, as discovered by subsequent observational follow-ups by our research assistant.

Domestic violence was infrequently observed in the course of our fieldwork, although cases were obtained through informant interviews. Corporal punishment of children is acceptable as long as it is not excessive. In general, community violence does not appear to be pronounced. Of eighty arrests recorded at a local police headquarters from 1981 through 1984, no homicides and two rape attempts were included. Commonly, cases involved illegal brewing or theft of items such as cows, food, or household possessions. There were, however, several house burnings, which we have observed elsewhere can result in deaths, even of babies. Public rowdiness and fighting while drunk occasionally appeared among the cases recorded, as well as episodes of physically threatening to "beat" or "bewitch" someone. There were also several cases of beating and robbing people on the road at night. Stealing from absent victims, however, was the most frequent crime, composing 35 percent of the cases.

Cases of child abuse and neglect appear to have been quite rare in the past. Wagner, writing about the Abaluyia in the 1930s, noted the importance of having children for both men and women. So strongly was fertility emphasized that a young girl could increase her chances of marriage by becoming pregnant. A man usually welcomed and adopted his illegitimate child, who was often thought by his siblings to be their father's favorite child. Infanticide, although rare, did sometimes occur in cases of maternal death during delivery. This was done through fear that without his or her mother the child would have no place in society. Overall, the general picture that emerges from Wagner's description is one in which women and men both enjoy prestige and have social power as a consequence of significant economic roles as producers of children and crops, and as performers of other instrumental activities. Men, however, actually allocated land to women as wives and passed on property to their sons, thus giving men, overall, greater economic power than women. Nevertheless, in comparison to the present, when land is now owned by men as *individuals,* past arrangements were such that women had control and even monopoly of crop production and distribution of surplus (Nasimiyu, 1985). Moreover, in the modern era cash crops are controlled by men, which, along with the decline in economic advantage associated with having children, has worked to erode further the power of women.

Child Abuse: A National Problem

In recent years Kenyan scholars, politicians, and other concerned citizens have sponsored or attended seminars or workshops on the subject of child abuse. In December 1982, for example, such a workshop was sponsored by the World Health Organization in collaboration with the University of Nairobi (Onyango and Kayongo-Male, 1983). The workshop included a Minister of Parliament and specialists from the fields of pediatrics, psychiatry, and sociology. The topics of concern included: child labor, battered child syndrome, sexual abuse, institutional child abuse and neglect, government attempts to reduce child abuse, and legal and policy issues. One paper from the seminar is specifically relevant to our present concerns; therefore, we will briefly discuss it here.

Bwibo (1982:11), a Kenyan pediatrician, states, "Recent figures show that in 1980–81, twenty-one children with battered child syndrome were admitted to Kenyatta National Hospital, of whom five died." Of significance to our present discussion, Bwibo notes that victims of child abuse frequently included: (1) "The babies of single mothers thrown along the road, dropped in pit latrines or dust bins, (2) the babies whose hands are burnt because they stole a piece of money from the homes" (1982:11). His cases included male and female abusers who included, in addition to parents, stepparents and child caretakers. There is no systematic data available on gender, but our strong impression is that women are substantially overrepresented in the pool of abusers. Women are the primary child caretakers, and in their gender-related status as "co-wives" and single mothers are frequently reported (e.g., in the press) as abusive.

Press reports of child torture, burning, scalding, battering, prolonged confinement, and the like are not uncommon. Editorials are encountered with such titles as "Our Sad Problem of Battered Children," and "State Urged to Tighten Laws on Child Abuse." Table 1 provides a sense of the type of instances one is likely to encounter in the news media. Our material, obtained from the newspapers, revealed the following information concerning child

TABLE 1

Sample Headlines from Kenyan Newspapers

Boy Found Buried in Mole Hole
2 Month Old Girl Abandoned at Bus Stop
5 Month Old Boy Rescued from a Church Latrine
Baby Wrapped in Paper Bag Abandoned
2 Month Old Girl Abandoned in Hospital
Unwed Teenager Mother Abandons 4 Month Old Baby
2 Year Old Boy Abandoned is Rescued from Ants
2 Day Old Boy Rescued from Ditch
4 Month Old Infant Abandoned in the Rain
Infant Dumped into Toilet Pit
Newborn Boy Abandoned in Primary School
5 Day Old Girl Found in Maize Plantation
Mother Abandons 2 Week Old Girl
8 Month Old Infant Found in Sewage
2 Week Old Baby in Plastic Bag Found on Wayside
Dog Digs Out Baby's Body
Mother Throws Three Year Old Boy into Latrine
One Year Old Boy Abandoned by Grandmother
Unmarried Mother Throws 2 Day Old Baby into Pit Latrine

abuse in Kenya. Looking at the age and sex of abusers, we found that adult women are reported more frequently as abusers. Of the sixty-two cases of abuse/abandonment we discovered, abusers were adult females in thirty-nine cases (62.9 percent), adult males in sixteen cases (25.8 percent), female children in three cases (4.8 percent). In four cases the sex of abusers was not reported. Of the seventy-six children mentioned in these cases of abuse/abandonment, twenty-six were males (34.2 percent) and twenty-nine were females (38.2 percent). In twenty-one cases, the sex of the children was not given. Thus, it appears that both boys and girls are victims of abuse in similar proportions. Only one case of incest (father-daughter) was discovered by us in our reading of the Kenyan papers. There were six cases of rape by nonrelatives and two cases of physical threats and beatings by male teachers. The only other males involved were the fathers of the abused/neglected children. Two grandmothers (one paternal, one maternal) and one stepmother were the only female relations, other than the children's mothers, who were abusers.

Twenty of the thirty-nine cases involving mothers were cases of unwed or single parents abandoning their children or attempting infanticide of an illegitimate newborn. Thus, both Bwibo and the media indicate that a common form of child abuse in Kenya involves getting rid of an unwanted infant or child by abandonment or attempted or actual infanticide. Our extended study of a student who attempted to kill her newborn is, therefore, to be construed as a particular case of what is, sadly, a common national occurrence.

Child Abuse and the Rural Extended Family: Case Illustrations

The importance of the extended family as a support network in child care, especially in time of crisis, was revealed in two cases of child abuse briefly described now and in a third case to be discussed in more detail. This last case also provides insight on the modern powerless status of young women in a society no longer as favorable as previously to the economic potential of women and children in a fully agrarian context.

Case 1

A 52-year-old woman has been living in the village for ten years. She married in 1950 when her husband brought two cows to her parents. Soon after their marriage, they moved to Taita (the coast) where they cut sisal to earn a living. They lived on the coast for twenty-four years, during which time she gave birth to three sons. Their marriage was fine until the mid-1960s, when she left work due to deteriorating strength. After this time, for the next several years, her husband became violent—beating the children when they asked for such things as food, clothing, and school fees. She, too, was beaten whenever she tried to protect the children. This pattern continued until 1974, when she came where she is now maintained on land owned by her brother. She earns money herself by selling pottery. When she came here, her sons were thirteen, five, and three years old. Her husband came to the village for a short time, during which she conceived a daughter. He ran away permanently, however, when he was warned by his brother-in-law that he would be arrested by the police for his violent beatings. His wife reports that he did not have a drinking problem, but was not a Christian. He never felt remorseful after his beatings, but would leave for several days. He felt he had done a "good job of discipline." Her legs still bother her, and her thirteen-year-old son has a permanently swollen hand that was twisted by his father ten years ago.

Two factors should be emphasized in this case. First, the informant believes that her husband's violence coincided with her own discontinuation of work. The resulting diminution of the family budget could very well have produced stress which then triggered violent reactions in her husband. Second, the informant's brother continues to serve as an important resource person for her and her children. From the standpoint of these children, their mother's brother intervened to disrupt violence which could very well have continued in his absence. We see, therefore, both economic and social support factors (i.e., extended family) implicated in the pattern of child abuse illustrated in this case.

Case 2

A woman in her fifties has been living here with her two sons and a granddaughter since 1982. She is divorced and has another son who lives elsewhere. The latter is the father of her granddaughter, who is ten years old. This girl is very pretty and a student in primary 2. She has a scar on her forehead where she was beaten with a cooking stick by her stepmother three years ago. Her father had lived in Mombasa in the 1970s, where he had three children (two are now dead) with a woman labelled as a prostitute. He subsequently married another woman, with whom he has had a son and a daughter. This wife became jealous on those occasions when he would ''slip out'' and would aggress against her husband's ''outside'' child. When interviewed, the child said she would be beaten about four times a month, but never when her father slept at home. She got along well with her siblings, but she was the only one ever beaten. Her father would beat her stepmother whenever he discovered that she had beaten his daughter. The stepmother was remorseful about beating the child, as indicated by her frequently taking the child to hospital for treatment. The child now lives with her grandmother, who was happy to take her because she has no daughters. The stepmother sometimes brings her clothes, but neither she nor the father provides any other assistance. The natural mother frequently visits but is closely monitored by the grandmother for fear that she would steal the child.

This example, like the previous case, shows the positive role of the extended family in alleviating child abuse. Were it not for her grandmother, this young girl probably would still be vulnerable to family violence. The stepmother is mentioned frequently by informants as one who is often aggressive to her stepchildren as a result of conflicts with her husband or co-wives. There do not appear to be any economic problems contributing to child abuse in this case. My informant said that ''the only problem was jealousy.'' Wife beating, if not too severe, is sanctioned, and indeed expected, by both husbands and wives. Wives have told Janet Kilbride that beating was proper when the wife ''deserved'' it. Wives, however, are never permitted to beat their husbands.

Case 3

That the attempted infanticide mentioned previously and described here is abusive was easily determined by the range of negative affect it elicited during audience appraisal. Anger, rage, fear, and the like clearly qualify the episode as an instance of child abuse, an extreme violation of community standards about proper child care. Such expressions of negative affect were displayed by school officials, nurses, police officials, and others as the public responded to Sarah.

Sarah is now on three years' probation and would like to return to school to continue her education (although this would be against school regulations). This sixteen-year-old became pregnant by a man she hardly knew, a married man visiting the rural area from the city. Until this incident, she had been an average student, in terms of school rank and attendance. Sarah comes from a polygynous family and has been raised by her stepmother (who is childless) and her father. Her own mother and father were divorced some time ago. The girl and her maternal family members revealed that she did not get along well with her stepmother and seems to be, in the opinion of her brother, the victim of mistreatment by her stepmother. He also believes a stress factor was lack of money for school fees. In recent years, her mother's brother had provided school fees for her. Sarah did not report her pregnancy to anyone due to "fear." According to her, she did not even realize she was pregnant until her seventh month. She waited about thirty minutes after giving birth before deciding to kill her baby. During this time she considered such questions as, "Where will I take the baby?" and "How can I get my school fees back for this term?" (There is a no refund policy.) In the days and weeks after she attempted infanticide, Sarah's mother and her maternal relatives proved to be a key resource group as they visited her in hospital and in jail. To my knowledge, her father and stepmother did not write a letter, much less visit their daughter after being informed of the incident and being asked to come see their grandson. Sarah's maternal uncle in particular, at considerable cost and time, looked after his niece and her newborn during this time of duress.

This case shows, as do the others, the important function of the extended family in alleviating, if not preventing, family violence. It is quite possible that were the unfortunate young mother without her family's financial and emotional support, she would have tried again to mistreat her child. It would seem that the young girl's lover has no expected ethical role to play. Sarah reported that she had no immediate plans to tell the father of the infant about the birth of their son, nor did anyone ask about him. This "moral absence" for men, as we shall see, represents a distinct change from the past.

Our three cases, taken together, show the significance of the social support concept in child abuse theory. Economic, family composition, and personal factors, too, are important to formulating multicausative theory.

Premarital Teen Pregnancy: Case Studies

The case of Sarah is, of course, an instance of child abuse as understood in modern Kenya. Fortunately, most cases of teenage pregnancy do not end in attempted or successful infanticide. Essentially the same social conditions that are responsible for Sarah's case, however, result in numerous cases of unwanted teen pregnancies. Sarah perceived herself as a mistreated step-daughter, as did her brother. This is one psychological factor that accounts for her particular case. Most teen girls who conceive an unwanted child, how-ever, pass the problem on to the child's maternal grandparents (their parents).

Because of contradictions in their own lives many men simply deny pa-ternity or otherwise fail to provide in any way for their children, if conceived in circumstances economically unfavorable to them (e.g., not married, mar-ried to someone else, still a student, etc.). A common scenario is for a teen-age girl to get pregnant accidentally and then leave her unwanted child at home to be cared for by her parents when she marries. This is often due to her husband's refusal to accept another man's child and forbidding her to have anything to do with this child. The following three cases derived from our field materials are typical.

Case 1

A young man in his early twenties and a "form 4 leaver" (i.e., a high school graduate) had a child whom he originally denied was his, although he knew he was the father. He "disappeared" for three months, but when he came home he found his nineteen-year-old girlfriend at his home and preg-nant. He refused to give her child support, so she went to the local govern-ment assistant administrative chief and then to court. He has now agreed to marry her if he gets a job, although he hasn't seen his two-month-old daugh-ter since birth. The girlfriend's parents are taking care of their own daughter and new granddaughter. His own parents are not annoyed because they know he has no money. He believes it could even happen again. He could impreg-nate another young lady.

Case 2

A fifty-two-year-old man lives with his wife, six sons, and a daughter. Two sons and two daughters have married and live elsewhere but one daughter-in-law's children also live with him. In addition, he has a total of seven grandchildren living with him, because each of the two daughters who has married left behind a child born before their marriages. These two grand-children were not accepted by their mothers' husbands. In each case the al-leged father denied his paternity in court. One was fined 3000 shillings, but he never paid. These two children call their grandfather "father" and he "loves them as his own children." One is in Form 3 (high school junior), and the other grandson is in Primary 5 (fifth grade). He is concerned, however, because his wife does not love these two children. She gives them less food and lots of work to do. He has told his wife to treat them better, but he feels most grandmothers are like that and look down on such unwanted grandchildren. It should be noted that these grandparents still have seven of their own children living with them.

Case 3

A woman in her fifties is one of three wives. She lives on several acres along with her co-wives. Still living at home are a total of twenty-four children of the three wives. Two sons also live in the compound with their own families. Problems associated with school fees and clothing are acute in this compound, since the husband is not a wealthy person. My informant, in addition to her nine resident children, also supports two grandsons who are eight and ten years of age. Her daughter left them behind when she married. She had been made pregnant by two different men, one a teacher. These men had "disappeared" long ago. Her daughter has been told by her husband not ever to go home, and she sends no help. She has had three children with her husband. Her father, already hard pressed, has paid school fees for his grandchildren, but clothing and bedding are a big problem.

These three cases serve to illustrate what proved to be of major existential import to residents of the village. Numerous informants volunteered the opinion that "unwanted grandchildren" were of profound problematic significance, perhaps even more than "unwanted children," since many young women seem to feel no anxiety (as they, also, expressed to me) about leaving their own "illegitimate" children with their mothers. The traditionally indulgent grandmother, as a consequence of a more general female powerlessness, often must now realize her traditional moral obligations in a context of economic poverty. Sometimes choices must be made between supporting one's own children or one's grandchildren, since many grandmothers themselves have young children. Our census material (Kilbride, 1986) revealed that more than half of the sixty-five homes in our census contain at least one resident grandchild. Twenty-two of these thirty-three homes do not have the grandchild's father living at home.

Unwanted Children and Moral Delocalization: An Applied Conclusion

Theory: Moral Delocalization

In his book *The Moral Order* (1983), R. Naroll shows through worldwide empirical correlation that when "moral nets" (family, neighborhood, etc.) are weak or weakened, around the world, such consequent behaviors as alcohol abuse, child abuse, youth stress, and the like are exacerbated. Naroll proposes that "a universal theory" of human behavior be further refined through research, with subsequent results evaluated, toward the eventual creation of a better worldwide moral order. We believe that the present direction of modernization in Kenya represents a threat of erosion of the extended family and community, conceived of as a moral net. Should this direction not be reversed, then the risk to what are still "children of value" will no doubt worsen (Kilbride and Kilbride, 1990). More precisely, in Kenya today, many men no longer are economically able to consistently display loyalty to neighbor, kinsmen, their children, or to women heretofore interdependent with them. Overall, the cash economy as presently constituted has caused a disproportionate rate of male migration to urban places. The rural scene has seen a concomitant increase in female isolation and burdensome economic responsibilities. Nevertheless Kenyans, particularly males, still want many children, such that Kenya has one of the highest population growth rates in the world (circa 4.2 percent per year). This is so even though children are nowadays expensive, particularly their clothing and schooling. The present, when viewed from the vantagepoint of the precolonial era, is on the whole both economically and—we argue here—morally "delocalized."

A process of "moral delocalization" closely paralleling that of economic delocalization can be observed in Kenya. Powerful, "modern" religious, educational, and legal institutions in Kenya declare that, for example, polygamy is "wrong," abortion is "illegal," "unnatural" birth control is "sinful" and that only women are legally responsible for "illegitimate" children. Moreover, many believe that women should be "punished" for premarital pregnancies. The present moral climate is largely derived from outside Kenya and, arguably, serves to reinforce macroeconomic patterns associated with the world capitalist system whose local manifestation has been described as economic delocalization (cf. Wallerstein, 1974). Today's publicly approved morality would have seemed quite foreign to previous generations of Kenyans, as indicated in the work of Wagner (1949, 1956). Elsewhere Wagner writes, "When I asked some elderly pagans whether pregnancy or the birth of an illegitimate child would decrease a girl's chances to find a husband they seemed genuinely surprised at my question. . . . they merely insisted that such a girl would marry soon as she would no longer care to reject suitors" (1949:381). In the circumstance where a man suspects he is responsible for a pregnancy, we learn that "While courting her he will as a rule deny being responsible for her condition until after the child is born . . . he would have to pay the full amount of marriage cattle if the girl died in childbirth. He therefore wants to see if everything goes well. When the child has been born he will be quite willing to marry the girl as he had been before (1949:437)." We also learn from Wagner that "even a son begotten by a man in his *esimba* (bachelor hut) before he married his first wife and by a different girl has the full status of a firstborn son and inherits accordingly" (1949:121).

In modern Kenya moral responsibility has been delocalized. Moral codes previously localized in east African sexual practices were embedded in a system of moral obligations that maximized male and female sexual pleasure and social responsibility (cf. Kisekka, 1976). In a recent paper Worthman and Whiting (1987) document for a Kikuyu community in Kenya that the pool of "unwed mothers" appears to be increasing, particularly among those who have significant amounts of formal education (e.g., the more modern). The modern school and associated values have replaced the traditional *ngweko* rituals as a major peer socialization setting. The *ngweko* custom (Kenyatta, 1938) was a form of lovemaking involving an apron used by girls to protect their private parts. Sometimes sexual relief was experienced, but "petting" would appear to have been the ideal. Worthman and Whiting state that boys were ostracized from further participation in *ngweko* by their peers if they broke the rules. The Church of Scotland mission disapproved of *ngweko*, so most of the educational functions of the practice have been lost. Worthman and Whiting conclude, "By means of a sacred ceremony, the parental generation transferred to youth the responsibility of regulating premarital sex and initiating the process of mate selection . . . When this system had been secularized by edict and the introduction of Western schooling, both the regulation of premarital sex and mate selection appear to have been destabilized, at least temporarily. We suspect that this effect of modernization is not unique" (1987:163–64).

Today young women in the modern monetized economy can no longer assume they can achieve social power solely through the reproduction of children and through their agricultural labor. The threat of "lack of school fees" is a most serious one in modern Kenya. One distinct disadvantage that renders women particularly powerless relative to men is their assumed singular culpability for bearing children "out of wedlock." Girls, not boys, are dismissed from school for getting pregnant. Girls are not permitted to return to school following cases of attempted infanticide. In my research many boys revealed to me that they did not acknowledge paternity in cases where they knew the child to be their own. In the case of the attempted infanticide discussed, not one person (family or other) considered the lover's behavior to be in any way morally problematic. Male refusal to accept one's illegitimate child, disapproved by traditional standards (where paternity was welcome), is common in the modern context. It has become so common that Sarah did not even view the father (her lover) to be a potential source of help for her and the baby—so much so that she did not even tell him she was pregnant or had delivered. This modern moral gender imbalance represents an "ethical delocalization" where local, traditional values more favorable to women have been replaced by standards from outside (as in the Church of Scotland example). In Kenya, the burden of child rearing in a modern society falls disproportionately on the shoulders of women, particularly on grandmothers, especially in the case of unwed mothers and some married women who "leave behind" their children after marriage. Overall, the Kenyan situation is not unusual in the developing world where, because of a colonial legacy and modern economic forces, women have experienced a loss of social power (Etienne and Leacock, 1980; Freeman, 1988). The micro/macro interaction of traditional with modern practices (delocalization) has also proven to be unfavorable for children, as we have shown here.

Applied Policy

Theoretically, our research overall consistently provides case support for the system support network theory of child abuse etiology. We have seen that the extended family in Kenya is a significant, traditionally derived support group that rallies around children who are abused or neglected. The system support network approach is, when attempted, also an important applied means for the prevention of child abuse in the United States. A parent-aide program has, for example, been established in Los Angeles for abusive parents "to provide them with someone in the community who would fulfill the role of good neighbor" (Kent, 1979:621). Salaried aides were recruited from among a pool of university students and unwed mothers. The program proved quite effective in relieving stresses associated with child care, loneliness, or what constituted for the participants a general social, physical, and economic isolation from other people.

The extended family persists as a traditional institution of considerable moral import as a social support institution. Elsewhere (Kilbride, 1986) the author has stated his hope that the extended family should be, whenever possible, supported in Kenyan legal code and national legislative regulations. Moreover, grandmothers (and possibly grandfathers too) could be profitably organized by government and churches, for example, into rural clubs or associations to be subsidized for their now-individualized and unrecognized efforts in child care. This strategy would be consistent with a localized, African-derived "kinship" idiom and is not precluded by modern "monetary" conditions. How precisely these and similar moral-economic choices are sorted out in Kenya as public policy will provide anthropologists with a continuing research opportunity to simultaneously combine theoretical, applied, and methodological concerns in a unified research effort (Pelto and Pelto, 1978).

Based on our work to date we have elsewhere suggested several public policy steps to our Kenyan hosts (Kilbride and Kilbride, 1990:241–49). Our suggestions included, foremost, a national and international recognition of East Africa's relatively powerless structural position in the global, capitalistic economic order. For this reason state and private resources are not sufficient to cope with the massive problems posed by modern life. Nevertheless, whenever possible Kenyans could, we believe, work not only to retain extended family institutions but also to promote what we call their traditional "child-centered" ideology as the basis for a modern child-centered public policy. Indeed, we also believe that we in the United States have much to learn from the Kenyan experience.

"Rugged individualism," so common in American life and now advancing in East Africa, does not, in our judgment, compare very favorably with social interactionism, particularly insofar as children are concerned. Let us keep in mind the challenge made by the noted psychologist David Elkind, "The child is a gift of nature, the image of the child is man's creation" (1987:6).

V

Methods for Special Purposes

Introduction to Part Five

Scientific anthropology should not be wedded to a single method, but should have as one of its strengths the potential to employ a variety of methods to address most appropriately the range of issues that can arise in sociocultural research. In this way, methods can be more sensitively adjusted to the research problem under consideration. The two papers in this section illustrate this important strength of scientific anthropology. The methodology used must be in keeping with the problem under investigation.

These contributions are especially relevant because they are at polar extremes in terms of their emphasis on qualitative ethnographic data and quantitative multidimensional data. This difference is primarily a result of the problem being addressed. Although both papers deal broadly with the problem of cultural preservation, they took quite different approaches.

Paredes, whose research is directed at issues related to Native American identity and cultural change, uses ethnographic and ethnohistorical research methods to answer both theoretical and practical questions regarding the Poarch Creek Indians of south Alabama. Paredes' task was twofold. On the one hand, he wanted to assist the Poarch Creeks to achieve recognition as a federally recognized Indian tribe. His second objective was to assist the group in their social and cultural revitalization movement. In both cases the most appropriate research strategy involved historical and qualitative methods.

Quantitative methods were much more appropriate for the work of Roberts and Carlisle who utilized cluster analysis and multidimensional scaling to reconstruct the lost historic town of Roanoke, West Virginia. The problem in this case was to generate information from the memories of former residents of the town to carry out accurate historic preservation. Their task was to derive the cognitive and expressive domains regarding buildings in the lost town. This called for the utilization of the data-gathering and analytical techniques of cognitive anthropology. The combination of cluster analysis and multidimensional scaling was especially appropriate for addressing this issue in a systematic manner.

10

"Practical History" and the Poarch Creeks: A Meeting Ground for Anthropologist and Tribal Leaders

J. Anthony Paredes

In 1971 I began research on a small, obscure, remnant American Indian community of about 500 people in south Alabama. The group is now recognized by the United States government as the Poarch Band of Creek Indians and has approximately 1800 tribal members, including many emigrants as well as those still living in the historic Poarch Creek Indian homeland near Atmore, Alabama. When I began my research the Poarch Creeks had been reported in the anthropological literature in only two brief articles (Speck, 1947, 1949) and a few passing references to them elsewhere. I was the first scholar to undertake intensive study of these people. The work continues.[1]

The initial research objective was to identify the mechanisms by which the Poarch Creek community had maintained its integrity and identity as "Indian" despite the virtual disappearance of native culture and language, absence of federal or state protection of their status as Indian, little or no contact with other Indians until quite recently, and, at least by the 1970s, intimate and prolonged interaction with non-Indians, including intermarriage.

Through key informants and casual interviews I soon learned that since the 1940s various elements of the community had actively pursued a movement of social and cultural revitalization (cf. Paredes, 1974) aimed at overcoming long-standing problems of extreme poverty, ignorance, poor health care, social discrimination, and psychological debasement. Following this initial discovery, new objectives were added to my research:

- Understanding the recent historical background against which these ongoing changes were taking place;

- Specifying the historical details of the processes by which the Poarch
  Creek community had come into existence in the first place;
- Determining the motivations of the leaders of the group;
- Assessing how ordinary community members were responding to ongoing
  processes of change.

Research Methodology

My initial research methods were mainly straightforward, "old-fashioned" ethnography. In an earlier essay (Paredes, 1976) I described these methods in some detail. To summarize here, during the winter and spring of 1972 I visited the Poarch community one weekend per month. These trips provided the opportunity to become better acquainted and establish rapport with young adults met in my initial visits in 1971 and to conduct the first of some fifty-five tape-recorded, oral history interviews, starting with the elders to whom the younger people directed me. During the summer of 1972 I lived in the community for some three months, continuing the oral history interviews, mapping the local hamlets, doing genealogical interviews, conducting a key-informant inventory of households, and participating in and observing as many aspects of community life as possible. In addition, I took numerous photographs, began to explore what kinds of archival information on the community might be available in the local courthouse, and spent many hours "just visiting," doing what we ethnographers like to call "unstructured interviews." During the academic year 1972–73, I continued occasional weekend visits to the community. Again in the summer of 1973, full-time residence in the community provided further opportunities for the kinds of research activites begun in 1972. I also undertook a full-scale demographic, economic, and attitudinal household survey of the community. This was endorsed by the Poarch Creek Council (not yet called the "Tribal" Council); a member of the Band employed by a multicounty Community Action Program was assigned to help me complete the interviews that summer and through the following year. By 1974 my stays in the community had become limited to only a few days at a time. (Brief visits continue, however, to the present; in 1990 I attended my nineteenth consecutive Poarch Creek Thanksgiving Powwow.)

By 1975 it was clear that the research was having beneficial results for the Creeks themselves. In the 1976 essay I described the process that the Peltos were to characterize as "ordinary ethnography" producing " 'plain' ethnographic data" (Pelto and Pelto, 1976:321–22). Further, I showed how ongoing longitudinal ethnographic research was providing unanticipated applications and practical benefits for the people studied. This present essay extends that theme through an account of ethnohistorical research I was to undertake later with a more self-conscious, ever-keener perception of the practical applications that the research might and, indeed, did have for the Poarch Creeks.

Extolling the virtues of older ethnographic and ethnohistorical methods should not be taken as disparagement of modern, quantitative, hypothesis-testing methods and modern, sophisticated techniques for sociocultural data collection and analysis. In a modest way, such methods and techniques were also used in the Creek research. For example, from my original household survey in the Creek community, we (Paredes and Joos, 1980) had the data to examine variations in personal optimism in relation to household economic conditions, as Schensul, Pelto, and I (Schensul et al., 1968) had done with rural Minnesotans of the 1960s living in circumstances similar in certain respects to those of the Alabama Creeks in the 1970s. Failing to achieve the same statistical results with the Creek material, we compared the optimism measure to quantitative data from the survey on perceptions of community history, a type of data not collected in the Minnesota research, but which was central for my interests in the Creeks. In short, those who saw the Poarch community as having improved during the recent past were those most likely to be optimistic about their personal futures. The results were pleasing and pointed in new theoretical directions, toward a more comprehensive model for understanding greater complexity in the intersection of several dimensions of intracultural diversity in perceptions of personal well-being. Nonetheless, in this instance it was the products of more old-fashioned, descriptive methods of ethnography and ethnohistory that proved most useful in meeting practical ends for the Creeks, thus reaffirming the point that methods must be in keeping with the nature of the research problem.

Neither is drawing a contrast between "old-fashioned" and "modern" methods in cultural anthropology meant to imply that the former are somehow exempt from considerations of objectivity, validity, reliability, and the like. Such scientific considerations are, of course, the point of all those old Boasian and Malinowskian maxims and admonitions about "being there," cross-checking informants, "getting everything," recording native texts, penetrating ethnocentric biases (cf., e.g., Boas, 1889), taking voluminous field notes, keeping a diary, long-term residence in the field, direct observation v. "hearsay evidence," repeated exposure to cultural routines, learning the native language, building rapport, "getting inside the native's skin," collecting artifacts, taking photographs, drawing diagrams, etc., and, in general, detailed documentation of observations (on the last, see especially Hsu, 1979:530). Nor should the ironic usage of "old-fashioned" be taken to mean that in fact the older, so-called "qualitative" methods of ethnography properly belong only to some antique natural history phase in the evolution of anthropological science (one could argue, as a matter of fact, that sociocultural anthropology has never fully matured as plain "natural history"). Indeed,

Kirk and Miller (1986) make much of the importance of long-term qualitative field research as a *discovery* method and as the "best check" on validity available in modern social science, despite, in their view, historic inattention to matters of reliability in ethnography. Apart from the question of the continued utility of older ethnographic field methods in social science specifically, Gould (1988:v), in his introduction to Jane Goodall's *In the Shadow of Man*,[2] celebrates the value of prolonged, careful field observations for science generally:

> We think of science as manipulation, experiment, and quantitification done by men dressed in white coats, twirling buttons and watching dials in laboratories. When we read about a woman who gives funny names to chimpanzees and then follows them into the bush, meticulously recording their every grunt and groan, we are reluctant to admit such activity into the big leagues. We may admire Goodall's courage, fortitude, and patience but wonder if she represents forefront science or a dying gasp from the old world of romantic exploration. Let me try, in this short introduction, to explain why the conventional stereotype is so wrong, and why Jane Goodall's work with chimpanzees represents one of the Western world's great scientific achievements.

So be it.

Putting aside matters of ethnographic field methods, *per se,* my later intensive archival researches on Creek ethnohistory, commenced in 1978, produced, in addition to eventual practical consequences, some "pure" scholarly results. With more detailed knowledge of the past gained through painstaking searches of public documents, the present Poarch Creek situation could be articulated to broad historical patterns in much more concrete ways than previously had been possible. For instance, with this background it was possible to elucidate rather directly the role of kinship and descent in the whole process of ethnic revitalization among the Poarch Creeks (Paredes, 1980). In this work, too, the results of "ordinary ethnography" provide a dimension of understanding, when conjoined with documentary research, that is missing from a "pure history," as might be constructed by a traditional historian without an anthropological grounding.

Continuing research and analysis of the Poarch Creek materials notwithstanding, the intertwining of research process and application in my relationships with the Creeks is further revealed in this present essay. What follows is derived from two separate reports written twenty-three months apart in the last stages of the Poarch Creeks' eventually successful petition for status as a federally recognized Indian tribe with all the political, legal, and economic advantages accompanying that status.

The Branch of Acknowledgment and Research (formerly the Branch of Federal Ackowledgment, and before that the Federal Acknowledgment Project), Bureau of Indian Affairs (BIA), reviews each recogniton petition in a time-consuming and meticulous process according to rigorous standards contained in regulations adopted in 1978 (see Greenbaum, 1985). As of September 1987, of twenty-five petitions reviewed, only seven tribes had been federally recognized through the process established by the 1978 regulations. The Poarch Band of Creek Indians, officially recognized in 1984, was one of those.

The first part of what follows originally carried the title of this present essay and was presented at the 1982 Annual Meeting of the American Society for Ethnohistory in Nashville, Tennessee, in a session on "unrecognized" American Indians seeking federal acknowledgment. That paper described my efforts for the Band in its bid for federal recognition. In October 1982, with a grant to the Poarch Band from the Department of Health and Human Services' Administration for Native Americans (ANA) (for which I had written most of the grant proposal), we were about to begin the final research effort to document the Band's case for federal recognition. The paper is presented here much as it was read at the meeting; I hope to convey some of the urgency and excitement I felt on the brink of that final push—an admittedly peculiar and ironic use of the hoary "ethnographic present," but one that is now especially appropriate for our purpose of emphasizing the theoretical and practical results of research in this volume.

The second part of this section consists of excerpts from the final report on the "status clarification" grant from the ANA, which I wrote for the Poarch Band Tribal Council in September of 1984. In that report I described the completed work which had been only just beginning when I spoke at the ethnohistory meeting two years earlier.

October 1982: The Theoretical and the Practical Entwine

In part, this is an update of my 1976 article in which I described how by-products of my research proved useful to the Poarch Band of Creeks and suggested that the research process itself may have had beneficial effects on the efforts of tribal leaders to improve and strengthen their community. Without planning to do so, I became, in the words of one of the commentators on that article, "a catalyst and resource person in an open-ended, continuing process of defining community problems and developing skills and techniques for coping" (Lurie, 1976:320).

My purpose here is to describe how my casual role as a helper to the Creeks evolved into a more formal relationship as a result of the Federal Acknowledgment Project (FAP), a relationship that already has proven beneficial to me and, I hope, will prove of practical benefit to the Creeks. The essence of this new role is my continuing ethnohistorical research on the nineteenth century background of the present-day Poarch Band of Creek Indians. However, it is a kind of research that is guided not only by my own interests but also by the requirements for federal recognition, hence the term "practical history."

The research discussed here is indeed "practical history" of the most critical sort. My anthropological goals must take into account forthright awareness that the research is itself part of a much larger sociopolitical process involving the hopes and aspirations of several hundred Poarch Creeks engaged in their most important dealings with the United States in 150 years. To emphasize the political nature of anthropological involvement in federal recognition research, it must be noted that even the name that we use to designate a group may have political significance. I am careful to specify here the "Poarch Creeks" rather than the more general term "Eastern Creeks" which appeared in the title of my 1976 articles. This is because since then a number of other organizations have come to the fore as self-designated Eastern Creek Indians; one of these submitted a petition for federal recognition that has been rejected. The Poarch tribal chairman, Eddie Tullis, is concerned that his people should disassociate themselves from the "Eastern Creek" label because of the possibility that the term has been discredited by the activities of others claiming Creek Indian identity in the Southeast.

Despite my involvement with the Poarch Band of Creeks since 1971, during the preceding twenty-five years they were doing very well without me. Led by the late Chief Calvin McGhee, the Poarch Creeks won improved educational facilities for their people and a land claim suit against the federal government. In these efforts and even earlier, the Poarch Creeks proved very adept at using the courts, public officials, and legal counsel. Hence, it is no surprise that they turned first to lawyers in their initial efforts to secure federal recognition, begun in 1975—before the federal acknowledgment project began. Specifically, they sought the aid of the Pine Tree Legal Assistance Program, based in Maine, which tribal leaders had come to know through their participation in intertribal activities. Even at that stage, however, the leaders of the Band put an attorney in touch with me, and as I described in my 1976 paper, he drew from my expertise in a statement submitted to the BIA. This early petition sought to restore a federal trust relationship that, in the argument of the attorneys, had been improperly ended in 1924 with the issuance of a fee-simple patent for the one remaining parcel of land Poarch Creek ancestors had held under terms of the 1815 Treaty of Fort Jackson (cf. Anderson, 1978). Apparently, nothing was ever done in response to that 1975 petition.

Since 1975 there has been an ever-growing commitment by the Poarch Creeks to secure a firm place for themselves within the larger context of intertribal relations and federal Indian policy. To this end the Poarch Band applied for and received several grants from a variety of agencies to support community programs. Moreover, in 1977, after careful review of their credentials, the Poarch Band of Creeks was admitted to full membership in the National Congress of American Indians. At present [1982], Poarch Creek tribal chairman Eddie Tullis serves as the Southeastern Area Vice President of the NCAI. [In 1988 another Poarch Creek, Buford Rolin, was Treasurer of NCAI.] With the issuance of the Federal Acknowledgment Project guidelines, the Band leadership began in early 1979 to prepare a petition for federal recognition under these regulations. Again, they turned to legal counsel, through the Native American Rights Fund. Again, I was called upon for informal assistance. This time, though, I was armed with more documentary evidence than I had had earlier.

From the very beginning of my research I recognized that, despite the existing scholarship on the Creeks of preremoval times, and despite the historical and genealogical research done in connection with the Creeks' land claim, there was an important information gap in the late nineteenth century, beyond the recollection of my oldest informants. As early as my first summer of fieldwork, in 1972, I did some archival research in the local courthouse and here, for example, found the records on the 1924 fee-simple patent, to which I was able to direct the attorneys in 1975. In their own legal research the attorneys found more records on Poarch Creek treaty lands.

Over the years, while continuing basic ethnographic research, I remained concerned about the need for 19th and early 20th century historical data in order to understand processes of change and interethnic relations in the Poarch community. My interest was further stimulated when in 1975 the young attorney for Pine Tree Legal Assistance gently chided me and anthropologists in general for not being more attentive to the documentary history of the groups they study. Finally in 1978, after failing to interest any historians in the work, I obtained a summer grant [from the now-defunct Rockefeller/FSU Center for the Study of Southern Culture and Religion] and set out to do the documentary research. Working largely through local courthouses in south Alabama and in the Federal Records Center in Atlanta, I was surprised to find what a large body of information I was beginning to amass from marriage records, newspapers, wills, land transactions, federal census schedules, and World War I draft registrations. However, I had not yet begun to tap what information might be available in state archives and in the Indian records of the United States. As concerns the latter, I was very pessimistic that I would find anything that would be useful, given the fact that earlier the U.S. government had hardly taken cognizance of the Poarch Creeks, federal protection of some of their lands notwithstanding. Even so, I now had not only the results of my basic ethnographic work and numerous oral history interviews, but also documentary historical information when the Creek leaders asked me to come to Poarch in early summer 1979 to consult with them and their lawyers, without pay, about preparing a petition.

On that day in 1979 a variety of activities, including a public meeting between the attorneys and members of the Poarch community, delayed my meeting with tribal leaders and attorneys until late at night. Among those activities were private consultations with individual attorneys, particularly the woman who would actually be preparing the FAP petition. I alerted her to possible local county records pertaining to a controversial school case within the community in the 1950s of which I was aware, but which was generally kept secret from latter-day outsiders.

Even though the case had caused hard feelings within the community, I was of the opinion that the outcome demonstrated conclusively that even in its earlier, less regularized form the tribal council had exercised "political influence or other authority over its members" as specified in the criteria for federal acknoweldgment. That night when we discussed the matter and the senior attorney concurred with my judgment, despite some councilmen's initial desire to let the incident lie in the past, the group agreed that the outcome of the case was a good piece of evidence to support the petition. Nonetheless, I was firm in my assertion that reference to the case was a matter for the council to decide, regardless of the opinion of the attorney or myself. In the end the documents were located and copies retrieved by an attorney, and I was provided with copies. These documents contributed both to my scholarly understanding of the Creeks and to building the petition for federal recognition. (Incidentally, by having the attorney retrieve these somewhat sensitive documents, neither I nor the tribal council risked damaging our relations with local people.) Partly because of the sensitive nature of some of the points that I would raise, I was rather insistent that attorneys and tribal leaders meet with me as a group to make my consultation. We continued until well past midnight.

The critical matter to be demonstrated in the petition was the continuous existence of the Band as an organized group with some form of leadership and political authority over its members. Though I suggested a variety of types of data that might be used, I was careful to identify pitfalls and the documentary difficulties involved, the present self-evident identity and organization of the Band notwithstanding. Tribal chairman Tullis said it best toward the end of my comments, stating, in effect, "the problem is to find written records to prove what we've always known." Afterward, another of the Creeks complimented me for "telling it like it is." I raised no false hopes, and at that stage established my role of scholarly advisor for what the tribal council and I saw as ultimately a matter that properly belonged in the hands of attorneys. Despite this, we were aware that before a final judgment might be made by BIA solicitors, a positive recommendation would have to come from the scholarly team in the Federal Acknowledgment Project. Thus, in the succeeding months I was frequently contacted by the attorneys for advice and assistance in preparing the petition. Nonetheless, an ethnohistorian's enthusiasm for work in a recognition case must be tempered by an awareness that research results must meet not only scholarly rules of evidence, but also legalistic tests of validity as well.

Late in 1979 a draft of the Poarch petition was completed. The Band asked me to proofread and suggest additions to the petition. I did so. In January 1980 the petition was finally submitted to the Bureau of Indian Affairs. At this stage I was still in the background and not actively involved in the Band's bid for federal recognition. In their view the petition was yet another in a series of legal instruments prepared by attorneys at the Band's behest for correcting the wrongs of the past. Even so, Band leaders knew they could rely on me for behind-the-scenes advice in the real legal business of making a petition. Neither they nor I saw any reason for me to become involved in the mainstream of the action. In a few months this was to change.

By the summer of 1980 it was much clearer both to me and to the Band that the Federal Acknowledgment Project staff were, indeed, scholars. With an anthropologist, George Roth, on the FAP staff, my identity as an anthropologist greatly increased my stock as a source to be drawn upon directly and publicly by the tribal leadership. In the spring a preliminary review of the Band's petition by the FAP staff found the petition suffered from "significant deficiencies." These were precisely in the nineteenth century gap I had earlier identified, and of which I had forewarned the council on that summer night the year before. Initially the tribal council sought my informal advice on how to remedy these deficiencies. I gave recommendations on how to reorganize existing data in combination with membership genealogies, which the newly-hired tribal archivist, a Band member, was very adeptly compiling. Also, I suggested other kinds of records that I had not yet explored that might be consulted. After some weeks, with funds from the newly-formed Alabama Indian Affairs Commission, the tribal council contracted with me to do the job. For the first time in my then eight-year association with the Band, I was specifically hired to do research for them. I was provided with travel money for a trip to the state capital and to the National Archives in Washington, D.C., and a consultant fee for ten days' work.

My ten days of consulting were spent searching for relevant documents in Washington and Montgomery. I found a surprising amount of material, especially in the BIA-Indian correspondence. For the most part these records merely confirmed and amplified what I had learned from older Creek informants. Even so, from the standpoint of "practical history," such records filled in details and provided independent written corroboration of what I had learned from informants, even though the records were themselves sometimes incomplete. For example, a series of letters on behalf of the Poarch Creeks received by the Bureau during the 1930s were subsequently destroyed but were still catalogued by index slips in the central files of "Letters Received."

Sometimes completely new and useful information emerged from documents even though they were not explicitly labeled "Indian" records. For example I did not know what kind of information might be contained in homestead files, but knew that some of the Poarch Creeks had acquired new lands in the later nineteenth century by homesteading. Once I had them in hand, I immediately discovered that these records contained information on the sale of improvements on lands, length of occupancy, and the identity of applicants' witnesses. The latter data made possible a partial reconstruction of social networks among Band ancestors in the nineteenth century. I could not have found those records so quickly, though, if I had not first found out about the homesteaders through fieldwork with informants. Similarly, were it not for my prior knowledge of the present-day Poarch community, its early twentieth century history, and important persons of the past, several hours poring over nineteenth century county commission minutes would have been useless. As it was, I was able to combine disparate bits of seemingly trivial information with data from ethnographic fieldwork to confirm informants' recollections and cast new light on community organization and leadership in an earlier era.

Throughout the fall of 1980, I worked on my report for the Band. Thanks to electrostatic copying machines and the U.S. mail, I continued to assemble copies of documents from a variety of sources, including, from the American Philosophical Society, Frank Speck's very brief field notes from his short trip to Poarch in 1941. Through interlibrary loans I was able to examine on microfilm a great deal of government correspondence pertaining to the Creek Indians in the nineteenth century. Countless hours spent over a microfilm reader grew tedious, yet here and there was a sentence or two embedded in a lengthy letter that made the search worthwhile. Most notable in this regard was my discovery in an 1845 government contractor's dreary letter a statement establishing that the Poarch Creek Indians had lived in their present area "since the first settlement of the state." During the fall, I was also in frequent telephone contact with the tribal archivist, Gail Thrower, who assisted me in retrieving additional information from local sources, even checking dates on tombstones in local cemeteries.

In January 1981 I completed my report for the Band, designated as a supplement to the petition. To my delight I was able to use nearly every scrap of new information found in previous months, often not merely as isolated bits of information but as points of evidence in arguments constructed to remedy deficiencies in the original petition. As the archivist commented, "You sure got a lot out of such a little bit of information." I would not have been able to make those arguments using documents, were it not for the other data I had from oral history interviews, household surveys, genealogical interviews, and participant-observation research done in the early 1970s. As historians discover the spoken word they make much of the need to prepare for an oral history interview by previous documentary research; in the kind of research described here, however, it was ethnographic research entered into cold, as it were, that laid the essential groundwork for a meaningful archival search.

Lest I appear immodest, I emphasize that for the Band's original petition the attorneys did an excellent job researching the early history of the Creeks and deftly pulled together many important federal records in their legal research on the Band's history, particularly their lands. Moreover, in my own archival research since 1980 I have been guided in a very precise manner by the Band's needs and the specifics of the federal acknowledgment criteria and guidelines. These limitations have served me well as an anthropologist, for they have forced me to focus upon specific documentation of historical fact. Clever as we anthropologists may be in developing conceptual models, theoretical analyses, and inferential arguments, there is no substitute for the concrete, "close to the ground" documentary verification that can emerge from painstaking efforts to build a "practical history" that meets not only anthropological standards but also legal and administrative requirements of proof as well.

I cannot resist recounting one of my archival discoveries that illustrates rather dramatically the profound, practical ramifications our work might have for American Indian peoples. In September 1931 an Episcopal minister to the Poarch Creeks wrote to the Commissioner of Indian Affairs seeking federal assistance for the Band. This triggered a series of communications attempting to determine who these Indians were. Eventually, in 1935, a Bureau of Indian Affairs officer wrote to anthropologist Duncan Strong of the Bureau of American Ethnology, inquiring about the Poarch Creeks. (By then the Indian Reorganization Act of 1934 was in full swing; all these letters are now placed in the National Archives' IRA file on Creeks.) Duncan Strong wrote back promptly that neither he nor Dr. John R. Swanton (a distinguished ethnologist) knew anything about these people, but added some speculations from Swanton about who they might be—speculations that were reasonable, but far from the mark. Besides, Strong noted, neither he nor Swanton could find the town of Atmore on the map! The statement is very perplexing since Atmore is clearly shown on both the U.S. Geological Survey map and the Rand McNally road atlas of the day. Strong's reply to the BIA appears to have closed any further consideration of the Poarch Creeks. On receipt, Strong's 1935 letter was hand-inscribed with a prophetic marginal notation instructing, "Hold for future study."

September 1984: Plainly Practical

In late 1983 the BIA's Branch of Federal Acknowledgment prepared a 118-page, three-part report of findings (cf. Fritz, 1984) on the Poarch Creeks' petition. On the basis of that report the Poarch Band of Creeks achieved, in August 1984, the primary goal for which they had applied for Status Clarification Project funds: formal acknowledgment as an Indian tribe by the United States of America. Presented here is a summation of the contribution that the Band's Status Clarification Project made to achieving federal recognition and an overview of specific activities generating the data.

The Band's decision to seek, and subsequently receive, a status clarification grant has proven in retrospect to have been very timely. Although a petition was already submitted to BIA before the Status Clarification Project began, the final reports of the federal acknowledgment staff drew significantly upon data produced specifically by the Status Clarification Project. Table 1 cites in detail specific portions of the government's report that were based upon data gathered in the course of the Status Clarification Project. In sum, approximately 13 percent of the forty-four page historical report (exclusive of summary) and 8 percent of the thirty-seven page anthropological report (exclusive of summary) were based upon information produced specifically by the Band's Status Clarification Project. [Likewise, large portions of the report relied upon the 1981 petition supplement, published articles, and papers I had written earlier.] Although at first these percentages might seem small, the specific information filled critical gaps in the evidence for federal recognition that would otherwise have been void.

Such items as an 1875 obituary for Peggy McGhee (*The Alabama Baptist*, vol. 2, no. 39, p. 3, col. 4), the testimony in an 1852 inheritance dispute (*Weatherford vs. Weatherford et al. - 20 Ala* 548), or the list of witnesses in an 1897 assault case (*State Subpoena Docket - D, Escambia County Circuit Court*, p. 13), taken out of context, might seem inconsequential, but it was precisely these kinds of data, discovered and assembled in the course of the Status Clarification Project, that proved essential to the Band's satisfaction of the criteria for federal acknowledgment.

Important pieces of information used by the BIA in making its favorable determination on the Band's petition were not found until after the Branch of Federal Acknowledgment (BFA) staff had already begun its full review of the petition and, in some cases, had even begun writing their report of findings. The incorporation of these "late-breaking" bits of information into the BIA's findings was made possible by frequent contact between Project researchers and BFA staff, both by telephone and in person. More important, copies of newly discovered documents (or notes thereon) were submitted directly to BFA staff in later stages of their report preparation. Often archival information submitted to BFA was accompanied by letter commentaries that in themselves constitute brief interim reports on status clarification [copies of these letters were compiled and appended to the full final report of the Status Clarification Project for the Tribal Council]. Some of this material was submitted as late as November 10, 1983, just fourteen days before the BIA's positive recommendation was announced publicly at the Band's annual Thanksgiving Powwow, on November 24, 1983.

The archival information produced by the Status Clarification Project resulted from many months of tedious and sometimes discouraging, seemingly fruitless searches of manuscripts, microfilm, public documents, and published sources at a dozen repositories in Alabama, Florida, Georgia, and Washington, D.C.

A brief account of procedures used in searching Alabama Supreme Court cases serves here to illustrate the effort entailed in tracking potentially relevant sources. First, the *Alabama Digest* and the *Southern Reporter* [standard court-case registries] were consulted to identify all Alabama Supreme Court cases involving Indians, Indian treaties, and Indian lands, or persons with surnames common among Band members during the critical time period (essentially all of the nineteenth century), resulting in a list of more than 200 cases. Next, each of these cases was checked in the published reports of the Alabama Supreme Court and the Alabama Court of Appeals to determine whether the case had any bearing on the history of the Poarch Band or its members specifically, resulting in the identification of approximately eighty-eight cases by surnames and thirty-eight "Indian cases" potentially relevant to Alabama Indian history generally, Band history specifically, or family history of Band members individually. Of these cases, twenty-five were identified as most promising, and a request was made to the Alabama Supreme Court clerk to retrieve the full, original transcripts of these cases, most of which were housed in the Alabama Department of Archives but required that the actual search be made by Court personnel according to state regulations and practices. Of the twenty-five requested cases, transcripts of eleven were actually retrieved. One of these was *Weatherford vs. Weatherford et al.* Before the transcript could be examined, however, the document required restoration, since at some time in the past the volume containing the desired information had been water-damaged and, thus, the pages could not even be separated without special treatment by the conservation laboratory at the Alabama Department of Archives. Once the pages could be separated it became obvious

TABLE 1

Portions of Branch of Federal Acknowledgment Report on
Poarch Band of Creeks Based on Data Generated Specifically
by the Band's Status Clarification Project

Page	Paragraph*	Historical Report Lines	Number of Lines
7	3	10–15	6
9	2	12–16	5
9	3	1–11	11
10	1	1–8	8
14	3	20–25	6
15	2	15–22	8
15	3	all	22
16	1,2	all	16
18	5	1–2	2
19	1	1–2	2
20	4	3–9	7
20	5	4–9	6
25	4	1–5	5
26	3	1–13	13
26	4	all	17
27	1	all	2
28	4	15–16	2
28	5	1–5	5
29	1	all	3
29	4	all	10
30	1	37–41	5
31	2	all	14
31	3	1–8	8
32	4	all	15
33	1	all	5
35	3	all	10
36	1	all	11
36	2	all	14
38	1	all	29
40	4	all	7
Total			274

that the full transcript was of even more importance than the published summary of the case had indicated; a microfilm was made of the approximately 100 pages of handwritten transcript. Tribal archivist Gail Thrower meticulously read and made notes on the microfilm copy; these and a copy of the

TABLE 1 *(Cont.)*

Page	Paragraph*	Anthropological Report Lines	Number of Lines
4	1	13–16	4
4	2	4–8	5
4	2	12–15	4
6	3	7–10	4
9	5	all	7
9	6	all	11
11	1	2–5	4
11	2	5–7	3
11	4	all	10
11	5	all	6
12	2	all	9
12	4	2,4	2
12	5	1–4	4
14	5	all	12
14	6	1–4	4
17	6	all	8
18	1	all	2
22	3	6–8	3
22	4	4–7	4
23	4	5–12	8
30	2	5–8	4
33	2	5–9	5
33	3	all	9
33	4	all	12
Total			144

*Any portion of a paragraph appearing on a page was numbered as a separate paragraph.

microfilm itself were transmitted directly to the BFA staff. *Weatherford vs. Weatherford et al.* proved to be a "goldmine" of information directly relevant to the origin of the Poarch Band within the larger Creek Nation of the early 1800s; thus, information from this case was pivotal at several points in the BFA's positive findings.

In addition to archival research for specific documents to provide evidence that the Band met the criteria for federal recognition, the Poarch Band's Status Clarification Project included a detailed historical demography analysis. Graduate assistant Charles Stevens, under the direction of principal investigator Paredes, conducted these researches. This activity required developing a coding system and the transposition to computer forms of data

from microfilm copies of the original U.S. census schedules for the vicinities
where Band ancestors lived during the period 1850–1900. The data were then
subjected to computer-assisted analyses. The most detailed of these analyses
was a systematic comparison of Poarch Band ancestors with their non-Indian
neighbors in the 1900 census; the results demonstrated quantitatively that during this census (which, not coincidentally, serves as the primary base document for tribal membership) Band ancestors were a population distinct from
others in their vicinity within a number of demographic and social parameters. These research results have been presented in a 180-page master's thesis
(Stevens, 1983) and in papers presented [by Stevens] at the American Anthropological Association and the Mid-South Sociological Conference. Copies of all these documents were transmitted to both the Band and to the
Branch of Federal Acknowledgment. Although none of these items are directly cited in the BFA's final report, this aspect of the Status Clarification
Project produced important quantitative results for understanding the demographic development of the Band during a period for which there is the least
documentary historical evidence.

Conclusion

The Poarch Band quickly began to reap the benefits of federal recognition. By 1986 funding from the Bureau of Indian Affairs, the Indian Health
Service, other federal agencies, and a variety of public and private sources
provided the Band with a budget of nearly $2,000,000 to support tribal gov-
ernmental operations, a health center, social services, law enforcement, a
housing project, and education. In addition, in April 1985 a Band-owned,
1500 seat, state-of-the-art, high stakes "Bingo Palace" opened for business
on tribal land; in November 1985, with a federally secured loan the Band
bought a Best Western Motel on the nearby interstate highway. With a payroll
already over 250 employees by 1986 the Band has become one of the largest
employers in the county (cf. Paredes, 1992). All this had been achieved by a
group that did not even have an official separate corporate mailing address
in 1971.

Along with realizing new opportunities that came with federal recognition, the Band maintains many of its programs and activities from earlier
eras, most notably the Thanksgiving Powwow, begun in 1970, that attracts
thousands of visitors (and dollars) each year and was designated in November
1985 by the Southeastern Tourism Society as one of the "Top Twenty Events
in the Southeast." At the 1987 Powwow the "Senior Princess" performed the
musical selection she had presented as the first-ever Poarch Creek entrant in
the Miss National Congress of American Indians competition the preceding
September: a rendition of "In the Sweet Bye and Bye" in the Muskogee

(Creek) language, learned only a few months earlier in the Band-sponsored cultural awareness program taught by a traditionalist Creek Indian brought from Oklahoma.

In April 1987, the Poarch Band of Creeks dedicated, with prayers in English and Muskogee, a new, million-dollar, federally funded tribal center to house offices of tribal government and its services. Soon tribal police headquarters, courts, and fire stations were to follow. By late 1987 the Band was making the final preparations—including an archaeological impact assessment—for a museum and tourist attraction (including bingo) in a more populous part of the state, on tribal lands acquired a few years earlier with federal historic preservation funds. The plans for this new venture have been surrounded by a considerable amount of internal and external controversy, in part because of the historic nature of the site. The controversy has received ample notice in the public media, the first serious negative publicity that the Band leadership has encountered since beginning its astounding ascent from poverty, obscurity, and powerlessness in the 1940s.

All the projects, programs, enterprises, and buildings (fitted out with computers and other high-tech equipment) of the Poarch Band of Creeks in the 1990s stand as monuments to more than forty years of efforts by these people to improve their lot and revitalize their tribal heritage, latter-day controversies and criticisms notwithstanding. As it happened, I came along quite serendipitously at just the right time for the Creeks. My research was to serve not only my own anthropological interests but also the practical interests of the Creeks.

As described here, the ethnohistorical research done on my own and at the behest of the Poarch Band clearly was critical to the success of their petition for federal recognition. Also, statistical data from the 1973 household survey and from a similar survey done by the Band itself in 1981 with my assistance (and much of the analysis done by my students) provided the necessary documentation of needs for some of the first federal grants that the community received, facts still sometimes recalled and acknowledged by some long-time tribal leaders. Sometimes, however, benefits to the Creeks have come from surprisingly humble sorts of data—the kind of old-fashioned "stuff" of anthropology that P. J. Pelto (personal communication) has informally touted with ironic humor as "mere description."

Despite the emphasis on ethnohistorical research in this essay, ethnographic documentation of the *contemporary* community was also essential for federal recognition. Early in the official review of the Poarch petition, BIA anthropologist George Roth was trying to verify and document the present-day residential community among current Band members at Poarch. After Roth had made a field trip to Poarch headquarters, I asked him if he had found what he needed. He said that he had and announced almost triumphantly (it seemed to me) that he had even found a fairly recent, detailed, hand-drawn settlement pattern map of the community. For a second I was confused and taken aback that I had not known about the map, but I quickly realized that the item in question was a copy of my field map, which I prepared in the summer of 1972 and made available to the Tribal Council several years later!

Epilogue

In October 1988 I went to Poarch for a banquet at the Creek Indian Restaurant and the first joint meeting of the Creek Indian Arts Council and Board (such meetings continue in the 1990s). The previous summer I had agreed to serve on the advisory board, a body composed largely of non-Indian dignitaries, e.g., a banker from Wetumpka, Alabama (site of the controversial new development), the president of the junior college at the local county seat, and members of the staff of the Alabama Department of Archives and History. We received a presentation from members of the architectural firm preparing the design for the museum/tourist complex to be built at Wetumpka—complete with the results of the archaeological impact assessments done by Auburn University. Then, we turned to the agenda in the carefully arranged portfolio provided to each of us by the Band. The principal business at hand was discussing recruitment of a professional curator for the museum (salary range $24,000 to $30,000 annually). Sitting there, I could not help but reflect on the contrast between the tasteful, small-town business-chic ambience of this meeting and the humble beginnings of the Poarch Creeks' quest for a better place in the modern world. Meanwhile, there is still a book-length analysis to be written explaining how all this happened. And my closest Creek friends still remind me from time to time that I have not yet written "The Book."

11

Domain Analysis of Lost Scenes from Roanoke, West Virginia: An Aid to Modeling in Historic Preservation[1]

John M. Roberts and Ronald C. Carlisle[2]

In 1981, the memories of twenty former inhabitants of Roanoke, West Virginia, (Figure 1) were utilized to reconstruct a schematic view of fourteen buildings in what had been the central behavior setting of the town (Figure 2). By that time Roanoke was uninhabited, but the setting of the town did not disappear under the waters of Stonewall Jackson Lake, a man-made flood control lake built by the U.S. Army Corps of Engineers, until 1984.

Prior to 1981, historical information on Roanoke was assembled, and architectural drawings and photographs were made of some of the town's structures. This effort, however, had not included the mapping of buildings into appropriate cognitive and expressive domains. In a measure, the low-budget research reported here served both to reduce this ethnographic deficiency and to illustrate steps that could be taken in the future with some similar venture in historic preservation.

In this research, which combines both qualitative and quantitative approaches, similarities among buildings (as perceived by the town's former inhabitants) were used in mapping fourteen homes, stores, and other structures into a three-dimensional space that was ethnographically interpretable. At the same time the respondents ranked the structures on a small set of attributes. The analysis of these data placed the structures within a cultural context and was used to develop a model historic preservation strategy. This strategy would be helpful if it was desirable to select a small number of these structures for preservation or for interpretation in an exhibit based on photographs, architectural drawings, and other documentation.

Obviously, it would have been preferable to study Roanoke as a living community, but it was not possible to do so. This research shows that one can

FIGURE 1

Location of Roanoke, West Virginia

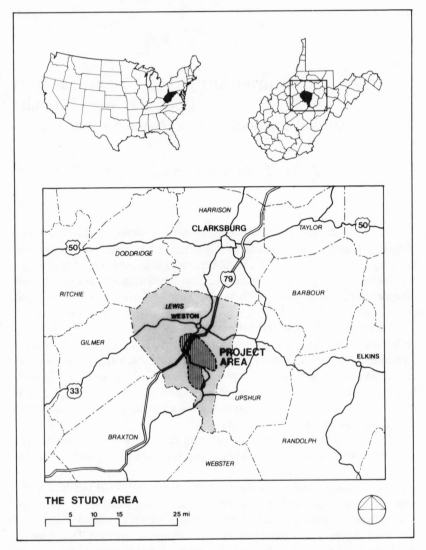

THE STUDY AREA

salvage ethnographic information of value (despite the fallibility of human memory) even after the architectural settings themselves are essentially lost. In the larger sense, our argument is that innovative sociocultural research has a place in the formulation of historic preservation policy.

FIGURE 2

The Layout of the Fourteen Buildings that Form the Roanoke National Register of Historic Places District

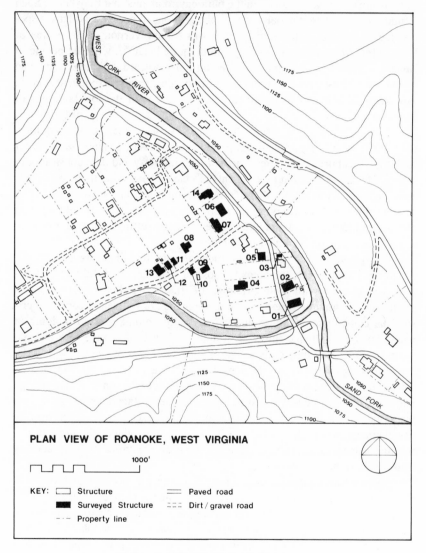

PLAN VIEW OF ROANOKE, WEST VIRGINIA

1000'

KEY: ▢ Structure   ═══ Paved road
     ■ Surveyed Structure   ═ ═ ═ Dirt / gravel road
     – ·– Property line

Cultural Attitudes Toward Structures

Although the field of cultural anthropology has given little attention to the complexities of historic preservation, it is easy to see why historic preservation should be one of its concerns. The matter is too complicated to consider here, but a few points are germane.

It is a commonplace that Americans can be involved with the structures (both historic and nonhistoric) in the built environments that they know. Such attitudes can be shared widely, as with the millions of people who have a special regard toward such national shrines as Mount Vernon or the Statue of Liberty (cf. Meinig, 1979), or they can be quite local, as with the people of Roanoke, who held similar affective attitudes toward buildings they had known on a daily basis for years or even decades. Every respondent used in this study thought it reasonable to be concerned with the lost buildings of Roanoke.

The psychology of historic preservation, of course, is more complex than this. Virtually everyone has experienced the loss of a valued setting after such forces as hurricanes, fires, earthquakes, highway and dam construction, urban redevelopment, and other agents of change have done their work. It is easy for most adults to recall some architectural setting, such as a church, school, childhood home, or store, that was once known intimately but that has since disappeared. Years later, these vanished settings can still evoke interest, nostalgia, or even a form of mourning.

Frequently, such personal attitudes toward buildings are unacknowledged until some crisis threatens the loss of structures and the mental landscapes associated with them (Meinig, 1979). Indeed, historic preservation groups and community preservation movements are frequently rooted in crisis. The constituents of these groups may rally around one old building or many, but the challenge imposed by the possibility of change to a familiar townscape or scene frequently sets in motion a process of evaluation and decision making about historical "significance." The process is seldom dispassionate for those who share the affective experience of a sense of community. Persons who have never paused to inventory their attachments to a building may find themselves defending it from the wrecker's ball, oftentimes by vague appeals to its "historical worth." Nostalgia heightens the sense of impending loss and can promote the mundane to the realm of the irreplaceably historic (Lowenthal, 1975).

All of this suggests that the historical attachments of individuals and communities are more involuted and complex than is immediately apparent (a familiar circumstance for the cultural anthropologist). The form, intensity, and outward expression of this experience of place, or "topophilia" as Tuan has termed it (Tuan, 1974), is itself a historical phenomenon. The "personal constructs" (Fitzgibbon, Pomeroy, and Green, 1985) by which new landscapes and scenes are judged are molded by past personal experience. These attachments and perceptions, which are shared among community members to a greater or lesser degree, have wider connotations for decision making in community and urban redevelopment projects, city planning, historic preservation efforts, and in other undertakings that affect the architecture of America. Understanding the psychological dynamics of human interaction with the built environment is thus of more than passing descriptive or historical interest. The reconstruction of lost cultural domains has a place in this general enterprise.

Cultural anthropologists are latecomers to this area of intellectual concern. Geographers, landscape architects and planners, historians, psychologists, and other scholars have created a large literature on the relationship between the physical environment and human cognition and affect. Much of this literature, however, deals with the interpretation of landscape aesthetics: that is, how and why people react to certain landscape scenes the way they do (Higuchi, 1983; Pearce and Waters, 1983; Fitzgibbon, Pomeroy, and Green, 1985). Comparatively fewer studies have specifically examined the affective dimension of the architectural environment (but consider Price, 1964; Solomon, 1966; Rickert, 1967; Canter, 1969; Rapoport, 1969, 1982; and Bastian, 1975).

When it comes to the analysis of scenes, though, cognitive psychology offers the most promise for development in anthropological domain analysis. The following quotations from Mandler (1984) suggest the possibilities that this field has for domain analysis of the present type; that is, analysis based on the memories of respondents: Mandler (1984:87) has commented:

These studies suggest that much of our knowledge of large-scale spaces is topological rather than Euclidean in character and furthermore is often fraught with inconsistencies.

Mandler (1984:77–78) has also noted that:

it is assumed that a scene schema is hierarchically organized. Good evidence for this assumption is supplied by studies showing that less detail is required to recognize an individual object when it is placed in a scene than when it is presented in isolation . . . Only a sketch of an object is required to recognize it if it fills a slot in a scene schema. Thus a scene schema contains objects, and the objects in turn can be conceived as schemas in their own right. This hierarchical character of scenes is roughly comparable to that of stories or scripts. A story schema too must have certain constituents but these need not be elaborated, in fact, need only be hinted at, for recognition of their role to occur . . . When we look in more detail at the nature of the hierarchical structures of scenes, we find little information on which to rely. It does seem, however, that the level of objects in scenes is roughly equivalent to the "basic" level of actions in scripts. When people are asked to list the parts of ordinary scenes, such as a school, park, restaurant, or beach, most of the things they list are basic-level objects . . . Although people have remarkably good memory for scenes, in general they encode or remember little about the descriptive (figurative) details of what the basic-level objects look like . . . This finding is comparable to remembering the gist of stories and events rather than their details. Subjects do much better at remembering what objects were in the scene, that is, at remembering inventory information. In addition, they remember fairly accurately spatial relation information (in a relative, or perhaps topological sense, not necessarily metric information), just as they remember the temporal relations in scripts. There are also privileged spatial dimensions (for example, vertical information is remembered better than horizontal information), reminiscent of the advantage that causal relations have over temporal relations.

Finally, Mandler (1984:90–91) notes:

Many of the spatial relationships in scenes, then, are determined by knowledge about the human interactions that take place in them. It is possible to document the relative contributions of knowledge about places and knowledge about event-related interactions to accuracy of scene recognition. Scene knowledge consists of inventory and spatial relation information that allows us to recognize a place as a living room or a playground. Event-related knowledge in pictures of scenes consists of inventory and spatial relation information that implies human interaction.

The memories of the Roanoke informants permitted them to perform the photograph sorting tasks that yielded the similarity matrix for the hierarchical clustering and multidimensional scaling solutions presented here. The informants also scaled the buildings on eight variables and produced relevant auxiliary information. The memories of these informants made it possible to augment an ethnographic description of a now-lost cultural domain and to offer a tentative strategy for historic preservation. Before discussing our research in detail, we review a few points about the primary format by which historic properties in the United States are currently recognized, the National Register of Historic Places.

The National Register Process

The National Register of Historic Places is one of the principal vehicles through which the historical significance of elements existing in the American landscape is formally recognized. Established by passage of the National Historic Preservation Act of 1966, the National Register identifies and evaluates the historical, architectural, and/or archaeological significance of nominated properties under one or more of four criteria: (a) the property reflects a historical event or theme of importance in American history; (b) the property is associated with a historically prominent person; (c) the property shows architectural prominence and importance; and (d) the property is important for the information that it possesses or is likely to yield. No matter under which of these criteria a property is nominated, the nomination form is also evaluated according to whether the resource appears to be of national, regional, or local significance. The simultaneous application of four criteria by three geographical ranges produces a 4×3 or twelve-cell field within which any given property may be proposed for inclusion in the Register.

Evaluations are conducted at both state and federal levels, based upon forms prepared by nominators. The forms describe the nominated property, discuss its proposed significance, and establish a property boundary. At the state level, an advisory board made up of informed individuals (usually architects, historians, archaeologists, geographers, etc.) evaluates each proposal and may recommend listing to the Keeper of the National Register.

No matter under which criteria a property is nominated, or at what geographical level, the process involves an evaluation of presented data by persons who may themselves have no intimate familiarity with the property in question. As a general rule, evaluator identification with a property and with its proposed significance is maximized for properties that are associated with nationally significant events or people and minimized for properties of local significance. A specific definition of "local significance" (such as that applied to Roanoke) may be impossible to formulate for evaluators who have never participated in the affective field of a specific small-town community or crossroads village. Nor are the missing pieces likely to be contributed by the kinds of historical or architectural information called for on the National Register nomination forms. Indeed, such properties may appear to the outside observer to be quite ordinary and lacking in distinction.

The present study offers one technique through which it may be possible to establish some criteria of local significance by eliciting information from informants that is not currently collected in the course of National Register nomination form preparation. In essence, the study strives to create an operational definition of local significance by tapping local knowledge and opinion about what was important in Roanoke's built environment and what was not. The approach has obvious limitations but offers an approach to creating an approximately local definition for buildings of "local significance" by incorporating ethnographic information into the National Register evaluation process.

The wider implication of this concern is that the techniques of cultural anthropology are relevant and applicable to establishing historical significance (or insignificance), particularly where architecturally naive or nonelite structures are concerned. By obtaining such information, persons outside the cognitive domain of these structures may be able to participate more fully in the topophilic experience. At the same time, these ethnographic techniques of data collection and analysis can extend the quality and enhance the character of information available about locally significant candidate sites. This process may therefore strengthen a case for significance under criterion d, that is, that sites are important (significant) for the information that they are likely to yield.

The Lost Setting: Roanoke, West Virginia

The rural community of Roanoke, West Virginia, once stood within the area now encompassed by the Stonewall Jackson Lake project in Lewis County, north-central West Virginia (see Figure 1). Weston, the county seat of Lewis County, is 1.5 miles north of the project area, which is crossed by U.S. Routes 19 and 79.

Figure 2 shows the layout of Roanoke as of about 1980. The village was on the west bank of the West Fork River, which was dammed to produce Stonewall Jackson Lake at the point where the Sand Fork joins the river. Figure 2 also gives the spatial arrangement of the fourteen buildings (numbered and shown in solid black) within the core section of the village that once nestled in the sharp bend of the West Fork River. These buildings define the study area.

Most of Roanoke's founding families were of English, Irish, or German extraction, and many families remained in the area for generations. By 1876, Roanoke was a bustling local center for lumber, cattle, and farming. Trains made daily runs through the village in the 1890s connecting it with Weston and other neighboring towns and villages. Roanoke developed a rich and varied community life—decidedly local but with various voluntary associations, churches, and a surprisingly large list of occupations for so small a town (Bauman and Coode, 1983).

Roanoke exported wool and timber, but while the railroad remained, livestock, particularly beef cattle and turkeys, was its main export. By the 1940s, however, the railroad had been abandoned; trucks rumbling along the paved highways outside Roanoke provided similar services, but trucks also isolated the small town and dampened the sense of community integration that the railroad through town had provided. Very few farmers in and near Roanoke could now make a living by farming alone. Young men were called away to war and were attracted to a world of wider horizons. Radio and television became the constant companions of those left behind, reminders of a world outside the West Fork River country.

Thus began a slow decline, a community aging process not unique to Roanoke. How long this process might have continued if left to itself is hard to say, but with each young person who left and with each older person who died, Roanoke was fading from the scene like so many other once-thriving small towns of America. It was a place whose time had come and gone, but gradual attrition was not Roanoke's ultimate fate. Construction of the Stonewall Jackson Dam and impoundment of the West Fork River would submerge Roanoke and several other small West Virginia villages. A series of environmental studies were first required to inventory, evaluate, and record the cultural resources of the project area (Gilbert/Commonwealth, Inc., 1980). The agent of change had itself created an opportunity to assess "environmental dispositions" (Taylor and Konrad, 1980:286) in this one example of small-town America. Much of Roanoke subsequently was recommended for inclusion in a locally significant historic district (Gilbert/Commonwealth, Inc., 1980). The selected buildings formed an architectural and historic core within Roanoke and eventually were determined eligible for listing in the National Register of Historic Places. A later project (Carlisle, 1983) recorded the architecture and history of a portion of the project area, including Roanoke.

Roanoke was described in the initial study as a "community with a compact core and loose edges" (Gilbert/Commonwealth, Inc., 1980:62), and the core area (see Figure 2) was equated with its historic district, composed of buildings of various types. These buildings were thus a "given" in our research from the outset.

The historical and oral historical investigations were altogether important and comprehensive given the time constraints of the project, but in the end they represented the perspectives of outsiders. The present venture augmented these data with a perspective drawn from former residents of this vanished community.

The Problem of Information Loss

This research was carried out in the presence of major losses in relevant information. Indeed, historic preservation data bases are commonly limited or restricted. In a sense, any preserved structure is only a "found" model of an original scene. Thus, although a colonial mansion may still stand, it may no longer dominate a large estate and cannot be viewed in its original context. Similarly, when a historic house is surrounded by more contemporary commercial or industrial buildings, it is difficult to convey the realization that the house, for example, may have been the focal point of a residential neighborhood. Viewers of such structures must cooperate if they are to envisage the original scenes, but artful preservation can greatly facilitate such leaps of imagination.

The loss of the physical features of an original setting, of course, is not the only form of loss. Nothing is more ephemeral than the knowledge and attitudes of the people for whom the structures were once part of a daily scene. In the absence of written records, especially, this information is steadily lost as people forget, move away, or die, and at best it can only be partially reconstructed on the basis of such evidence as still survives.

It is in this cultural area that domain analysis can add perspective. If the structures still exist in living memory (as may be the case for structures or multiple resource properties such as Roanoke), memory, fallible as it is, can still yield ethnographic estimates or approximations of historical significance. Since the more true-to-life the representation of an original scene is, the more rewarding the viewer's experience is likely to be, these estimates are potentially useful in the work of historic preservation and in the interpretation of historic properties.

Research Methodology

Informants were interviewed a year or two after most of them had left Roanoke (many resettling in nearby Weston, West Virginia). This informant pool therefore consisted of people who were still accessible from among a more widely scattered population of the town's former residents. Since both time and resources were limited for this research, it was not feasible to employ a sampling design that took the total former population into consideration.

Interviews were conducted with twenty former residents (ten males and ten females) who (after the expenditure of some effort) were found to be living in the general region. The men had, on the average, spent 40.1 years of their lives in Roanoke, and their mean age was 63.6 years with a range of 19 to 84 years. The women, on the average, had spent 40.0 years of their lives in Roanoke, and they had a mean age of 63.2 years with a range of 29 to 79 years. The length of residence, however, is somewhat misleading, since some informants were "in and out" of the community on an intermittent basis.

All respondents were familiar with the fourteen Roanoke buildings in this study, and their experiences of interaction in these buildings were generally high. They met Mandler's strictures for good scene recall, already given.

Each respondent was given a low-key, easy-going interview in his or her home or in an office at the local courthouse where he or she also performed the sorting task described below. Each respondent ranked the buildings from one (highest) to fourteen (lowest) on the basis of eight variables: personal value, missed (i.e., the respondents were asked to rank the buildings in the order in which they missed them), familiarity, interest, community importance, historical importance, beauty, and mysteriousness. No respondent objected to any task. Indeed, most of them seemed to find the work interesting and even evocative.

Pile sorting is an established technique that has been widely used in developing similarity matrices for use in hierarchical clustering and multidimensional scaling. The technique is flexible, quick, and undemanding of respondents, and it is useful, particularly for exploratory work such as this in a variety of ethnographic contexts.

Usually, cards carrying written expressions are sorted. In previous studies, these have included cards bearing the names of poolroom behaviors or the names of machine shop machines (Roberts and Chick, 1979, 1987). Photographs or even physical objects, such as parts produced on an engine lathe, have been sorted (Chick and Roberts, 1987). Occasionally, the card expressions have had geographical implications, as with tourist attractions (e.g., Kemper, Roberts, and Goodwin, 1983) or Japanese shrines (Roberts, Morita, and Brown, 1986).

In the present research, a black and white photograph of each building was mounted on a 5 × 8 inch card for use in the sorting and rank-ordering tasks. Depending upon the task, the fourteen cards were laid out in various orders by each informant. The same verbal instructions were given to all informants. They were cautioned to think of the real buildings (not the photographs) in their work. The photographs were simply intended to jog memories and to insure that all identifications of buildings were correct. Since many of the buildings had had multiple uses within living memory, reliance on linguistic identifications alone would have been less reliable than the use of photographs supplemented by linguistic tags.

For the sorting task, each informant was given the shuffled deck of fourteen card-mounted photographs and was asked to group them into two or more piles on the basis of the similarities he or she thought that the buildings had to each other. Respondents were permitted to make changes in their initial sortings until they were satisfied with the results.

Each pile sort yielded a 14 × 14 zero-one similarity matrix, and the twenty matrices were summed to produce a single aggregate similarity matrix that was processed through a hierarchical clustering program developed by D'Andrade (1978) on the basis of the U-statistic and through the KYST multidimensional scaling program. For the ranking task, the cards were simply laid out in rank order for each of the eight variables.

The Hierarchical Clustering Solution

The tree for the hierarchical clustering solution is presented in Figure 3. Note that the top seven structures constitute a core cluster (*K*). Architectural elevation drawings for buildings in this cluster appear in Plate 1. Next, there is a two-element outlying subcluster (*C*) followed by a five-element outlying subcluster (*J*). These structures are illustrated in Plate 2. In addition to the drawings, verbal descriptions of the structures are given in the following paragraphs. These are directly based (even word for word) on the descriptions provided by Michael and Grantz (1983).

The subcultures shown in Figure 3 have been named by the authors, but these are only working designations. Unfortunately, it was not feasible to elicit subcluster names from the respondents whose judgments led to the hierarchical clustering solution in the first place.

The core subcluster, designated *K* in Figure 3, contains seven elements collectively designated as "large secular structures." This subcluster is further divided into two subclusters, designated *F* and *I* in Figure 3, entitled respectively "flat-roofed and primarily commercial structures that are close to one another" and "two-story structures."

Subcluster *F*

This subcluster is divided into a doublet (Buildings 01 and 02) and a singleton (Building 03). The two structures in the doublet are described as "commercial structures (i.e., stores) but with some history of use as private dwellings."

Rinehardt Store/Marsh Home (Building 01). Construction of this one-story insulbrick-covered rectangular frame building took place between 1905 and 1930. The building contained five rooms, one of which was the general merchandise sales room. The other four rooms had unknown functions, although one was probably a general storage room. The building was also the residence of the storekeeper, Jesse Rinehardt, who sold building supplies, groceries, and such from about 1920 to the late 1930s. Later, it became the home of the Marsh family.

Whitesel Store/Independent Order of Odd Fellows Lodge (Building 02). This two-story rectangular frame building stood next to Building 01 and was probably built in the 1890s, possibly 1897. The largest of four rooms on the first floor was the store area. The second floor had five rooms, the largest of which was the meeting room of the Odd Fellows and the Rebeccas, the female counterparts of the lodge.

Poststore/Home (Building 03). This one-story rectangular frame structure was built about 1912. The first floor included a living room (formerly a barber shop), a kitchen (formerly part of a restaurant), and a bedroom.

FIGURE 3

Hierarchical Clustering Solution for Fourteen Buildings in the Roanoke, West
Virginia, Historic District Based upon the Responses of Twenty Former Residents.
Building Numbers are Given at Left. Letters Designate Clusters and Subclusters
Discussed in the Text.

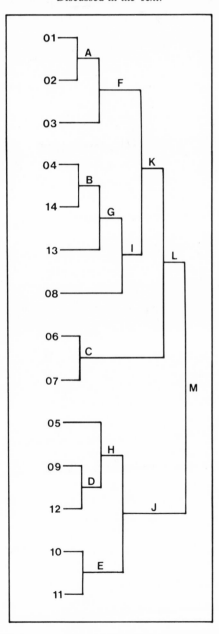

PLATE 1

Elevation Drawings of Seven Roanoke, West Virginia, Buildings Included in Cluster *K*, Large Secular Structures. From Top to Bottom, the Building Numbers Represented are 01, 02, 03, 04, 14, 13, and 08.

 01 - Rinehardt Store/Marsh Home

 02 - Whitesel Store/Independent Order of Odd Fellows Lodge

 03 - Post Store/Home

 04 - Feeny Home

 14 - Smith/Fox Home

 13 - Mullooly/Gillooly/Hawkins Hotel/Home

 08 - Dr. M. E. Whelan Home

PLATE 2

Elevation Drawings of Seven Roanoke, West Virginia, Buildings Included in Subcluster *C*, Church and Church Parsonage, and Subcluster *J*, Single-Story Structures. From Top to Bottom, the Building Numbers Represented are 06, 07, 05, 09, 12, 10, and 11.

06 - Roanoke Methodist/Protestant Church

07 - Roanoke Methodist/Protestant Church Parsonage

05 - Posey Home/Bee Shoe Shop/Telephone Exchange

09 - Conrad/Brinkley Post Office/Home

12 - Malcolm Home

10 - Hawkins Store/Home

11 - Dr. M. E. Whelan Office

Subcluster *I*

This subcluster is divided into a doublet (Buildings 04 and 14) and two singletons (Buildings 13 and 08). The doublet and the first singleton (subcluster *G*) are termed "two-story dwellings, one with a previous commercial history." The doublet (subcluster *B*) is simply entitled "two-story dwellings." The doublet is described first.

Feeney Home (Building 04). The ca. 1885 Feeney home was a two-story, three-bay clapboard-sided, ell-shaped central chimney I house (see Kniffin, 1936; Glassie, 1968). The second floor had two bedrooms. The house was locally known as the residence of Thomas Feeney, who opened a well-known emporium in Roanoke in 1891. Feeney was a prosperous and widely recognized figure in Roanoke community affairs.

Smith/Fox Home (Building 14). The Smith/Fox home was a two-story ell-shaped frame structure with a gable roof. Originally, it may have been a clapboard-sided central passage I house. The first floor of the dwelling had six rooms. The second floor had five rooms. The structure was probably built for Porter Smith in the late nineteenth century. Smith was a gang foreman for the B & O Railroad. The Smiths sold the house to C. E. Fox, a timberman and woodsman in the Roanoke area, in the 1940s.

Mullooly/Gillooly/Hawkins Hotel/Home (Building 13). This ca. 1880–1882 structure had fourteen halls and rooms and served for many years as Roanoke's hotel. It was later used as a private residence. The hotel was a two-story, three-bay, ell-shaped frame I house with a medium-pitch gable roof. The first floor had seven rooms. The second floor rooms included two hallways, two bedrooms, and three storage rooms. The hotel may have been built in 1882 by William L. White, who operated it only until the middle of the following year. He sold the property to the Mullooly family, and they continued the hotel operations until James H. Bosley (see also Building 10) bought the property in 1920. In 1929, Charles Hawkins acquired it. Located along the old Weston and Gauley Bridge Turnpike (West Virginia County Route 23/5), the hotel was well known to both local residents and travelers.

Dr. M. E. Whelan Home (Building 08). The most architecturally elaborate private residence in Roanoke, the ca. 1888 Dr. M. E. Whelan residence remained in the family of Roanoke's well-known physician until it was purchased by the government for the Stonewall Jackson project. The home was a two-story, ell-shaped frame structure with gable roofs covered with slate partially laid in a decorative scale-like pattern that matched the roof of the office next door (Building 11). The first floor included a hallway, a parlor, a living room/bedroom/sitting room, a dining room, and a kitchen. A grand stairway led to the second floor, which included a hallway, three bedrooms, and an unfinished attic. The house had ornate mantles and wood paneling. Together with the doctor's office (see Building 11), Dr. Whelan's home was a focal point of Roanoke community life.

Subcluster C

This subcluster includes a church and church parsonage, i.e., the religious component of the village. Together, they form an outlying subcluster that joins subcluster K to yield a larger subcluster, L, "large and/or important structures."

Roanoke Methodist/Protestant Church (Building 06). This church was dedicated in July 1886 and was built by the parishioners from poplar timbers and siding. It was remodeled in the 1950s. It was a two-story, rectangular frame structure with a gable roof and belfry; lancet windows were found in the southwest and northeast elevations. The first floor had four rooms; the second floor had two rooms. Informants particularly recalled the ministry of the Reverend Lloyd Miller (ca. 1945–60), who lived in the adjoining church parsonage (see Building 07). Mr. Miller also preached in the nearby communities of Oil Creek, Peterson Siding, and Crawford, West Virginia, so services in the Roanoke church were limited to one or two per month. The church congregation numbered about 100 contributing members at its peak in the 1920s.

Roanoke Methodist/Protestant Church Parsonage (Building 07). The ca. 1886 parsonage was a one-story, rectangular frame bungalow with a medium-pitch gable roof and hipped roof porches at both front and rear. The structure contained eight rooms.

Subcluster J

This remaining subcluster, designated "single-story structures," is a true outlier. It is divided into two other subclusters, H, designated "single-story, bungalow-style structures primarily used as dwellings but in two cases with a prior commercial background," and E, termed "single-story, white, gable-roofed structures that are close to each other and which have some previous commercial history." Subcluster H is further divided into a doublet and a singleton. The doublet, D, is described as "single-story dwellings, though one has a remote history of use as a post office." The doublet is described below.

Conrad/Brinkley Post Office/Home (Building 09). This one-story, ell-shaped, insulbrick-covered structure with shed-roof addition was possibly constructed around 1900. Before World War I, one room in the building

Roberts and Carlisle

served as the Roanoke post office, and the rest of the structure was postmaster John Conrad's home. The building was afterwards inhabited by the Brinkley and Phillips families. The last private owners, the Perrines, used the building as a rental property.

Malcolm Home (Building 12). The Malcolm home was a one-story rectangular frame building built by Charles Malcolm in the 1950s as a residence for his mother. It was originally a five-room rectangular structure to which a five-room addition was subsequently made. The building was included within the Roanoke National Register of Historic Places district in 1981, but it was subsequently excluded due to its relatively recent construction date.

Subcluster *H* also contained a singleton, described below.

Posey Home/Bee Shoe Shop/Telephone Exchange (Building 05). This one-story, insulbrick-covered frame bungalow was constructed in the early twentieth century. It was primarily remembered by informants as a residence, and contained six rooms in 1981. In earlier years, however, it had only two rooms and housed Zeke Bee's shoe shop on one side and the local telephone exchange on the other side. The first floor included a kitchen, a room that was previously the telephone exchange, a bathroom, and three bedrooms.

Until telephones became common, Roanoke residents made and took their calls from the People's Telephone Company exchange in this structure. Zeke Bee was remembered as a colorful local character, and the area around his shop was often jokingly called "Zekeville" by residents. More recently, the building was remembered as the home of Robert and Anna Posey.

Subcluster *J* also contained the doublet *E*.

Hawkins Store/Home (Building 10). The Hawkins store/home is a one-story, rectangular frame structure with a medium-pitch gable roof. The structure had three rooms and possibly was built between 1920 and 1925 by James H. Bosley. Bosley also owned the hotel in Roanoke (see Building 13). The store was used for selling cattle feed, but Bosley also dealt in local poultry and eggs. Charles Hawkins acquired the store and hotel from Bosley in 1929 and sold sugar, animal feed, bread, and other staples. When Hawkins died, his son-in-law, Charles Malcolm (see also Building 12), continued to operate the store, which was later converted into a residence.

Dr. M. E. Whelan Office (Building 11). This one-story structure was built before 1880 by physician and prominent Roanoke citizen, Dr. M. E. Whelan (see also Building 08) as his medical office. This office was a one-story three-bay rectangular frame building with a gable roof. There were two rooms. Their exact functions are unknown, but it is likely that the front room was the examining room, and the rear room may have been the private office of the doctor. During his early years in Roanoke, Dr. Whelan apparently also lived in the office for a time before his next-door home was built. After Dr. Whelan's death, the office was converted by his widow into a rental dwelling, but the respondents usually continued to refer to it as the doctor's office.

Results

Judging from the "error" count in the program, the Feeney home (Building 04) and the Smith/Fox home (Building 14) were sorted most consistently by the informants. The two buildings also constitute the tightest cluster. In contrast, the Roanoke Methodist/Protestant Church parsonage was least consistently sorted, and the church-parsonage subcluster was the least well defined of any of the subclusters. The Hawkins store/home was also sorted less consistently than the other buildings except for the parsonage; the Hawkins store/home and Dr. M. E. Whelan's office subcluster is the second loosest subcluster.

If the drawings of the church and the parsonage are examined, it is plain that the two buildings are very different in architecture. They are undoubtedly linked because of their religious association, but clearly, some of the sorters simply treated the parsonage as an unimpressive dwelling.

Table 1 gives the ratings for the fourteen structures on eight variables. The structures are listed in the order that they appear in Figure 3, and simple inspection shows that the average rank orders of the variables are so highly correlated that it is not necessary to give a correlation table.

The ratings, however, have ethnographic interest. When two structures are compared, the results serve to round out the general ethnographic picture of Roanoke.

The Multidimensional Scaling Solution

The similarity matrix derived from the card sorting was used for a multidimensional scaling solution (Table 2). The three-dimensional solution defines a space into which the structures can be plotted. This probably represents the simplest formulation of a domain that could be useful in historic reconstruction. Again, the dimensions were named by the authors, and it is regrettable that the respondents could not have been used for this task.

Dimension I appears to be an impressiveness or weight dimension that tends to range from large-sized buildings to small ones. Dimension II pertains to the use of the structures, for it seems to range from residential to nonresidential structures. Finally, Dimension III can be interpreted as a reality dimension for it seems to range from unworldly to worldly; in pragmatic terms

TABLE 1

Ranks and Average Ranks on Eight Variables for Fourteen Structures in Roanoke, West Virginia*

BUILDING NAME	Building Number	Variables							
		Personal Value (N = 18)		Missed (N = 18)		Familiarity (N = 19)		Interest (N = 18)	
		Rank	Avg. Rank	Rank	Avg. Rank	Rank	Avg. Rank	Rank	Avg. Rank
Rinehardt Store/Marsh Home	01	(08)**	8.00	(10)	8.83	(08)	8.06	(11)	8.58
Whitesel Store	02	(13)	10.56	(13)	11.11	(12)	10.22	(13)	10.32
I.O.O.F. Lodge*	03	(01)	3.17	(02)	3.67	(02)	4.33	(03)	5.11
Post Home/Store	04	(10)	8.61	(08)	7.89	(10)	8.89	(10)	8.32
Feeney Home	14	(11)	8.78	(11)	8.94	(09)	8.78	(08)	7.84
Smith/Fox Home	13	(09)	8.50	(07)	7.78	(11)	9.67	(6.5)	7.16
Hotel	08	(12)	9.83	(12)	9.67	(13)	10.83	(12)	9.63
Dr. M. E. Whelan Home*	06	(14)	13.22	(14)	12.94	(14)	12.72	(14)	13.11
Roanoke Methodist/Protestant Church* Church Parsonage	07	(06)	7.11	(09)	7.94	(05)	5.61	(09)	8.26
Posey Home/Bee Shoe Shop/Telephone Exchange	05	(03)	4.39	(03)	3.83	(03)	4.72	(04)	5.63
Conrad/Brinkley/Post Office/Home	09	(07)	7.50	(06)	7.17	(07)	6.28	(05)	6.37
Malcolm Home*	12	(02)	4.00	(01)	3.11	(01)	3.33	(01)	2.68
Hawkins Store/Home*	10	(04)	5.61	(04)	5.89	(04)	5.44	(6.5)	7.16
Dr. M. E. Whelan Office	11	(05)	5.72	(05)	6.22	(06)	6.11	(02)	4.84

continued

TABLE 1 (*Cont.*)

Ranks and Average Ranks on Eight Variables for Fourteen Structures in Roanoke, West Virginia*

Variables

BUILDING NAME	Community Importance (N = 18)		Historical Importance (N = 18)		Beauty (N = 18)		Mysterious (N = 17)	
	Rank	Avg. Rank	Rank	Avg. Rank	Rank	Avg. Rank	Rank	Avg. Rank
Rinehardt Store/ Marsh Home	(12)	9.61	(09)	8.33	(04)	5.06	(13)	10.00
Whitesel Store								
I.O.O.F. Lodge*	(13)	11.94	(12)	11.33	(07)	6.22	(11)	9.41
Post Home/Store	(03)	4.50	(06)	6.33	(01)	2.00	(07)	8.06
Feeney Home	(06)	7.11	(10)	8.61	(11)	10.78	(10)	9.35
Smith/Fox Home	(07)	7.33	(07)	7.78	(11)	10.78	(09)	8.82
Hotel	(08)	7.56	(11)	9.50	(13)	11.56	(12)	9.52
Dr. M. E. Whelan Home*	(11)	8.72	(13)	11.72	(11)	10.78	(14)	11.18

continued

TABLE 1 (Cont.)

Ranks and Average Ranks on Eight Variables for Fourteen Structures in Roanoke, West Virginia*

| | | | | | Variables | | | | |
| BUILDING NAME | Community Importance (N=18) | | Historical Importance (N=18) | | Beauty (N=18) | | Mysterious (N=17) | |
	Rank	Avg. Rank	Rank	Avg. Rank	Rank	Avg. Rank	Rank	Avg. Rank
Roanoke Methodist/ Protestant Church*	(14)	13.94	(14)	12.33	(14)	13.22	(04)	5.65
Church Parsonage	(10)	8.44	(02)	4.50	(08)	7.06	(02)	4.06
Posey Home/Bee Shoe Shop/ Telephone Exchange	(02)	4.00	(04)	4.83	(03)	4.67	(03)	5.18
Conrad/Brinkley/ Post Office/Home	(04)	5.61	(05)	5.17	(09)	8.28	(05)	5.77
Malcolm Home*	(01)	2.61	(01)	1.78	(06)	5.61	(01)	2.77
Hawkins Store/Home*	(05)	5.83	(03)	4.78	(02)	3.78	(06)	6.82
Dr. M. E. Whelan Office	(09)	7.78	(08)	8.00	(05)	5.22	(08)	8.41

*Asterisk denotes one of five structures that define Roanoke's cultural domain as determined in the study.

**Rank proceeds from a low of 1 to a high of 14. For example, a rank of 1 under "personal value" means least personal value, and a score of 14 means greatest personal value.

TABLE 2

Multidimensional Scaling Solution for the Fourteen
Structures in Roanoke, West Virginia

| | Dimensions | | |
| | I | II | III |
Building Name	Weight	Use	Unworldly
*Whitesel Store/International Order			
of Odd Fellows Lodge	0.969	0.616	-0.014
Rinehardt Store/Marsh Home	0.789	0.751	-0.217
*Roanoke Methodist/Protestant Church	0.714	0.027	0.945
*Dr. M. E. Whelan Home	0.619	-0.609	0.169
Smith/Fox Home	0.600	-0.728	-0.153
Feeney Home	0.390	-0.574	-0.229
Mullooly/Gillooly/Hawkins Hotel/Home	0.300	-0.602	-0.504
Post Store/Home	0.177	0.311	-0.738
Dr. M. E. Whelan Office	-0.233	0.882	0.470
Roanoke Methodist/Protestant Church Parsonage	-0.468	-0.278	0.729
*Hawkins Store/Home	-0.644	0.589	-0.418
Posey Home/Bee Shoe Shop/Telephone Exchange	-0.999	-0.237	0.178
Conrad/Brinkley Post Office/Home	-1.010	-0.047	-0.185
*Malcolm Home	-1.204	-0.108	-0.034

*Asterisk denotes one of five structures that define Roanoke's cultural domain as
determined in the study.

it may represent a continuum from the nonsecular to the secular. Note that the
doctor's office and house are skewed somewhat toward the nonsecular.

The multidimensional space is portrayed in Figure 4. The five structures discussed in the following section are named, but the remaining structures are simply indicated. Their coordinates, of course, are given in Table 1.

Discussion and Potential Application

The preservation of historically significant structures often has many
motivations. Since there is almost never enough money to permit extensive
preservation of entire districts or historic communities, it may be desirable to
develop strategies for selecting a minimum number of structures that will satisfy historically motivated preservation needs by modeling the historic domain of the larger community. Ordinarily, both informational and expressive
attributes must be taken into consideration. In the following exercise, five
Roanoke structures were selected on the basis of informant sorting and ranking as the minimum number among the fourteen buildings within the Roanoke
historic district. These five structures in essence sample the historic domain

FIGURE 4

Multidimensional Scaling Plot for the Fourteen Buildings in the Roanoke Historic
District. The Plot Graphically Displays the Data Presented in Table 2. The Five
Structures Discussed in the Exercise are Labeled.

MULTIDIMENSIONAL SCALING PLOT

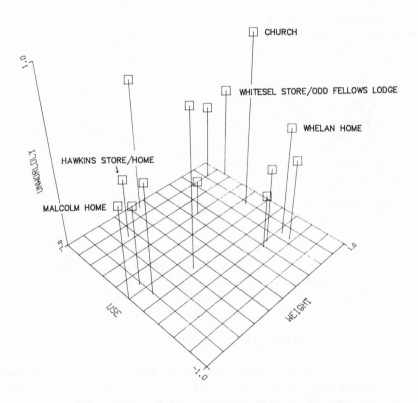

of Roanoke, at least as that domain is represented through the composite evaluations of the informants. An attempt was made to combine historic significance, aesthetic considerations, and cultural representativeness into a single
selection.

The approach developed here suggests just one strategy that could be
helpful in defining the boundaries and community composition of historic

districts or multiple property nominations to the National Register where knowledgeable community informants are still available as sources of information. Admittedly, the techniques used in this exploratory venture can be improved, but the general perspective should endure.

In making preservation choices, there is often a tendency to overrepresent buildings in the "large, important structures" cluster (e.g., *L*, Figure 3) in the definition of historic districts. Indeed, many of the buildings now listed on the National Register are just such impressive structures. The pilot work conducted in Roanoke, however, suggests that although buildings such as the town church and the architecturally impressive doctor's home (which even outsiders might identify as being at least locally "historic") are legitimate components of the Roanoke cultural domain, other, less architecturally elaborate structures are equally part of that domain. These latter buildings clarify the borders of the district and are of potential assistance in site/district interpretation.

The Roanoke study reaffirms the idea that the concept of what is historic includes a nostalgic composite of affective dimensions, some of which are more easily elicited and interpretable than are others. It is not new, of course, to suggest that historic preservation, if it is to be in any sense representative, should preserve, for example, not only the "iron baron's house," but also the iron worker's home and the mills that brought them together. What is comparatively new, however, is a technique rooted in cultural anthropology for selecting *which* houses and *which* mills or parts of mills might be chosen as representatives of a larger cognitive whole.

In Roanoke, if only five buildings could be selected that would model the town in ways that exemplified the cognitive and expressive understandings of its inhabitants, that selection might be guided by a set of principles derived from the analysis of the structural domain. These principles might include the following:

1. Each major cluster should be represented.
2. The center and both ends of each major dimension should be represented.
3. Ranges in judged attitudes, such as buildings of community importance, beauty, and mysteriousness should be represented.

Obviously, with a small number of buildings it is necessary to compromise in the application of these principles. The set of five buildings described below, however, constitutes one instance of such an application. The attributes for each building included within the sample domain are broadly listed below. Ratings extend from low (1) to high (14).

Whitesel Store/International Order of Odd Fellows Lodge (Building 02)

I (weight) .969; II (use) .616; III (unworldly) .014. *A* commercial structures < *F* flat-roofed and primarily commercial structures < *K* large secular structures < *L* large important structures. Personal value, missed, interest, and community importance (13). Familiarity and historical importance (12). Mysteriousness (11). Beauty (07).

Roanoke Methodist/Protestant Church (Building 06)

I (weight) .714; II (use) .027; III (unworldly) .945. *C* religion associated < *L* large important structures. Personal value, missed, familiarity, interest, community importance, historical importance, and beauty (14). Mysteriousness (04).

Dr. M. E. Whelan Home (Building 08)

I (weight) .619; II (use) .609; III (unworldly) .169. *I* two-story structures < *K* large secular structures < *L* large important structures. Mysteriousness (14). Familiarity and historical importance (13). Personal value, missed, and interest (12). Community importance and beauty (11).

Hawkins Store/Home (Building 12)

I (weight) -.644; II (use) .589; III (unworldly) -.418. *E* single-story, white, gable-roofed structures with commercial history < *J* single-story structures. Interest (6.5). Mysteriousness (6). Community importance (5). Personal value, missed, and familiarity (4). Historical importance (3). Beauty (2).

Malcolm Home (Building 12)

I (weight) -1.204; II (use) -0.100; III (unworldly) -0.034. *D* single-story dwelling < *H* single-story, bungalow-style structures < *J* single-story structures. Personal value (2). Missed, familiarity, interest, community importance, historical importance, beauty, and mysteriousness (1).

Figure 4 shows that the selected buildings roughly model the full space. Figure 3 gives the distribution of the selected buildings among the subclusters. Finally, the values for the eight variables given in Table 1 were considered in making point selections.

No attention was paid to the physical proximity of buildings in making the selection. In a real design, it conceivably might be necessary to move some buildings if the array were to be used, for example, as an outdoor museum.

It is impossible, of course, to recreate without distortion the domain defined by fourteen buildings with only five structures, but the chosen five illustrate dwellings, stores, and religious structures (considering the Whitesel store/Odd Fellows lodge as a representative of something of a secular religion) in a variety of architectural styles. The structures also fit in a range of community attitudes.

The choice of these five structures is least surprising in the cases of the Whitesel store/Odd Fellows lodge, the Dr. M. E. Whelan home, and the Roanoke Methodist/Protestant church. The approach illustrated here, however, would aid in discriminating between the Whitesel store/Odd Fellows lodge and the Rinehardt store/Marsh home if only one or the other of them could be preserved. The former occupies a more solid position within the Roanoke cultural domain. The Malcolm home and the Hawkins store/home, on the other hand, stand out because of what they are *not*. In the case of the Malcolm home, this emic evaluation coincides with the outsider's view and may help to explain why this building was subsequently removed from the Roanoke historic district. It would be inaccurate, however, to consider these buildings to be "noncontributing" to Roanoke's larger cultural domain. They clearly do occupy a place in that domain, and the assessment of the attitudes of former residents contributes to understanding what that place is. Such knowledge could allow for a more informed choice in defining the boundaries of a historic district and in its interpretation.

Conclusion

The foregoing treatment illuminates some aspects of the cultural domain associated with fourteen buildings that make up the historic district of Roanoke, West Virginia. Although the idiom of simple quantitative analysis might be foreign to former residents of the town who knew the core area of the village, it is unlikely that the taxonomy given in the clustering solution or the space defined by the multidimensional scaling solution would either surprise them or strike them as being uninterpretable.

Persons outside the system of Roanoke community life might well have selected either the same or different buildings for preservation on an impressionistic basis. Still, a more methodologically rigorous process of selection may, at times, be desirable in order to formulate as valid a definition of the original cultural domain as possible. The major point of this article is that such a process is possible. This merits some additional discussion.

It may, for example, be impossible to reconstitute an exact original domain when substantial physical changes—in this case, architectural loss— have occurred. A study of machine shop syncretism seems to support the inference that attitudes held by machinists toward their original manual machines may change once computer-controlled machines are introduced. These changes even occur in the minds of machinists who have not yet learned how to operate the new equipment (Roberts and Chick, 1987). It is as though the older, more familiar engine lathe becomes somehow "less beautiful" or desirable in the eyes of the machinists once the new machine is on the shop floor.

There may be parallel changes in attitudes associated with building loss. In practical terms, our affective ties to a "historic" building may be altered by destruction or substantial alteration of the surrounding architectural context, even when that context is composed of so-called "noncontributing structures." Attitudes held by the informants toward the fourteen Roanoke buildings already may have been altered at the time of the fieldwork simply because of the loss of nearby buildings that were not included within the proposed historic district. Thus, scaling projects based on the residual fourteen structures may only produce an approximation of the original cultural domain.

The human capacity to "read" expression in others comes into play when visitors assess examples of historic preservation. If the preserved structures model, even to a small degree, the original semantic space, it facilitates the development of an appraisal and a response on the part of the visitor that approximates, at least roughly, the response of the original participants in the domain. It can be argued that only when a set of preserved structures accurately models the original domain can such empathies be developed in those outside the community, for example, by people who had never participated in the experience of Roanoke as a living community.

This is not to say that historic structures are not judged by visitors on the basis of idiosyncrasies or by the standards of the contemporary culture. Such judgments occur all the time. Application of the preservation strategy discussed here, however, offers the possibility that a visitor to a historic site may be able to develop a psychological or cultural perspective on the original historic domain that is concordant, at least roughly, with the perspectives of the inhabitants of a house, town, farm, or village. The possibilities for a richer array of responses on the part of site visitors may be increased proportionately if such approaches to preservation are adopted in settings for which a variety of informants are still available, as in the documentation of the rapidly fading industrial heritage of First World countries, for example.

Applied cultural anthropologists have not been greatly involved in problems of historic preservation, but they have many fine qualifications for just this task. Furthermore, the need for such applications is so widespread in the United States, particularly as a result of the demise of the infrastructure of traditional heavy industry, the abandonment of small towns, the construction of new roads, housing developments, and recreational facilities, that the opportunities and need for careful and meaningful selection in the preservation process are very great.

VI
Epilogue

Introduction to Part Six

In this final section of the book, Professor Pertti J. Pelto reviews the trends of anthropological research methodology and applications over the past two decades. He concludes that the future utility and credibility of anthropological research in policy matters will require even greater attention to scientific research methodology as we try to address the complex social and cultural issues of this final decade of the twentieth century.

12

Anthropological Research Methods and Applications: Taking Stock

Pertti J. Pelto

The appearance of this volume provides a suitable moment for assessing some of the trends in sociocultural research methodology and application of which this set of papers is a part. It is now twenty years since the appearance of the first edition of *Anthropological Research* (Pelto, 1970). Recently a new textbook by H. R. Bernard (1988) provided an update on the rapidly developing field of research methods.

During the 1980s many changes were taking place in the culture(s) of anthropological research. Economic conditions in our profession continued to point many newly graduated Ph.Ds into jobs outside of academe. New directions in applied anthropology developed; and the nature of expectations in the wider public (including other disciplines) shifted with regard to anthropologists' research activities. Increased interdisciplinary teamwork has contributed to sharing of research methodologies across disciplinary lines; major developments in both qualitative and quantitative research have spread in networks that frequently ignore disciplinary boundaries. If economic forces have played a major role in affecting trends in research methods, so did technological developments, especially in the world of computers.

I will not attempt a comprehensive review of all these developments here. That task will require a considerable research effort, in order to better understand the very important trends in anthropological research, especially of the past two decades.

The Microcomputer Age

The advent of powerful, low-cost microcomputers ranks as the primary factor contributing to the explosion of interest in research methods currently affecting anthropology. During the 1960s and 1970s the increased use of mainframe computers only nibbled around the edges of sociocultural research, even as computerized data processing transformed the working styles of archaeologists and physical anthropologists. At the beginning of the 1980s a handful of anthropologists were experimenting with the first commercially available microcomputers (particularly the Apple computer). However optimistic some of them may have been concerning these machines, nobody imagined that within a decade the microcomputers would be capable of replacing mainframe computers for data analysis in all but the largest, most complex research projects.

By 1985 large numbers of anthropologists had joined other social science researchers in using microcomputers for writing field notes, proposals, letters, and all manner of other text materials. In these uses the microcomputers simply took over tasks for which typewriters had been the standard equipment. However, the accumulation of large amounts of computerized writing naturally led to the idea that new methods could be found for the tedious, often disorganized processes of analyzing qualitative data.

The memory capacities of the first generation of microcomputers were too small to accommodate any but the simplest statistics. All that changed quickly. By 1985 both the SAS and SPSS statistics programs—mainstays in mainframe computing—had become available for the micros, and scores of other programs for statistical analysis were entering the marketplace. Powerful statistics programs such as SYSTAT (1988, 1989) could be operated with (the now old-fashioned) machines that use two floppy-disks. Database systems and spreadsheets proved to be useful tools for management of data sets, at least for more enterprising researchers. Anthropologists with large and complex data sets, particularly archaeologists, were quick to adapt the new microcomputer technology to fieldwork. In the second half of the decade hard disks with twenty, thirty, forty megabyte storage capacities had become commonplace even in laptop computers.

The effects of the microcomputers on anthropological work should be studied with care, for this revolution in research technology is far from complete. Here I will simply list a few hypotheses for future investigation, particularly in reference to sociocultural research:

1. Ease of use of microcomputers has resulted in at least a twofold expansion of basic field notes (among researchers using microcomputers), with a concomitant increase in field note detail.
2. Database systems and related software have contributed to improved data organization and management among researchers using microcomputers in fieldwork.

3. Computerized data entry in the field has resulted in a shortening of the lag time between data collection and initial data analysis, even in cases where no statistical analysis is attempted in the field.
4. Availability of easy-to-use statistical programs for microcomputers has led to adoption of quantified statistical methods among anthropologists who were not users of statistics in their earlier research.
5. Complex methods of pattern analysis, previously used only by specialists (e.g., multidimensional scaling, property fitting) will be increasingly used by anthropologists as they become routinized in easy-to-use software programs.
6. The common language of microcomputers, along with common software programs, is leading to increased interdisciplinary communication in research methods.
7. In the 1990s easy-to-use statistical programs for microcomputers will lead to improved communications between highly experienced quantitative anthropologists and the many other anthropologists who heretofore had little probability of entering the arena of complex numerical analysis.
8. The power now available in newest generations of microcomputers is facilitating the development of new approaches to statistical analysis. One such development is that of permutation tests, or randomization tests, that permit researchers to explore empirically the P values of relationships in field data sets without having to deal with all the assumptions associated with conventional parametric statistics. As Behrens notes in his review of these procedures, "randomization tests are valid for any sample regardless of its size or the manner in which it was selected! The reason for this is . . . a randomization test generates its own probability distribution empirically" (Behrens, 1989:400).
9. Major developments will take place in the 1990s in the area of text analysis, including use of various expert systems, hypertext, and a new generation of text searching software.

The Construction of Primary Data

Basic issues in anthropological methodology were explored in a conference sponsored by the National Science Foundation in 1985. The discussions focused on the "Construction of Primary Data in Cultural Anthropology." The participants noted that, given the rapid changes now happening in even the most remote research sites, "each of us has the responsibility to make sure that data are collected in such a way as to document fully the influence of the particular situation on the results of the research and in such a way that others can use them" (Bernard et al., 1986:383).

That conference led to the development of a Summer Institute, also funded by the NSF, which has been held at the University of Florida since 1987. The three-week Summer Institute has evolved a training program that critically examines the construction of qualitative and quantitative data, accompanied by orientation to some easy-to-use software programs for anthropologists. A major aim of the 1985 conference and subsequent Summer Institutes has been to increase anthropologists' awareness of the methodological issues involved in the processes whereby raw field observations are transformed into primary data for both qualitative and quantitative analysis. The Institute also includes suggestions for improvements in the contents of methodological training in anthropological programs.

A major product of the Summer Institute has been the development of special software (ANTHROPAC) for anthropologists. Steve Borgatti, the designer of this set of programs, has added new components to the program each year, reflecting recent methodological developments as well as new additions to the contents of the summer training. Programs such as ANTHROPAC provide tools and techniques for pattern analysis of data; at the same time they help to make more explicit (and open to replication) the processes used by fieldworkers to "create order" from the chaos of research observations (Borgatti, 1989, 1990).

Increased use of microcomputers in fieldwork, including the burgeoning use of laptop computers for field notes, brings anthropologists to a new confrontation with the epistemological issues of *data construction*. Methodologists in anthropology and other disciplines have long been aware of the importance of *operational definitions* in all systematic research (cf. Pelto and Pelto, 1978:38–53). Recently, various "postmodernist" theorists have emphasized the central role of social construction of data, not only in the social sciences but in biological and physical sciences as well. The more extreme postmodernist claim appears to be that the "creation of order" in research, including laboratory research, produces organization of phenomena that "in no way preexists . . . [the research process]." (Latour and Woolgar, 1979:246).

Methodologists at the 1985 NSF Conference, both qualitative and quantitative, emphasized the central importance of this idea, noting that "construction of primary data . . . [is] an interactive process between a researcher, a theory, and the research materials under study, whether they be people in the field or documents to be examined. Moreover, we acknowledge that data construction goes on after one leaves the field." (Bernard et al., 1986:383).

The position taken by most methodologists is that awareness of the processes of "social construction of primary data" should lead to more careful documentation of the *actual processes of data collection and data analysis,* so that other persons, including those in other disciplines, can understand and critically assess the sources of specific data statements—the descriptive and analytic generalizations that purport to come from empirical observation. The total obfuscation of these processes, in some examples of "interpretive anthropology," would seem to be illogical. Why go out to fieldwork at all, if the ethnographic reporting is to be a totally subjective rendition, in which any order or pattern results solely from the ingenuity of the researcher's interpretations?

Contrary to widely held notions in anthropology, most quantitatively oriented researchers in the social sciences, particularly in anthropology, are acutely aware of the extent to which field data are "constructed" in the interaction between the researcher and the field experience. All anthropologists observe the "real world" of the field situation through the lenses of theory, personal interests and predilections, and selected methods of data collection. The observations from fieldwork are translated and filtered through the researcher's language system, and then further transformed as the data are analyzed "back home." A central methodological issue in both qualitative and quantitative research is to make those steps of translation and "filtering" more and more explicit and open to critical review by other researchers. In that process the researcher assumes that there are regularities, patterns of culture and behavior, among the people studied. The "constructed data" are more or less successful approximations of those patterns.

Although the use of microcomputers would seem, on the one hand, to contribute further "artificiality" to the ways in which researchers "create order" among natural phenomena, there is the possibility that use of computers, with both qualitative and quantified data, may be able to contribute to the interperson, publicly accessible explication and replicability of our data analysis. Until the 1980s there was little possibility that anthropological data could be shipped and shared in a manner that permitted reevaluation of specific data analyses.

Now such reanalysis, through data sharing, is a distinct possibility. The data themselves can be easily transferred as computer files. At least some of the main steps and features of data analysis can be described in relation to specific software programs, so that other researchers can follow the pathways of data processing to find out if they reach the same conclusions, the same generalizations, as the original researcher.

New Developments in Applied Anthropology

In contrast to the "technological determinism" I postulated in relation to microcomputers, forces for change of a quite different sort emanate from recent developments in applied anthropology. A major factor in this sector is

the growth in numbers of practicing (applied) anthropologists. After the hal-
cyon days of the 1960s, academic openings for anthropologists became increasingly scarce. Somewhat to the surprise of the pessimists, large numbers
of anthropologists found employment in government agencies, the business
world, and in international organizations. Regional organizations of practicing anthropologists have been formed, as well as the rapidly growing National Association of Practicing Anthropologists (NAPA). This new
generation of non-academic researchers has strong methodological interests,
not least because the products of research must make sense to practical,
policy-making administrators.

Throughout the 1980s research by anthropologists came to be in increasing demand at the World Bank, UNICEF, WHO, various public and private health agencies, multidisciplinary development programs, and other
settings. In the world of applications, the pace of research is often quickened;
data are needed quickly.

Rapid Ethnographic Procedures

The demand for quick results from ethnographic work is one of the major influences current in the applied social sciences. In earlier decades anthropologists often argued that ethnographic work for applied projects
required many months, in order to provide the "holistic background" necessary for understanding local cultural and social processes. That style of applied ethnographic work has been increasingly criticized for its slowness and
failure to respond to specific questions raised by the programs the research
was intended to serve.

Pressures for rapid appraisals developed in several different areas of applied social sciences throughout the 1970s. Researchers working in the agricultural sector appear to have been the first to develop specific methods and
guidelines that were subsequently widely disseminated and adopted. Unpublished working papers on these concepts were circulating in the 1970s, and
workshops were held on the topic (for example) at the Institute for Development Studies, University of Sussex. Beebe commented that "Publication of
the book *Farming Systems Research and Development Guidelines for Developing Countries* (Shaner et al., 1982), and distribution of Robert Rhoades's
(1982) paper 'The Art of the Informal Agricultural Survey,' were extremely
important contributions to the evolution of the concept of Rapid Appraisal
which focuses on agriculture" (Beebe, 1987). The history of rapid appraisal
in rural development was reviewed in depth in a Ford Foundation-sponsored
conference held in Thailand in 1985, subsequently published in a monograph
of *Proceedings of the 1985 International Conference on Rapid Rural Appraisal* (Grandstaff et al., 1987).

In medical anthropology there were similar developments, though they took a somewhat different form. Large-scale, multidisciplinary research projects were developed, which required systematic and focused ethnographic components to be carried out in a few weeks of intensive work. In one such project, T. Marchione was commissioned to prepare a field manual for ethnographic research in infant feeding practices, to be carried out by researchers from the Population Council, Cornell University, and Columbia University School of Public Health (Marchione, 1981). The field manual suggested approximately ten weeks of ethnographic reconnaissance, with a sample of thirty to fifty informants. The informants were to be selected from the same communities in which a later, structured interview survey was to be carried out. A similar project, concerning infant feeding practices in northern Cameroon, was carried out over a six-week period in 1982, using a field manual designed by G. Pelto for the Educational Development Council (Pelto, 1984).

"Rapid anthropological assessment" became widely known in the community health and nutrition sector after the publication of the "RAP Manual" *(Rapid Assessment Procedures)* by Scrimshaw and Hurtado (1987). The publication provides "anthropological approaches to improving programme effectiveness" in nutrition and primary health care. The "data collection guides" in the RAP manual provided brief (1–2 page) outlines for data collection on socioeconomic status, definitions of health and illness, household composition, diet of sick children, use of health resources, and other topics.

Throughout the later part of the 1980s a number of applied anthropologists have been involved in writing guidelines or manuals for ethnographic data collection in various sectors of health/nutrition research, as well as in topical areas such as marine resources, forestry, animal husbandry, and aspects of horticulture. The original "RAP Manual" of Scrimshaw and Hurtado has been adapted to specific topics such as AIDS and epilepsy; Gretel Pelto has recently developed a comprehensive manual for data collection on acute respiratory illness for the World Health Organization (Pelto, 1990); and Bentley and associates developed a field guide for "rapid ethnographic assessment " in a program involved with dietary management during childrens' diarrheal episodes. "Because the data were urgently required for subsequent phases of research, the time allotted for data collection and analysis for each site was six weeks" (Bentley et al., 1988:110).

Rapid assessment or rapid ethnographic reconnaissance takes many forms. The main impact of these methodological developments is not, however, primarily concerned with the *speediness* of research. The various manuals, field inventories, and guidelines all point toward demystifying ethnographic field work. The aims are to make specific products and processes of field research more available to programmatic users and to collaborating researchers from other disciplines. At the same time, these topically specific methodological tools make possible a testing and comparing of different methodologies. Specific guidelines for data collection with key informants provide a format for comparisons with survey data as well as with other strategies of qualitative research.

The various forms of rapid assessment place heavy emphasis on key informant interviewing and direct observation (cf. Beebe, 1987; Scrimshaw and Hurtado, 1987). At the same time, the techniques often involve small-scale quantified research, including both structured interviewing and structured observations. The various guidelines commonly specify minimum numbers of informants and respondents, and suggest ways to increase representativeness of observations.

The selection of key informants is yet another area for which greater systematization is taking place. Johnson has recently published a set of guidelines for this, *Selecting Ethnographic Informants* (1990). The book gives examples of informant selection based on the use of theory-driven frameworks, as contrasted with selection that utilizes an emergent, data-driven method. He points out that once the representativeness of informants has been assured, "articulateness, willingness to participate, trustworthiness and other personal attributes then become screening devices. At this point, personal attributes can drive the selection process with less risk of potential bias" (Johnson, 1990:88).

Understanding Qualitative Data

Two separate, distinct trends are pushing anthropologists (and others) toward reexamination and codification of qualitative research methods. The spread of interest in rapid assessment and other ethnographic contributions to farming systems research, primary health care systems, and other forms of development projects is contributing to development of specific approaches for both short-term and longer-term collection of data. In the area of cultural belief systems, for example, medical anthropologists are refining techniques for systematic exploration of "explanatory models" of specific illnesses (Kleinman, 1980). Specific research methods include various forms of free listing, card sorting, triad sorting, interviewing in relation to illness episodes, and collection of illness histories (cf. Bentley et al., 1988; Kendall et al., 1990; G. Pelto, 1990; Weller and Romney, 1988).

Rapid (or not so rapid) appraisal in farming systems, on the other hand, can involve eliciting of lists of crops, local (emic) definitions of types of soils/lands, modes of cultivation, variations in labor allocation, and other domains. Specific research techniques outlined in Weller and Romney (1988) would be quite suited to some of these data topics, but seem not as well known among anthropologists involved in agricultural development. On the other hand, researchers interested in agricultural practices make extensive use of mapping, collection of seasonal and annual activity calendars, group interviews concerning gender division of household tasks, and other techniques especially suited to farming systems topics (Chambers, n.d.; Beebe, 1987; Grandstaff et al., 1987).

New interest in analysis of qualitative data arises from a quite different direction. As mentioned, the advent of microcomputers has focused attention on the possibilities for development of sophisticated software programs for use in analyzing field notes and other complex textual materials. Some researchers now use programs such as NOTEBOOK for maintaining field notes in a systematic, easily accessed manner. ZY-INDEX, ANYWORD, GOFER, and other word-search oriented programs are coming into use for searching or scanning large bodies of field notes. These programs are capable of finding words or combinations of words as directed by the researcher; hence they can be used in connection with whatever individual coding systems investigators devise for data retrieval. In keeping with the new tendencies for interrelating of qualitative and quantitative data, Wellman has described a system for integrating textual materials with statistical analysis (Wellman, 1990).

Miles and Huberman are prominent among a fairly large number of researchers, mostly nonanthropologists, who have developed systematic approaches to qualitative data analysis during the 1980s. Their book, *Qualitative Data Analysis,* addressed the question: "What methods of analysis can we employ that are practical, communicable, and non–self-deluding—in short, *scientific,* in the best sense of that word?" (Miles and Huberman, 1984:15). Although some anthropologists appear to be defining qualitative research in nonscientific or even antiscientific terms, a major trend of the 1980s has pointed toward greater specificity, greater precision, and increased replicability of results from qualitative materials.

Communications and Data Sharing in the Electronic Era

The use of BITNET and other national and international electronic mail systems became an important resource for researchers in the later 1980s. Social scientists joined other researchers in electronic exchange of data sets, manuscripts, and research ideas. Informal conferences are now easy to organize through BITNET, and electronic bulletin boards have added to the exchange of research materials.

World Cultures, initiated by Douglas White, is the first electronic anthropological journal. The publication is distributed in the form of floppy diskettes, and consists to a large extent of cross-cultural data sets, as well as discussions about cross-cultural research methodology. The advent of electronic publishing is of particular significance because of the greatly increased possibilities for sharing of qualitative and quantitative data among researchers at different locations.

Graduate Training in Research Methods

Graduate training in research methods among departments of anthropology is rather uneven, in both quantity and quality (cf. Trotter, 1988). However, it appears that the "good old days," when graduate students were sent to do doctoral fieldwork without prior research training, are becoming a thing of the past. Most programs in anthropology now include some training in methodology, though the contents appear to vary a great deal, depending on the research styles of the different faculties. Plattner recently published a trial inventory of basic methodological skills that all departments should offer their graduate students. This inventory, incorporating ideas from over twenty "discussants," included both qualitative and quantitative methodologies, and specified "the use of a microcomputer for word processing and data manipulation, including familiarity with the syntax of one or more basic operating systems . . . " (Plattner, 1989).

His basic inventory is instructive because it consists in large part of basic skills that apply to all sectors of sociocultural anthropology. Interviewing skills, direct observation, learning the local language, data recording and coding, and other aspects of qualitative research are the foundations of all ethnographic work. In addition, Plattner comments, "All cultural anthropologists should be familiar with the elements of quantitative data collection and analysis. Graduate training in cultural anthropology should include the development of a research design for quantitatively testing a hypothesis." (Plattner et al., 1989).

In proposing that all graduate programs should offer training in the full array of ethnographic methodology, Plattner's statement suggests that the individual research tools and techniques are relatively independent of specific theoretical frameworks. The supposed associations between methodological techniques and theoretical formulations are to a large extent "historical accidents." Life histories, pile sorts, paired observations may call up images of specific theoretical formulations, but they can equally well serve the purpose of researchers with distinctly different conceptual models. Of course, the same point can be made for all the secondary data sources—censuses, newspaper accounts, trade documents, court cases, vital statistics, church records—they, too, are frequently utilized in a variety of competing theoretical paradigms.

The main point is that training in anthropology should include a full range of specific ethnographic skills, so that newly graduated practitioners, whether inside or outside of academe, can produce data and analyze them effectively, in ways that make the stuff of anthropological reporting credible to a wider public.

Workshops, Summer Institute, and Other Training

Although we place most emphasis on methodological training within graduate programs, specialized instruction in microcomputer techniques, statistics, and other research tools is now offered in a variety of workshops and other short-term training situations. Some of these training programs are offered in the context of North American anthropology (e.g., NAPA Workshops; the Summer Institute at the University of Florida), but a new burgeoning of training workshops is aimed at developing increased research skills in Third World countries. Short-term (one- or two-week) working sessions are especially common in international health research. WHO and other agencies have sponsored a series of workshops on research design for studies of diarrhea, acute respiratory infections, AIDS, and other topics in which medical anthropologists are involved. The Ford Foundation has initiated a new series of training workshops in research on women's health issues in India. To an increasing extent these workshops are aimed at improving the blending of qualitative ethnographic work with the quantified survey research of epidemiologists. In some instances anthropologists have been surprised to find that epidemiologists and other health care researchers have quite sophisticated experience with techniques of direct observation and informant interviewing.

Many of the workshops have been held in Third World locations, specifically for promoting the data-gathering skills and research design sophistication of social science researchers in developing countries. Microcomputer technology plays an increasing role in these efforts. In contrast to the situation in earlier decades, in which increased computerization contributed to the marginalization of social research in the Third World, the advent of microcomputers makes statistical analysis (and other kinds of analysis) more accessible to small research groups, even low-budget nongovernmental organizations (NGOs). For example, in the case of women's groups in India, funded by the Ford Foundation, the objectives of recent workshops have been to enhance the quality and quantity of ethnographic work on issues of womens' health, partly by means of microcomputer technology. The first step is simply to develop extensive files of computerized field notes. Following that, the coding, indexing, and data retrieval can be systematized with easy-to-use software programs. In addition, some domains of women's illnesses can be explored, and patterns analyzed, using the ANTHROPAC program for systematic data analysis (e.g., using pile sorting and multidimensional scaling). These state-of-the-art research methods were not feasible for small-scale private organizations such as NGOs in days before moderate cost microcomputers became widely available.

Concluding Comments

This brief review has touched on only a small portion of recent developments in anthropological research methods and applications. Throughout the 1980s there have been many other publications and research activities that represent change in the ways that anthropologists go about their fieldwork. The incorporation of local people into "participatory research" deserves a larger discussion; many other innovations in the composition of fieldwork teams have been developed over the past decade. Among the more quantitatively oriented anthropologists there have been a whole series of methodological innovations during the 1980s. Cross-cultural statistical research has become much more sophisticated; quantitative study of intracultural diversity has become an accepted paradigm in diverse theoretical realms.

Although many of these methodological trends are focused on local and regional level data gathering, new methods are emerging for examining interactions between microlevel and macrolevel processes. For example, the work of DeWalt and Barkin concerning agricultural modernization in Mexico illustrates methodological tools for describing the ways that international technological and commercial developments reach down to local-level economic situations of farmers (DeWalt and Barkin, 1987; also cf. DeWalt and Pelto, 1985). A number of other researchers in various applied fields are developing research methods for dealing with these complex relationships.

Some developments of the 1980s have been quite subtle and gradual. The increased attention to research methodology in the reviewing of research proposals at NSF, NIH, and most other funding agencies might be difficult to document, but the trends seem clear. In earlier decades it was possible to submit anthropological proposals with practically no statement about data collection and analysis; now such proposals are rarely seen.

Anthropological research is gaining ground, however slowly, in influencing policy making among private and public agencies. Many factors are at work in these changes; but our increasing attention to research methodology—to careful design of primary data construction, plus systematic pattern analysis—can play a central role in increasing the credibility of our research products. Those increases in credibility depend on effective blending of qualitative and quantitative materials.

Notes and References

Introduction

References

Bernard, H. Russell
 1988 *Research Methods in Cultural Anthropology.* Beverly Hills, CA: Sage Publications.

Boas, Franz
 1973 The Limitations of the Comparative Method of Anthropology. In *High Points in Anthropology,* edited by Paul Bohannon and Mark Glazer, 84–91. New York: Alfred A. Knopf.

Boudon, Raymond
 1988 Will Sociology Ever Be a Normal Science? *Theory and Society* 17:747–71.

Bourdieu, Pierre
 1988 Vive la Crise! For Heterodoxy in Social Science. *Theory and Society* 17:773–76.

DeWalt, Billie R., and Pertti J. Pelto
 1985 *Micro and Macro Levels of Analysis in Anthropology: Issues in Theory and Research.* Boulder, CO: Westview.

Evans-Pritchard, E. E.
 1973 Social Anthropology: Past and Present. In *High Points in Anthropology,* edited by Paul Bohannon and Mark Glazer, 358–70. New York: Alfred A. Knopf.

Geertz, Clifford
 1984 Distinguished Lecture: Anti Anti-relativism. *American Anthropologist* 86:263–78.

Johnson, Allen
 1978 *Quantification in Cultural Anthropology.* Stanford, CA: Stanford University Press.

Malinowski, Bronislaw
 1961 *Argonauts of the Western Pacific.* New York: E. P. Dutton.

Moles, Jerry A.
1977   Standardization and Measurement in Cultural Anthropology. *Current Anthropology* 18:235–58.

Murdock, George, et al.
1982   *Outline of Cultural Materials.* New Haven, CT: Yale University Human Relations Area Files.

Naroll, Raoul, and Ronald Cohen
1973   *A Handbook of Method in Cultural Anthropology.* New York: Columbia University Press.

Pelto, Pertti J.
1970   *Anthropological Research: The Structure of Inquiry.* New York: Harper and Row.

Pelto, Pertti J., and Gretel H. Pelto
1975   Intra-cultural Diversity: Some Theoretical Issues. *American Ethnologist* 2:1–18.

———

1978   *Anthropological Research: The Structure of Inquiry,* 2nd ed. New York: Cambridge University Press.

Robinson, William S.
1950   Ecological Correlations and the Behavior of Individuals. *American Sociological Review* 15:351–57.

Royal Anthropological Institute of Great Britain and Ireland
1951   *Notes and Queries on Anthropology,* 6th ed. London: Routledge and Kegan Paul.

Rudner, Richard S.
1966   *Philosophy of Social Science.* Englewood Cliffs, NJ: Prentice Hall.

Schweder, Richard A.
1973   The Between and Within of Cross-Cultural Research. *Ethos* 1:531–43.

Spiro, Melford E.
1986   Cultural Relativism and the Future of Anthropology. *Cultural Anthropology* 1:256–86.

Wallace, A. F. C.
1970   *Culture and Personality,* 2nd ed. New York: Random House.

Culture, Stress, and Depressive Symptoms

Notes

1. Collection of the data reported here was supported by NIMH Research Grant MH33943. The analyses described here were supported by NIMH Research Grant MH42553.

2. A more complete description of this research, along with descriptive data, is available elsewhere (Dressler and Badger, 1985; Dressler, 1987).

3. Very briefly, data to test this model were collected in a survey of a simple random sample of 285 households in the black community. All persons interviewed were: (a) heads of households; or (b) the spouse of a head of household, designated at random as the respondent in those households, where the head was married. Dressler and Badger (1985) provide descriptive data.

4. Two specific points should be noted. First, the model presented here does not include all the relevant controls for what amounts to a status inconsistency model; these are presented elsewhere (Dressler, 1988), and it can be demonstrated that the deletion of the control terms makes no difference to the results. Second, there is some redundancy between the economic status component of the lifestyle incongruity measure and the social class measure (i.e., both include information on household occupational ranks). It can be shown that this redundancy does not influence the results. These measures are used here, despite redundancy, because of somewhat better distributional properties.

References

Aneschensel, Carol S., and Jeffrey D. Stone
1982   Stress and Depression. A Test of the Buffering Model of Social Support. *Arch Gen Psychiatry* 39:1392–96.

Cassel, John
1976   The Contribution of the Social Environment to the Host Resistance. *American Journal of Epidemiology* 104:107–23.

Cohen, Jacob, and Patricia Cohen
1975   *Applied Multiple Regression/Correlation Analysis for the Behavioral Sciences*. Hillsdale, NJ: Lawrence Erlbaum Associates.

Cohen, Sheldon, and S. Leonard Syme (eds.)
1985   *Social Support and Health*. Orlando, FL: Academic Press.

Dohrenwend, Barbara S., and Bruce P. Dohrenwend (eds.)
1981   *Stressful Life Events and Their Contexts*. New York: Prodist.

Dressler, William W.
1985   Psychosomatic Symptoms, Stress, and Modernization: A Model. *Culture, Medicine and Psychiatry* 9:257–86.

————
1986   Unemployment and Depressive Symptoms in a Southern Black Community. *Journal of Nervous and Mental Diseases* 174:639–45.

————
1987   The Stress Process in a Southern Black Community: Implications for Prevention Research. *Human Organization* 46:211–20.

1988 Social Consistency and Psychological Distress. *Journal of Health and Social Behavior* 29:

Dressler, William W., and Lee W. Badger
1985 Epidemiology of Depressive Symptoms in Black Communities: A Comparative Analysis. *Journal of Nervous and Mental Disease* 173:212–20.

Dressler, William W., Jose Ernesto Dos Santos, Philip N. Gallagher, Jr., and Fernando E. Viteri
1987 Arterial Blood Pressure and Modernization in Brazil. *American Anthropologist* 89:389–409.

Farley, Reynolds
1985 Three Steps Forward and Two Back? Recent Changes in the Social and Economic Status of Blacks. *Ethnic and Racial Studies* 8:4–28.

Frazier, E. Franklin
1966 *The Negro Family in the United States.* Chicago: University of Chicago Press (original: 1939).

Ilfeld, Frederic W.
1977 Current Social Stressors and Symptoms of Depression. *American Journal of Psychiatry* 134:161–66.

Lazarus, Richard S.
1966 *Psychological Stress and the Coping Process.* New York: McGraw-Hill.

Paykel, E. S.
1979 Causal Relationships Between Clinical Depression and Life Events. In *Stress and Mental Disorder,* edited by J. E. Barrett. New York: Raven Press.

Pearlin, Leonard I.
1982 The Social Contexts of Stress. In *Handbook of Stress: Theoretical and Clinical Aspects,* edited by Leo Goldberger and Shlomo Breznitz, New York: Free Press.

Pearlin, Leonard I., M. A. Lieberman, E. G. Menaghan, and J. T. Mullen
1981 The Stress Process. *Journal of Health and Social Behavior* 22:337–56.

Pelto, Pertti J.
1970 *Anthropological Research: The Structure of Inquiry.* New York: Harper and Row.

Pelto, Pertti J., and Gretel H. Pelto
1978 *Anthropological Research: The Structure of Inquiry,* 2nd ed. London: Cambridge University Press.

Powdermaker, Hortense
1939 *After Freedom: A Cultural Study of the Deep South.* New York: Viking Press.

Rahe, Richard H., and Rasnom J. Arthur
   1978   Life Change and Illness Studies: Past History and Future Directions. *Journal of Human Stress* 4:3–15.

Scott, Robert, and Alan Howard
   1970   Models of Stress. In *Social Stress,* edited by Sol Levise and Norman A. Scotch. Chicago: Aldine.

Syme, S. Leonard, and Lisa F. Berkman
   1976   Social Class, Susceptibility, and Sickness. *American Journal of Epidemiology* 104:1–8.

Tausig, Mark
   1982   Measuring Life Events. *Journal of Health and Social Behavior* 23:52–64.

Turner, Jay R.
   1981   Social Support as a Contingency in Psychological Well-being. *Journal of Health and Social Behavior* 22:357–67.

Pattern Probability Models of Intracultural Diversity

Notes

1. We are grateful to J. S. Thomas and Mike Jepson for their support and efforts in the research. This research was made possible by grants from the Mississippi-Alabama Sea Grant Consortium (NA85AA-D-SG005), and by the Research and Public Service Council of the University of South Alabama.

2. The prevalence rate among this sample of shrimp fishermen (.50) is statistically significantly higher than (1) the national rate for males (.33); (2) white collar workers (.28); and (3) other blue collar workers (.42). More information can be found in Kline et al., 1989.

References

Acheson, James M.
   1981   Anthropology of Fishing. *Annual Review of Anthropology* 10:275–316.

Ague, C.
   1973   Nicotine and Smoking: Effects Upon Subjective Changes in Mood. *Psychopharmacologia* 30:323–25.

Aronoff, Joel
   1967   *Psychological Needs and Cultural Systems.* New Jersey: D. Van Nostrand.

Ashton, H., and R. Stepney
  1982 *Smoking: Psychology and Pharmacology.* London: Tavistock.

Birnbaum, A., and A. E. Maxwell
  1961 Classification Procedures Based on Bayes's Formula. *Applied Statistics* 9:152–69.

Black, P.
  1984 The Anthropology of Tobacco Use: Tobian Data and Theoretical Issues. *Journal of Anthropological Research* 40:475–503.

Bowers, Evelyn J., and I. Elain Allen
  1984 Cigarette Smoking: Example of Behavioral Regulation of Physiological Homeostasis. *New England Journal of Medicine* 99(2):108–9.

Cherek, D. R.
  1981 Effects of Smoking Different Doses of Nicotine on Human Aggressive Behavior. *Psychopharmacology* 75:339–45.

———
  1985 Effects of Acute Exposure to Increased Levels of Background Industrial Noise on Cigarette Smoking Behavior. *International Archives of Occupational and Environmental Health* 56(1):23–30.

Clark, R.
  1978 Cigarette Smoking in Social Interaction. *International Journal of the Addictions* 13:257–69.

Cohen, Sheldon, Tom Kamarck, and Robin Mermelstein
  1983 A Global Measure of Perceived Stress. *Journal of Health and Social Behavior* 24:385–396.

Damon, A., et al.
  1973 Smoking Attitudes and Practices in Seven Preliterate Societies. In *Smoking Behavior: Motives and Incentives,* edited by W. L. Dunn, 219–30. Washington, D.C.: Winston.

Danowski, F.
  1980 Fishermen's Wives: Coping with an Extraordinary Occupation. *Marine Bulletin* 37. Kingston, R.I.: University of Rhode Island Sea Grant.

Dredge, Paul
  1980 Smoking in Korea. *Korea Journal* 20:25–36.

Dunn, William L.
  1978 Smoking as a Possible Inhibitor of Arousal. In *International Workshop on Behavioral Effects of Nicotine,* edited by K. Battig, 18–25. Basel, Switzerland: S. Karger.

Eckert, P.
1983   Beyond the Statistics of Adolescent Smoking. *American Journal of Public Health* 73:439–41.

Elgerot, A.
1976   Note on Selective Effects of Short-Term Tobacco Abstinence on Complex vs. Simple Mental Tasks. *Perceptual and Motor Skills* 42:413–14.

Feinhandler, S.
1986   The Social Role of Smoking. In *Smoking and Society,* edited by R. Tolison, 167–87. Toronto, Canada: Lexington.

Fertig, J. B., and O. R. Pomerleau
1986   Nicotine-Produced Antinociception in Minimally Deprived Smokers and Ex-Smokers. *Addictive Behaviors* 11:239–48.

Gilbert, D.
1979   Paradoxical Tranquilizing and Emotion-Reducing Effects of Nicotine. *Psychological Bulletin* 86:643–61.

Grunberg, N.
1985   Nicotine, Cigarette Smoking and Body Weight. *British Journal of Addiction* 80:369–77.

Ikard, F., Dorothy E. Green, and Daniel Horn
1969   A Scale to Differentiate Between Types of Smoking as Related to the Management of Affect. *The International Journal of Addictions* 4:649–59.

Jepson, Michael, J. Stephen Thomas, and Michael C. Robbins
1987   The "Skipper Effect" Among Gulf Coast Shrimp Fishermen. *Sociology and Social Research* 72:20–24.

Kasl, S., and S. Cobb
1983   Psychological and Social Stresses in the Workplace. In *Occupational Health,* edited by B. Levy and D. Wegman, 251–63. Boston: Little, Brown.

Kleinke, Chris L., Richard A. Staneski, and Frederick Meeker
1983   Attributions for Smoking Behavior: Comparing Smokers with Nonsmokers and Predicting Smokers' Cigarette Consumption. *Journal of Research in Personality* 17:242–55.

Kline, Annette
1986   *Smoking as an Occupational Adaptation Among Alabama Shrimpboat Captains.* M.A. Thesis, Department of Anthropology, University of Missouri, Columbia.

Maril, Robert Lee
1983   *Texas Shrimpers.* College Station, TX: Texas A & M University Press.

McGinnis, J. Michael, Donald Shopland, and Clarice Brown
    1987   Tobacco and Health: Trends in Smoking and Smokeless Tobacco Consumption in the United States. *American Review of Public Health* 8:441–67.

Norr, James L., and D. C. Norr
    1978   Work Organization in Modern Fishing. *Human Organization* 37(2):163–71.

Overall, J. E., and C. M. Williams
    1963   Conditional Probability Program for Diagnosis of Thyroid Function. *Journal of the American Medical Association* 183:307–13.

Pearlin, L. I., et al.
    1981   The Stress Process. *Journal of Health and Social Behavior* 22:337–56.

Pelto, Pertti J., and Gretel H. Pelto
    1978   *Anthropological Research: The Structure of Inquiry.* New York: Cambridge University Press.

Poggie, J. J. Jr., and C. Gersuny
    1974   Fishermen of Galilee. *Marine Bulletin* 17. Kingston, R.I.: University of Rhode Island.

Polivy, Janet, Rick Hackett, and Peter Bycio
    1979   The Effect of Perceived Smoking Status on Attractiveness. *Personality and Social Psychology Bulletin* 5(3):401–4.

Pomerleau, O., and C. Pomerleau
    1984   Neuroregulators and the Reinforcement of Smoking: Towards a Biobehavioral Explanation. *Neuroscience and Biobehavioral Reviews* 8:503–13.

Pomerleau, O. F., D. C. Turk, and Joanne B. Fertig
    1984   The Effects of Cigarette Smoking on Pain and Anxiety. *Addictive Behaviors* 9:265–71.

Remington, Patrick L., et al.
    1985   Current Smoking Trends in the U.S. *Journal of the American Medical Association* 253(20):2975–78.

Russel, M.
    1976   Tobacco Smoking and Nicotine Dependence. In *Research Advances in Alcohol and Drug Problems* #3, edited by R. Gibbins et al., 1–47. New York: John Wiley.

Siegrist, J.
    1985   Psychosocial Coronary Risk Constellations in the Work Setting. In *Behavioral Medicine: Work, Stress, and Health,* edited by W. Doyle et al., 45–79. NATO Asi Series no. 19.

Silverstein, B.
1982   Cigarette Smoking, Nicotine Addiction, and Relaxation. *Journal of Personality and Social Psychology* 42:946–70.

Spielberger, C.
1986   Psychological Determinants of Smoking Behavior. In *Smoking and Society*, edited by R. Tolison, 89–134. Toronto, Canada: Lexington.

Sterling, T., and J. Weinkam
1976   Smoking Characteristics by Type of Employment. *Journal of Occupational Medicine* 18:743–54.

———

1978   Smoking Patterns by Occupation, Industry, Sex, and Race. *Archives of Environmental Health* 33:313–17.

Thomas, J. Stephen
1986   The Indochinese in Bayou La Batre, Alabama: A Preliminary Assessment of Social Impacts. *Alabama Sea Grant Extension Bulletin* #MASGP-86-008. Auburn University.

Thomas, John S., and Michael C. Robbins
1985   Social Status and Settlement Pattern Features: A Tojolabal Maya Example. *Human Organization* 44(2):172–76.

———

1988   The Use of Settlement Pattern Features to Determine Status Differences in a Tojolabal Community. *Geoscience and Man* 26:29–37.

Troyer, R., and G. Markle
1983   *Cigarettes: The Battle Over Smoking.* New Brunswick, NJ: Rutgers University Press.

Ugalde, A.
1970   Measuring Wealth in a Semi-Cash Economy. *Rural Sociology* 35:512–22.

U.S. Department of Health and Human Services
1985   Occupation and Smoking Behavior in the United States: Current Estimates and Recent Trends. *The Health Consequences of Smoking: Cancer and Chronic Lung Disease in the Workplace, a Report of the Surgeon General*, 19–96. Department of Health and Human Services #(PHS) 85-50207. Rockville, MD: Office on Smoking and Health.

———

1986   Prevalence of Cigarette Smoking: 30 Years of Change. *Smoking and Health, A National Status Report: A Report to Congress*, 17–60. Department of Health and Human Services # HHS/PHS/CDC 87-8396. Rockville, MD: Office on Smoking and Health.

Wack, J., and J. Rodin
1982   Smoking and Its Effects on Body Weight and the Systems of Caloric Regulation. *American Journal of Clinical Nutrition* 35:366–80.

Warburton, D. M., and K. Wesnes
1978   Individual Differences in Smoking and Attentional Performance. In *Smoking Behaviour: Physiological and Psychological Influences,* edited by R. E. Thornton, 19–144. London: Churchill Livingstone.

Wesnes, K., and D. M. Warburton
1978   The Effects of Cigarette Smoking and Nicotine Tablets Upon Human Attention. In *Smoking Behaviour,* edited by R. E. Thornton, 131–47. London: Churchill Livingstone.

1983   Smoking, Nicotine, and Human Performance. *Pharmacological Ther.* 21:189–208.

Wesnes, K., A. Revell, and D. M. Warburton
1984   Work and Stress as Motives for Smoking. In *Smoking and the Lung,* edited by G. Cumming and G. Bonsignore, 233–48. New York: Plenum.

Westman, M., Dov Eden, and Arie Shirom
1985   Job Stress, Cigarette Smoking and Cessation: The Conditioning Effects of Peer Support. *Soc. Sci. Med.* 20(6):637–44.

White, David R. M.
1977   Environment, Technology, and Time-Use Patterns in the Gulf Coast Shrimp Fishery. In *Those Who Live from the Sea,* edited by M. E. Smith, 195–214. St. Paul, MN: West.

Wills, Thomas Ashby, and Saul Shiffman
1985   Coping and Substance Use: A Conceptual Framework. In *Coping and Substance Use,* edited by Saul Shiffman and Thomas Ashby Wills, 3–24. New York: Academic Press.

Intracultural and Intrasocial Variability

Note

1. Due to logistical and other problems of the field situations in both Case I and Case II, it was not possible to obtain a registry of all fishermen and cooperative members from which a random sample could be drawn. The samples used in these studies are opportunistic, and thus only random samples from the hypothetical pop-

ulation of all samples that exist under similar conditions. This sampling procedure is not ideal, but it is a useful way around the difficulties imposed by many field situations (cf. Thomas, 1986:439–47).

References

Acheson, J. M.
1981 Anthropology of Fishing. In *Annual Reviews of Anthropology,* vol. 10, edited by B. J. Siegel, A. R. Beals, and S. Tyler, 275–316. Palo Alto, CA: Annual Reviews.

Acheson, J. M., J. J. Poggie, R. B. Pollnac, and J. Wilson
1980 The Tragedy of the Common: An Uncommon View. In *Social and Cultural Aspects of New England Fisheries: Implications for Management,* 803–12. Final report to National Science Foundation. University of Rhode Island, University of Maine Study of Social and Cultural Aspects of Fisheries Management Under Extended Jurisdiction.

Anderson, L. G.
1980 Estimating the Benefits of Recreational Fishing Under Conditions of Congestion: Comments and Extension. *Journal of Environmental Economics and Management* 7:401–6.

Apostle, R., L. Kasdan, and A. Hanson
1985 Work Satisfaction and Community Attachment Among Fishermen in Southwest Nova Scotia. *Canadian Journal of Fisheries and Aquatic Sciences* 42:256–67.

Bennett, J.
1969 *Northern Plainsmen: Adaptive Strategy and Agrarian Life.* Chicago: Aldine.

Brox, O.
1990 The Common Property Theory: Epistemological Status and Analytical Utility. *Human Organization* 49:227–35.

DeWalt, B.
1979 *Modernization in a Mexican Ejido: A Study in Economic Adaptation.* Cambridge: Cambridge University Press.

Gordon, D., D. W. Chapman, and T. C. Bjornn
1973 Economic Evaluation of Sport Fisheries—What Do They Mean? *Transactions of the American Fisheries Society* 103:293–311.

Gordon, H. Scott
1954 The Economic Theory of a Common-Property Resource: The Fishery. *Journal of Political Economy* 62:124–42.

Hardin, G.
   1968   The Tragedy of the Commons. *Science* 162:1243–48.

Malinowski, B.
   1931   Culture. *Encyclopedia of the Social Sciences,* 621–46.

———
   1939   The Group and the Individual in Functional Analysis. *American Journal of Sociology* 44:938–64.

Marchak, P., N. Guppy, and J. McMullan
   1987   *Uncommon Property: The Fishing and Fish Processing Industries in British Columbia.* Agincourt, Ontario: Methuen.

McCay, B. J., and J. Acheson
   1987   *Question of the Commons.* Tucson, AZ: University of Arizona Press.

McConnell, K. E., and J. G. Sutinen
   1979   Bioeconomic Models of Marine Recreational Fishing. *Journal of Environmental Economics and Management* 6:127–39.

Pelto, P. J., and G. H. Pelto
   1975   Intra-cultural Diversity: Some Theoretical Issues. *American Ethnologist* 2(1):1–18.

Pelto, P. J., and J. J. Poggie
   1974   Regional Models of Modernization: A Regional Focus. In *Rethinking Modernization,* edited by J. J. Poggie and R. N. Lynch. Westport, CT: Greenwood Press.

Poggie, J. J., and C. Gersuny
   1974   Fishermen of Galilee. *Marine Bulletin* No. 17. Kingston, RI: University of Rhode Island.

Pollnac, R. B.
   1974   The Sociocultural Correlates of Fishing as a Subsistence Activity. *Anthropology Working Paper No. 4.* University of Rhode Island, Department of Sociology and Anthropology.

———
   1985   Social and Cultural Characteristics in Small-scale Fishery Development. In *Putting People First,* edited by Michael M. Cernea. New York: Oxford University Press.

———
   1986   Peoples of the Sea and Coastal Zone: An Anthropological Perspective. In *Marine Science Information: An International Commodity,* edited by T. Grunby et al., 37–53. Port Aransas, TX: Marine Science Institute.

Pollnac, R. B., and J. J. Poggie, Jr.
1978 Economic Gratification Orientations among Small-scale Fishermen in Panama and Puerto Rico. *Human Organization* 37:355–67.

Pollnac, R. B., and J. J. Poggie, Jr.
1988 The Structure of Job Satisfaction Among New England Fishermen and Its Application to Fisheries Management Policy. *American Anthropologist* 90:888–901.

Schaeffer, M. B.
1954 Some Aspects of the Dynamics of Population Important to the Management of the Commercial Marine Fisheries. *Inter-American Tropical Tuna Commission Bulletin* 34:583–603.

Smith, C.
1981 Satisfaction Bonus from Salmon Fishing: Implications for Economic Evaluation. *Land Economics* 57:181–94.

Stevens, J. B.
1969 Measurement of Economic Value in Sport Fishing: An Economist's Views on Validity, Usefulness, and Propriety. *Transactions of the American Fisheries Society* 98:352–59.

Steward, J. H.
1963 *Theory of Culture Change*. Urbana, IL: University of Illinois Press.

Thomas, D. H.
1986 *Refiguring Anthropology*. Prospect Heights, IL: Waveland Press.

Wood, C., and T. D. Graves
1971 *The Process of Medical Change in a Highland Guatemalan Town*. Los Angeles Study Center, University of California.

Qualitative/Quantitative

References

Bernard, H. R.
1988 *Research Methods in Cultural Anthropology*. Beverly Hills, CA: Sage.

Pelto, Pertti J., and Gretel H. Pelto
1978 Anthropological Research: The Structure of Inquiry. 2nd ed. New York: Cambridge University Press.

Child Feeding During Diarrhea in North India

Notes

1. A distinction should be made between food "restriction" and "withholding." Food restriction often implies a shift in diet—some foods are withdrawn, whereas others are offered. Food withholding, however, implies that food in general is withheld, and quantities are reduced. The nutritional consequences of these possible behaviors may be very different.

2. The term for "untouchables," coined by Mahatma Ghandi.

3. A non-Hindu tribal group, previously pastoral. In Anangpur, they are generally better off and hold political power.

4. Neither Harijans or Gujars are by definition part of the Hindu classification system. However, the Hindu concepts of pollution and purity cut across all groups to some extent. In Anangpur, Harijan and Muslim families were restricted by Gujars in their use of wells.

5. Statistical analysis of the key variables showed that 200 interviews were more than enough to establish variability, even within villages. Although time constraints prevented us from conducting a "quick and dirty" survey to establish estimates of variability for some of the key factors, this would have been the preferred methodology.

6. Pelto et al. (1983) analyzed the relationship of the two dietary diversity scores with quantified nutrient intake data from Finland and Connecticut. The results showed strong correlations between these scores and intakes of protein and calories in Finland, with lower correlations for the Connecticut data. Four of five vitamins had good correlations in both settings, and of minerals, iron showed the strongest correlation in Connecticut, and phosphorus in Finland. It is likely that higher correlations would result in populations with more variation in nutritional status, such as India, where as additional ingredients are added to a staple, the nutritional adequacy of the diet increases. The diversity scores, then, should also be associated with food availability.

7. The increase in potato consumption during diarrhea episodes reflects their availability during the case monitoring data collection, and nonavailability during the survey.

References

Bennett, L.
1983   The Role of Women in Income Production and Intrahousehold Allocation

of Resources as a Determinant of Child Health and Nutrition. Workshop on Determinants of Infant and Young Children Feeding and Care. Geneva: World Health Organization, December.

Bentley, M. E.
1987 *The Household Management of Childhood Diarrhea in Rural North India.* Ph.D. Dissertation, University of Connecticut.

———

1988 The Household Management of Childhood Diarrhea in Rural North India. *Soc Sci Med* 27:75–85.

Bentley, M. E., G. H. Pelto, D. Schumann, W. Straus, G. A. Oni, C. Adegbola, E. de la Pena, and K. H. Brown
1988 Rapid Ethnographic Assessment: Application in a Dietary Management of Diarrhea Program in Nigeria and Peru. *Soc Sci Med* 27:107–16.

Bentley, M., R. Stallings, J. Elder, and M. Fukumoto
Maternal Feeding Behavior and Child Acceptance of Food During Diarrhea Convalescence, and Health in the Central Sierra of Peru. *Amer Jour Pub Health*, Vol 81, no. 1, Jan. 1991.

Bhan, M. K., N. K. Arora, O. P. Ghai, K. Ramachanran, V. Khoshoo, and N. Bhandari
1986 Major Factors in Diarrhoea Related Mortality Among Rural Children. *Indian J Med Res* 83:9–12.

Black, R. E., K. H. Brown, and S. Becker
1983 Influence of Acute Diarrhea on the Growth Parameters of Children. In *Acute Diarrhea: Its Nutritional Consequences in Children,* edited by J. A. Bellanti, Nestle Nutrition Workshop, Vol 2, 73–84. New York: Raven Press.

Brown, K. H., R. E. Black, A. D. Robertson and S. Becker
1985 Effects of Season and Illness on the Dietary Intake of Weanlings During Longitudinal Studies in Rural Bangladesh. *Am J Clin Nutr* 41:343–55.

Brown, K. H., K. L. Dickin, M. E. Bentley, G. A. Oni, V. T. Obasaju, S. A. Esrey, S. Mebrahtu and R. Y. Stallings
1987 Consumption of Weaning Foods from Fermented Cereals: Kwara State, Nigeria. Presented at Workshop on Household Level Food Technologies for Improving Young Child Feeding in Eastern and Southern Africa, Nairobi, Kenya, 11–16 October.

Brown, K. H., A. S. Gastañaduy, J. M. Saavedra, J. Lembcke, D. Rivas, A. D. Robertson, R. Yolken and R. B. Sack
1988 Effect of Continued Oral Feeding on Clinical and Nutritional Outcomes of Acute Diarrhea in Children. *J Pediatr* 112:191–200.

Burke and Allen
981 Paper presented at the American Anthropological Association.

Cattle, D.
1976 Dietary Diversity and Nutritional Security in a Coastal Miskito Indian Village, Eastern Nicaragua. In *Frontier Adaptations In Lower Central America,* edited by M. Helms and F. Loveland. Philadelphia, PA: Institute for the Study of Human Issues.

Chen, L. C.
1983 Interactions of diarrhea and malnutrition: mechanisms and interventions. In Diarrhea and Malnutrition: Interactions, Mechanisms, and Interventions, edited by L. C. Chen and N. S. Scrimshaw. New York: Plenum Press.

Committee on International Nutrition Programs
1985 *Nutritional Management of Acute Diarrhea in Infants and Children.* National Research Council, Washington, DC: National Academy Press.

Coreil, J., and E. Genece
1988 Adoption of Oral Rehydration Therapy Among Haitian Mothers. *Soc Sci Med* 27:87–96.

Dewey, K. G.
1981 Nutritional Consequences of the Transformation from Subsistence to Commercial Agriculture in Tabasco, Mexico. *Human Ecology* 9:151–87.

Freed, S. A., and R. S. Freed
1980 *Fertility, Sterilization, and Population Growth in Shanti Nagar, India: A Longitudinal Ethnographic Approach.* New York, NY: Anthropological Papers of the American Museum of Natural History, Vol 60, part 3:229–86.

Green, E.
1986 Diarrhea and the Social Marketing of ORT Salts in Bangladesh. *Social Science and Medicine* 24:357–66.

Hoyle, B., M. Yunus and L. Chen
1980 Breast-feeding and Food Intake Among Children with Acute Diarrheal Disease. *Am J Clin Nutr* 33:2365–71.

Kendall C., D. Foote and R. Martorell
1984 Ethnomedicine and Oral Rehydration Therapy: A Case Study of Ethnomedical Investigation and Program Planning. *Soc Sci Med* 19:253–60.

Khan, M., and K. Ahmad
1986 Withdrawal of Food During Diarrhoea: Major Mechanism of Malnutrition Following Diarrhoea in Bangladeshi Children. *J Trop Pediat* 32:57–61.

Kolenda, P. M.
1968 Region, Caste and Family Structure: A Comparative Study of the Indian "Joint" Family. In *Structure and Change in Indian Society,* edited by M. Singer and B. S. Cohn, 339–96. Viking Fund Publications for Anthropology, No. 47. New York: Wenner-Gren Foundation for Anthropological Research.

Kumar, V., C. Clements, K. Marwah and P. Diwedi
1985   Beliefs and Therapeutic Preferences of Mothers in Management of Acute
Diarrhoeal Disease in Children. *J Trop Pediatr* 21:109–12.

Leach
1967   Caste, Class and Slavery: The Taxonomic Problem. In *Caste and Race:
Comparative Approaches*, A. de Reuck and J. Knight, J. and A. Churchill.
London:17–27.

Mandelbaum, D. G.
1970   *Society In India* (volumes 1 & 2). Berkeley, CA: University of California
Press.

Martorell, R., J. Habicht, C. Yarbrough, A. Lechtig, R. E. Klein and R. A. Western
1975   Acute Morbidity and Physical Growth in Rural Guatemalan Children. *Am
J Dis Child* 29:1296–1301.

Minturn, L., and J. Hitchcock
1966   *The Rajputs of Khalapur, India*. Six Cultures Series, Vol III. New York:
Wiley and Sons, Inc.

Molla, A., A. M. Molla, S. A. Sarker, M. Khatoon and M. Rahaman
1983   Effects of Micronutrients During Disease and After Recovery. In *Diarrhea and Malnutrition: Interactions, Mechanisms, and Interventions*, edited by
L. C. Chen and N. S. Scrimshaw, 113. New York: Plenum Press.

Morley, D.
1973   *Paediatric Priorities in the Developing World*. London: Butterworths.

National Academy of Sciences
1981   *Management of the Diarrheal Diseases at the Community Level*. Committee on International Programs. Washington, DC: National Academy Press.

Nations, M
1982   Illness of the Child: The Cultural Context of Childhood Diarrhea in
Northeast Brazil. Ph.D Dissertation, University of California, Berkeley.

Nichter, M.
1988   From Aralu to ORS: Sinhalese Perceptions of Digestion, Diarrhea and
Dehydration. *Soc Sci Med* 27:39–52.

Pelto G., M. Bentley, P. Edlin and P. Pelto
1983   Relationship of Dietary Complexity to Nutrient Intake in Two Industrialized Food Systems. *Fed Proc Abstract*, 67th Annual Meeting, April, American
Institute of Nutrition, Chicago, Illinois.

Rowland, M.G.M., G. J. G Rowland and T. J. Cole
1988   Impact of Infection on the Growth of Children from 0 to 2 Years in an
Urban West African Community. *Am J Clin Nutr* 47:134–38.

Sarker, S. A., A. M. Molla, A. K. M. M. Karim and M. M. Rahman
1982 Calorie Intake In Childhood Diarrhea. *Nutr Rep Internat* 26:581–90.

Scrimshaw, S., and E. Hurtado
1987 *Rapid Assessment Procedures for Nutritional and Primary Health Care: Anthropological Approaches to Program Improvement.* UCLA Latin American Center and United Nations University.

Srinivasa, D. K., and E. Afonso
1983 Community Perception and Practices in Childhood Diarrhea. *Indian Pediat* 20:859–64.

Stevens, W. K.
1984 India's 'Forced March' To Modernity. New York: *New York Times Magazine*, January 22.

UNICEF
1985 *State of the World's Children.* Oxford: Oxford University Press.

Vijayaraghavan, K., Y. N. Mathur, D. H. Rao and S. Kumar
1985 KAP Studies On Diarrhoeal Disease In East Godavari District, Andhra Pradesh. Hyderabad, India: National Institute of Nutrition.

Patients' Use of Freestanding Emergency Centers

Notes

1. The term "alternative delivery services" is used by U.S. medical system participants to signify these new health care forms. Within anthropology, however, the term "alternative" has usually referred to medicines, therapies, or providers (e.g., chiropractic, homeopathy, or indigenous medicine) that are in contrast with or external to biomedicine (Salmon, 1984).

2. The research reported here was supported by the National Center for Health Services Research and Health Care Technology Assessment, DHHS, under grant number HS 05043. I would also like to thank Billie DeWalt, John van Willigen, Janet Bronstein, and Ann Millard for their helpful comments on earlier drafts of this paper.

3. The FEC was open twelve hours a day, and for the purposes of sampling, a typical day was divided into six two-hour blocks of time. The clinic schedule was stratified according to day of the week, and two time blocks were randomly selected for each day of the first week and two for each day of the second week, for a total of twenty-eight blocks of time. To ensure maximum distribution, each time period could only be assigned two times for week 1 and two times for week 2. Thus, all six time periods were sampled four times; four additional time periods were then chosen to

make up the necessary twenty-eight blocks (see Rylko-Bauer, 1985:111–14, 297). Problems in the field led to only two instances where changes had to be made from this original sampling plan.

4. Certain features of the FEC created problems for the sampling of patients and the administration of the questionnaire, which led to the development of a set of criteria for systematic sampling. These features included the unpredictability of patient flow, the relatively short amount of time spent waiting to see the doctor, follow-up visits by patients, and the fact that some patients might be in mental, emotional, or physical discomfort.

The first two points have been discussed in the text of the paper with regard to the sampling strategy. In addition, the short wait meant that there was often a limited amount of time available for filling out a questionnaire prior to the patient's visit with the doctor. Therefore, patients were contacted before they were called into the exam room, and were allowed to fill out the questionnaire at any time during their FEC visit. Almost half (46 percent) were able to finish the survey before they were called; 15 percent completed it in the exam room and 39 percent finished it in the waiting room after their visit was over. Although it is possible that patients might answer questions differently before as compared to after their exam, the chi-square test indicated that this variability did not significantly affect the distribution of responses on relevant variables.

As for the third feature, the Prompt Care Clinic did have some patients return for removal of stitches, changing of dressings, and similar problems. During the research period, seven patients who came at the designated sampling time were there for a recheck and had already filled out the questionnaire during their initial FEC visit.

Finally, the FEC treated urgent problems as well as minor complaints and routine health care needs, so that some patients either were not able to participate in the survey (e.g., if they had a serious illness or injury) or were not even approached for ethical reasons (e.g., if the patient was bleeding extensively or was obviously in pain or emotional distress). If such patients were not accompanied by a parent or spouse who could fill out the questionnaire on their behalf, then they were bypassed in favor of the next patient who walked in. This policy resulted in eleven patients who were bypassed.

Criteria Used For Sampling Patients in the FEC Survey

The sampling strategy involved taking a patient every thirty minutes. If a new patient did not appear at this designated time, then I took the next patient who did come in, and the subsequent half hour intervals were counted from that point.

If a patient could not be approached because he or she was called back into the exam room immediately upon entering, then I skipped him or her and took the next patient who came in.

If the "designated patient" had already filled out the questionnaire during an earlier visit, then I went on to the next patient who came in.

If the "designated patient" was in pain, discomfort, or otherwise appeared unable to participate, I skipped this patient and went on to the next one who came in.

If the patient was a child (under eighteen years) and accompanied by a parent or guardian, then the adult was asked to fill out the questionnaire on behalf of the patient.

If an adult patient was unable to fill out the questionnaire, and was accompanied by a parent or spouse, then this other person was asked to fill out the questionnaire on behalf of the patient.

If the "designated patient" refused to participate in the study, then I went on to the next patient who came in.

5. This supplemental data dealt with the amount of time respondents spent waiting to see the doctor, who accompanied the patients, etc. Demographic and health information was also recorded on all patients who came to the clinic during the sampling periods, based on observations and informal discussions. This was an unobtrusive way (as contrasted with examination of medical records) of determining that the sample was representative of the FEC patient population with regard to sex, race, and estimated age (see Rylko-Bauer, 1985:116–18).

The nonrandom selection of the FEC in this case study, and the fact that the sampling strategy was opportunistic, in the sense that the population from which this sample was drawn were those people who happened to come to the clinic during the survey period, means that the results are not generalizable, in a strict statistical sense, to the entire patient population of the Prompt Care Clinic or other FECs. It is also possible that persons who used FECs more often may be overrepresented in this sample. However, data on frequency of visits suggest a fairly even distribution on this variable. Almost half (48.9) percent of patients indicated that this was either their first visit or that they had come one time before to the clinic in the past twelve months, whereas 51.1 percent had been there two or more times (twelve of these coming five or more times in the past twelve months).

The relevance and validity of the study's findings to broader FEC populations is enhanced by the care that was taken to minimize bias at the various stages of the sampling process, by using a systematic method that approached randomness within the constraints of the research setting (as described in note 4).

The issue of generalizability is actually less important for case studies than is the idea of replicability. Yin (1984) points out that it is more appropriate to view a case study as one does an experiment, where the findings are generalizable to theoretical propositions rather than to populations. In both types of research strategies, methodological rigor and documentation are important so that future replication is possible.

6. The basic format of each question was as follows:

Compared to the emergency room (or doctor's office), I feel that the Prompt Care Clinic is

1	2	3
less expensive	about the same	more expensive

Appropriate responses were used for each dimension being measured. Patients were asked to circle the response that best completed the statement.

7. The time from 10:30 a.m. to 4:30 p.m. Monday through Friday was designated as being "during doctor's office hours." This is an arbitrary category, based on knowledge of the medical community and its standard practices. The rest of the time, from 4:30 p.m. to 10:30 p.m., Monday through Friday, as well as all day Saturday and Sunday, was designated as "after doctor's office hours."

8. The average value of 15.6 minutes was based on actual measurement of the amount of time patients waited from the moment of walking into the FEC to being called into the exam room. Extensive delays did occur occasionally, as reflected in the range of values from 2 to 110 minutes.

9. Respondents were asked to choose which of the following phrases best described how they decided to come to the FEC: (a) the trip to the clinic was part of my planned activities for today (chosen by 57.3 percent); (b) the trip to the clinic was a spur-of-the-moment decision while I was out taking care of other business (chosen by 42.7 percent).

10. The nature of the decision (i.e., planned or spur-of-the-moment) was significantly associated with (a) amount of time (self-reported) between illness onset and clinic visit ($\chi^2 = 12.884$, p $< .005$, 2df); (b) type of health problem brought to FEC ($\chi^2 = 13.395$, p $< .005$, 2df); (c) distance between respondent's home and FEC ($\chi^2 = 9.221$, p $< .01$, 2df).

11. For details on the ranking test, see Rylko-Bauer, 1985:300.

12. The interest generated by the development of FECs was evident from the large number (100) of letters that I received concerning the research following the announcement of my grant award by the agency. The requests for information (all of which I answered) came from social scientists, physicians, marketing firms, hospital administrators, public health officials, insurance carriers, etc.

References

Aday, LuAnn, Robert Andersen, and G. Fleming
1980 *Health Care in the United States: Equitable For Whom?* Beverly Hills, CA: Sage.

American Medical Association
1982 MDs Need to 'Hustle,' Family Physicians Says. *American Medical News* (May 28):3.

———
1985a   Satellite and Commercial Medical Clinics. Report of the Board of Trustees: Part I. *Journal of American Medical Association* 253(February 1):645–51.

———
1985b   Satellite and Commercial Medical Clinics. Report of the Board of Trustees: Part II. *Journal of American Medical Association* 253(March 1):1314–19.

———
1988   *Reference Guide to Policy and Official Statements.* Chicago: The Association.

Barger, W. K., and Ernesto Reza
1989   Policy and Community-Action Research: The Farm Labor Movement in California. In *Making Our Research Useful,* edited by John van Willigen, Barbara Rylko-Bauer, and Ann McElroy, 257–82. Boulder, CO: Westview.

Bernard, H. Russell
1988   *Research Methods in Cultural Anthropology.* Newbury Park, CA: Sage.

Beyer, Janice M., and Harrison M. Trice
1982   The Utilization Process: A Conceptual Framework and Synthesis of Empirical Findings. *Administrative Science Quarterly* 27:591–622.

Bohland, James
1984   Neighborhood Variations in the Use of Hospital Emergency Rooms for Primary Care. *Social Science and Medicine* 19(11):1217–26.

Bonham, Gordon Scott, and Larry S. Corder
1981   *National Medical Care Expenditures Study, Household Interview Instruments and Procedures 1.* DHHS Publication No. (PHS) 81-3280. National Center for Health Services Research, Public Health Service. Washington, DC: Government Publishing Office.

Boone, Margaret S.
1989   A Utilization Study Using Network Analysis: Maternal and Infant Health Policy Change in Washington, DC. In *Making Our Research Useful,* edited by John van Willigen, Barbara Rylko-Bauer, and Ann McElroy, 89–121. Boulder, CO: Westview.

Brewer, John, and Albert Hunter
1989   *Multimethod Research, A Synthesis of Styles.* Newbury Park, CA: Sage.

Brown, Lawrence D.
1985   The Managerial Imperative and Organizational Innovation in Health Services. In *The U.S. Health Care System: A Look to the 1990s,* edited by Eli Ginzberg, 28–47. Totowa, NY: Rowman and Allanheld.

Burns, Linda A., and Mindy S. Ferber
1981   Freestanding Emergency Care Centers Create Public Policy Issues. *Hospitals* 55(May 16):73–78.

Chatterton, Howard T., Nancy E. Clapps, and Stephen H. Gehlbach
1982   Patterns in Health Care Utilization in an Academic Family Practice. *Journal of Family Practice* 14(5):893–97.

Chesteen, S. A., S. E. Warren, and F. R. Woolley
1986   A Comparison of Family Practice Clinics and Free-standing Emergency Centers: Organizational Characteristics, Process of Care, and Patient Satisfaction. *Journal of Family Practice* 23(4):377–82.

Chyba, Michele M.
1983   Utilization of Hospital Emergency and Outpatient Departments, United States, January-June 1980. *National Medical Care Utilization and Expenditure Survey, Preliminary Data Report No. 2*, DHHS Publication No. (PHS) 83-20000. National Center for Health Statistics, Public Health Service. Washington, DC: Government Printing Office.

Cohen, Elliot L.
1983   Letter to the Editor. *Annals of Emergency Medicine* 12(3):113–114.

Cook, T. D., and C. S. Reichardt, eds.
1979   *Qualitative and Quantitative Methods in Evaluation Research.* Beverly Hills, CA: Sage.

Emmons, David W.
1988   Changing Dimensions of Medical Practice Arrangements. *Medical Care Review* 45(1):101–28.

Ermann, Dan, and J. Gabel
1985   The Changing Face of American Health Care. Multihospital Systems, Emergency Centers, and Surgery Centers. *Medical Care* 23:401–20.

Folland, S. T.
1987   Advertising by Physicians. Behavior and Attitudes. *Medical Care* 25:311–26.

Gesler, Wilbert M.
1988   The Place of Chiropractors in Health Care Delivery: A Case Study of North Carolina. *Social Science and Medicine* 26(8):785–92.

Gifford, Marilyn J., J. B. Franaszek, and Geoffrey Gibson
1980   Emergency Physicians' and Patients' Assessments: Urgency of Need for Medical Care. *Annals of Emergency Medicine* 9(10):502–7.

Gilbert, M. Jean
1989   Policymaking Roles for Applied Anthropologists: Personally Ensuring That Your Research Is Used. In *Making Our Research Useful*, edited by John van Willigen, Barbara Rylko-Bauer, and Ann McElroy, 71–87. Boulder, CO: Westview.

Goldstein, Michael S., et al.
1988   Holistic Physicians and Family Practitioners: Similarities, Differences, and Implications for Health Policy. *Social Science and Medicine* 26(8):853–61.

Gray, Bradford H., ed.
1986   *For-Profit Enterprise in Health Care.* Washington, DC: National Academy Press.

Hellstern, Ronald A.
1983   Letter to the Editor. *Annals of Emergency Medicine* 12(3):112–13.

Jonas, Steven, Roberta Flesh, Ronald Brook, et al.
1976   Monitoring Utilization of a Municipal Hospital Emergency Department. *Hospital Topics* 54:43–8.

Kasper, Judith A., and Marc L. Berk
1981   Waiting Times in Different Medical Settings: Appointment Waits and Office Waits. *National Health Care Expenditures Study Data Preview 6.* DHHS Publications No. (PHS) 81-3296. National Center for Health Services Research, Public Health Service. Washington, DC: Government Printing Office.

Katzman, Mitchell
1985   Freestanding Emergency Centers: Regulation and Reimbursement. *American Journal of Law and Medicine* 11(1):105–29.

Kerlinger, Fred N.
1973   *Foundations of Behavioral Research,* 2nd edition. New York: Holt, Rinehart, and Winston.

Kleiman, Michael B.
1981   Who Uses the Hospital Emergency Room: Correcting a Misconception. *Hospital and Health Services Administration* 26(Special Issue S1):63–71.

Kroeger, A.
1983   Anthropological and Socio-Medical Health Care Research in Developing Countries. *Social Science and Medicine* 17:147–61.

Levin, Jefrey S., and Jeannine Coreil
1986   "New Age" Healing in the U.S. *Social Science and Medicine* 23(9):889–98.

Ling, L. J., and I. Gold
1986   The Referral of Patients from Freestanding Emergency Centers to a Hospital Emergency Department. *Annals of Emergency Medicine* 15:923–26.

Mechanic, David
1979   Correlates of Physician Utilization: Why Do Major Multivariate Studies of Physician Utilization Find Trivial Psychosocial and Organizational Effects? *Journal of Health and Social Behavior* 20:387–96.

Miller, Karen E.
1983   An Economic Analysis of the Demand for Care in a Free-Standing Emergency Center. Unpublished Ph.D. dissertation, University of Texas at Houston.

National Association For Ambulatory Care
1985   FEC Factor II Data Released. *Ambulatory Care* 5(4):17.

National Center for Health Statistics
1982   *Current Estimates from the National Health Interview Survey: United States, 1980,* National Health Survey Series 10, Number 139. DHHS Publication No. (PHS) 82-1567. Public Health Service. Washington, DC: Government Printing Office.

Orkand Corporation
1979   *Preliminary Survey of Freestanding Emergency Centers.* Silver Springs, MD: The Corporation.

––––––
1983   *Study to Provide Updated Information on Emergicenters.* Health Care Financing Administration, TR-83W-018, PB83-211391, DHHS. Silver Springs, MD: The Corporation.

Parker, A. W., J. M. Walsh, and M. Coon
1976   A Normative Approach to the Definition of Primary Health Care. *Milbank Memorial Fund Quarterly* 54:415.

Pelto, Pertti J., and Gretel H. Pelto
1978   *Anthropological Research: The Structure of Inquiry,* 2nd ed. Cambridge, MA: Cambridge University Press.

Potter, Donald P.
1982   How the Michigan Hospital Association Views the Growth of Hospital Satellites. *Michigan Medicine* 81(8):77–8.

Reeves, Edward C., Billie R. DeWalt, and Kathleen M. DeWalt
1987   The International Sorghum/Millet Research Project. In *Anthropological Praxis,* edited by Robert M. Wulff and Shirley J. Fiske, 72–83. Boulder, CO: Westview.

Richards, Glenn
1984   FECs Pose Competition for Hospital EDs. *Hospitals* (March 16):77, 79, 80, 82.

Rizzo, D. A.
1988   Physician Advertising Revisited. *Medical Care* 26:1238–44.

Rogers, J., and P. Curtis
1980   The Concept and Measurement of Continuity in Primary Care. *American Journal of Public Health* 70:122.

Rossman, Gretchen B., and Bruce L. Wilson
1985   Numbers and Words: Combining Quantitative and Qualitative Methods in a Single Large-Scale Evaluation Study. *Evaluation Review* 9(5):627–43.

Roth, Julius A., and Dorothy J. Douglas
1983   *No Appointment Necessary.* New York: Irvington Publishers.

Rylko-Bauer, Barbara
1985   The Role of Freestanding Emergency Centers in the Delivery of Health Care: Perspectives on Change in American Medicine. Unpublished Ph.D. dissertation, University of Kentucky.

———

1988   The Development and Use of Freestanding Emergency Centers: A Review of the Literature. *Medical Care Review* 45(1):129–63.

Rylko-Bauer, Barbara, John van Willigen, and Ann McElroy
1989   Strategies for Increasing the Use of Anthropological Research in the Policy Process: A Cross-Disciplinary Analysis. In *Making Our Research Useful,* edited by John van Willigen, Barbara Rylko-Bauer, and Ann McElroy, 1–25. Boulder, CO: Westview.

Salmon, J. Warren, ed.
1984   *Alternative Medicines.* New York: Tavistock.

Schensul, Jean J.
1987   Knowledge Utilization: An Anthropological Perspective. *Practicing Anthropology.* 9(1):6–8.

Schwartz, Barry
1975   *Queuing and Waiting: Studies in the Social Organization of Access and Delay.* Chicago: University of Chicago.

Smith, A. G., and K. S. Louis, eds.
1982   Multimethod Policy Research: Issues and Applications. *American Behavioral Scientist* 26(1):1–144.

Stevenson, Gary
1983   FEC Acceptance, Growth, Cost Benefits Confirmed. *Emergence,* Special Issue, June 1983:S1–S6.

Stoner, Bradley P.
1985   Formal Modeling of Health Care Decisions: Some Applications and Limitations. *Medical Anthropology Quarterly* 16(2):41–46.

Tanner, R.
1982   Doc in the Box: Medical Care, Fast-Food Style. *Venture* (October):54–55.

Trotter, Robert T. II
1987   A Case of Lead Poisoning from Folk Remedies in Mexican American Communities. In *Anthropological Praxis,* edited by Robert M. Wulff and Shirley J. Fiske, 146–59. Boulder, CO: Westview.

van de Vall, Mark, Cheryl Bolas, and C. D. Kang
1976   Applied Social Research in Industrial Organizations: An Evaluation of Functions, Theory, and Methods. *Journal of Applied Behavioral Science* 12:158–77.

van Willigen, John, and Billie R. DeWalt
1985   *Training Manual in Policy Ethnography.* Washington, DC: American Anthropological Association.

Wall, Eric M.
1981   Continuity of Care and Family Medicine: Definition, Determinants, and Relationship to Outcome. *Journal of Family Practice* 13(5):655–64.

Weaver, Thomas
1985   Anthropology as a Policy Science: Part I, A Critique. *Human Organization* 44(2):97–105.

Weinerman, E. R., Robert S. Ratner, Anthony Robbins, et al.
1966   Yale Studies in Ambulatory Medical Care: Determinants of Use of Hospital Emergency Services. *American Journal of Public Health* 56:1036–56.

Weiss, Carol H., and Michael Bucuvalas
1980   Truth Test and Utility Test: Decision Makers' Frame of Reference for Social Science Research. *American Sociological Review* (April):302–13.

Werner, Oswald, and G. Mark Schoepfle
1987a   *Systematic Fieldwork, Volume I: Foundations of Ethnography and Interviewing.* Beverly Hills, CA: Sage.

———

1987b   *Systematic Fieldwork, Volume II: Foundations of Ethnography and Interviewing.* Beverly Hills, CA: Sage.

Yin, Robert K.
1984   *Case Study Research: Design and Methods.* Beverly Hills, CA: Sage.

Zola, Irving K.
1972   Studying the Decision to See a Doctor. *Advances in Psychosomatic Medicine* 8:216–36.

The Sociocultural Environment in the Genesis and Amelioration of Opium Dependence

References

Berger, L. J., and J. Westermeyer
1977   World Traveler Addicts in Asia; II. Comparisons with "Stay at Home" Addicts. *Amer. J. Drug Alc. Abuse* 4:495–503.

Geddes, W. R.
  1976   *Migrants of the Mountains* Oxford, Eng: The Clarendon Press.

Miles, D.
  1979   The Finger Knife and Ockham's Razor: A Problem in Asian Culture History and Economic Anthropology. *Amer. Ethnologist* 6:223–43.

Pelto, Pertti J.
  1970   *Anthropological Research: The Structure of Inquiry.* New York: Harper and Row.

Poshyachinda, V., Y. Onthum, C. Sithi-Amorn, and V. Perngparn
  1978   *Evaluation of Treatment Outcome: The Buddhist Temple Treatment Center, Tam Kraborg.* Bangkok, Thailand: Chulalongkorn University Institute of Health Research.

Suwanwela C., V. Poshyachinda, P. Tasanapradit, and A. Dharmkrong-At
  1977   *The Hill Tribes of Thailand: Their Opium Use and Addiction.* Bangkok: Institute of Health Research.

Westermeyer, J.
  1971   Use of Alcohol and Opium Among the Meo of Laos. *Amer. J. Psychiatry* 127:1019–23.

  1973   Folk Treatment for Opium Addiction in Laos. *Brit. J. Addictions* 68:345–49.

  1974a   Opium Smoking in Laos: A Survey of 40 Addicts. *Amer. J. Psychiatry* 131:165–70.

  1974b   Opium Dens: A Social Resource for Addicts in Laos. *Arch. Gen. Psychiatry* 31:237–40.

  1976   The Pro-heroin Effects of Anti-opium laws. *Arch. Gen. Psychiat.* 33:1135–39.

  1977a   Narcotic Addiction in Two Asian Cultures: A Comparison and Analysis. *Drug Alcohol Dependence* 2:273–85.

  1977b   Narcotic Addiction in Laos: An Overview. In *Current Perspectives in Cultural Psychiatry,* edited by E. Foulks, R. Wintrob, J. Westermeyer, A. Favazza, 191–202. New York: Spectrum Press.

  1978a   Indigenous and Expatriate Narcotic Addicts in Laos: A Comparison. *Culture, Medicine and Psychiatry* 2:129–50.

  1978b   Social Events and Narcotic Addiction: The Influence of War and Law on Opium Use in Laos. *Addiction Research* 3:57–62.

  1979   Influence of Opium Availability on Addiction Rates in Laos. *Amer. J. Epidemiology* 109:550–62.

1980a   Treatment for Narcotic Addiction in a Buddhist Monastery. *J. Drug Issues* 10:221–28.

1980b   Two Neo-Buddhist Cults in Asia. *J. Psychol. Anthropology* 3:143–52.

1980c   Sex Roles Among Opium Addicts in Asia: Influences of Drug Availability and Sampling Method. *Drug Alcohol Dependence* 6:131–36.

1981a   Opium Availability and Prevalence of Addiction in Asia. *Brit. J. Addictions* 76:85–90.

1981b   Three Case Finding Methods for Opiate Addicts Among the Hmong in Laos: A Comparison. *Internatl. J. Addiction* 16:173–83.

1982   *Poppies, Pipes and People: Opium and Its Use in Laos.* Berkeley, CA: University of California Press.

1983   Treatment of Opiate Addiction in Asia: Current Practice and Recent Advances. In *Research Advances in Alcohol and Drug Problems*, edited by R. Smart et al. 433–55 New York: Plenum Press.

1988   Sex Differences in Drug and Alcohol Use Among Ethnic Groups in Laos, 1965–75. *Amer. J. Drug Alcohol Abuse* 14:443–61.

Westermeyer, J., and L. J. Berger
1977   World Traveler Addicts in Asia; I. Demographic and Clinical Description. *Amer. J. Drug Alc. Abuse* 4:479–93.

Westermeyer, J., and P. Bourne
1977   A Heroin "Epidemic" in Laos. *Amer. J. Drug Alc. Abuse* 4:1–11.

———
1978   Treatment Outcome and the Role of the Community in Narcotic Addiction. *J. Nervous Mental Dis.* 166:51–58.

Westermeyer, J., T. Lyfoung, and J. Neider
1989   An Epidemic of Opium Dependence Among Asian Refugees in the U.S.: Characteristics and Causes. *British J. Addictions* 84:785–89.

Westermeyer, J., and J. Neider
1982   Variability in Opium Dosage—Observations from Laos 1965–75. *Drug Alcohol Dependence* 9:351–58.

Westermeyer, J., and G. Peng
1977a   Opium and Heroin Addicts in Laos; I. A Comparative Study. *J. Nervous Mental Dis.* 164:345–50.

———
1977b   Opium and Heroin Addicts in Laos, II. A Study of Matched Pairs. *J. Nervous Mental Dis.* 164, 351–54.

—————
1978 Comparative Study of Male and Female Opium Addicts Among the Hmong (Meo). *Brit. J. Addictions* 73:181–88.

Westermeyer, J., and C. Soudaly
1984 Lessons from a Methadone Treatment Program in Laos. *Drug Alcohol Dependence* 13:89–106.

Westermeyer, J., C. Soudaly, and E. Kaufman
1978 An Addiction Treatment Program in Laos: The First Year's Experience. *Drug Alcohol Dependence* 3:93–102.

Microlevel/Macrolevel

References

DeWalt, Billie R., and Pertti J. Pelto
1985 *Micro and Macro Levels of Analysis in Anthropology.* Boulder, CO: Westview Press.

Poggie, John J., Jr., and Robert N. Lynch
1974 *Rethinking Modernization: Anthropological Perspective.* Westport, CT: Greenwood Press.

Society and Land Degradation in Central America

Notes

1. The research reported here was supported by the International Sorghum/Millet Collaborative Research Support Program (INTSORMIL) through contract #AID/DSAN-G-0149, by a Fulbright Research Grant under their Central American Republics Research Program, and by two University of Kentucky Summer Research Fellowships.

2. A political economy approach has emerged as one of the major frameworks used to understand ecological change in the Third World (e.g., Spooner and Mann, 1982; Blaikie, 1984; Horowitz and Salem-Murdock, 1987; Little, 1987; Little and Horowitz, 1987; Painter, 1987; Schmink and Wood, 1987).

3. More detailed information on the methodology employed in this study may be found in Stonich, 1986.

4. Why landowners are more interested in growing pasture to feed livestock rather than growing basic grains or some other crop for export is made clear by comparing the potential returns on investment. Given the economic and environmental constraints in southern Honduras, there is a good chance that a farmer will not make any profit from growing grain (SRN, 1980:63). Estimates based on the "best case" scenario (i.e., where the market price is highest and the inputs lowest), a farmer would be able to make a profit of only about seventy-five dollars. This potential profit is not enough to entice most large landowners to produce grain beyond what they require for their own consumption. Those farmers with small holdings or those who are landless do have an incentive to produce their own grain. Many of the worker-days put into the production of crops is their own labor, and their own cash outlays are relatively minimal, whereas purchasing grains at retail prices involves a significant outlay of cash (DeWalt, 1985:177–88).

5. For a description of the household economic strategies of southern Honduran peasants see Stonich, 1986 (Chapter VI) and 1991a. The breakdown of households into the various strata in Table 2 is based on this study of the household economy, especially on the emergence of household survival strategies, which vary with respect to land tenancy. Also taken into consideration were the criteria employed in the classification of farms by size in the national agricultural censuses and in the technical reports of development assistance agencies.

6. The deviant situation of the largest landholder (seventy-five hectares) is due to the fact that he drove his herd of fifty cattle to a ranch in the lowlands, where he paid $3.00/head/month to graze his cattle during the dry season.

7. The extent to which cattle were allowed to graze in fallow fields was manifested to me when I attempted to choose a sample of fields in various stages of fallow in order to monitor floral growth. I was unable to find even one parcel that was not being used to graze cattle.

8. The various agricultural practices of each farmer subgroup combined to contribute to drastic rates in highland deforestation. There was, however, a major cause of deforestation that transcended all classes—the harvesting of fuelwood. Virtually every household used fuelwood for cooking. The majority of households (70 percent–80 percent) collected their own firewood, whereas the rest bought firewood from someone else in the community who had collected it locally. These figures are consistent with those of Jones (1982), who estimates that 94 percent of all households in the south (compared to 82 percent nationally) used fuelwood to cook. Jones also approximates that fuelwood use was 5.83 pounds/person/day.

References

ADAI (Ateneo de la Agroindustria)
    1987   Informe del Semenario "Lineamientos para un Mejor Aprovechamiento de la Ayuda Alimentaria," del 26 al 29 de Octubre, 1987. Doct no:42/87, Tegucigalpa, Honduras.

BANADESA
1987 Prestamos Otorgados por Sistema BANADESA, Boletin Estadistica BANADESA (mimeo). Tegucigalpa, Honduras.

BANTRAL
1987 Prestamos por Sistema BANCARIO, Boletin Estadistica BANTRAL—preliminar, (mimeo). Tegucigalpa, Honduras.

Bennett, John
1976 *The Ecological Transition: Cultural Anthropology and Human Adaptation.* New York and London: Pergamon Publishing Company.

Blaikie, Piers
1984 *The Political Economy of Soil Erosion in Developing Countries.* London: Longman.

Boyer, Jefferson
1983 *Agrarian Capitalism and Peasant Praxis in Southern Honduras.* Ann Arbor, MI: University Microfilms unpublished Ph.D. dissertation.

————
1984 From Peasant Economia to Capitalist Social Relations in Southern Honduras. *Southern Latin Americanist* 27:1–22.

CRIES (Comprehensive Resource Inventory Evaluation System)
1984 *Resource Assessment of the Choluteca Department.* East Lansing, MI: Michigan State University and the U.S. Department of Agriculture.

Crouch, Luis, and Alain de Janvry
1980 The Class Basis of Agricultural Growth. *Food Policy* Feb.:3–13.

CSPE/OEA (Secretaria Tecnica del Consejo Superior de Planificacion Economico y Secretaria General de la Organizacion de Estados Americanos)
1982 *Proyecto de Desarrollo Local del Sur de Honduras.* Secretaria Tecnica del Consejo Superior de Planificacion Economico y Secretaria General de la Organizacion de Estados Americanos. Tegucigalpa, Dic., Honduras.

de Janvry, Alain
1975 The Political Economy of Rural Development in Latin America: An Interpretation. *American Journal of Agricultural Economics* 57:490–99.

DeWalt, Billie R.
1983 The Cattle Are Eating the Forest. *Bulletin of the Atomic Scientist* 39:18–23.

————
1985 Microcosmic and Macrocosmic Processes of Agrarian Change in Southern Honduras: The Cattle Are Eating the Forest. In *Micro and Macro Levels of Analysis in Anthropology: Issues in Theory and Research,* edited by B. R. DeWalt and P. J. Pelto, 165–86. Boulder, CO: Westview Press.

DeWalt, Billie, and Kathleen M. DeWalt
1982 *Socioeconomic Constraints in the Production, Distribution and Consumption of Sorghum in Southern Honduras.* INTSORMIL, Farming Systems Research in Southern Honduras. Report No. 1. Lexington, KY: University of Kentucky Department of Anthropology.

1987 Nutrition and Agricultural Change in Southern Honduras. *Food and Nutrition Bulletin* 9(3):36–45.

DeWalt, Billie R., and P. J. Pelto, eds.
1985 *Micro and Macro Levels of Analysis in Anthropology: Issues in Theory and Research.* Boulder, CO: Westview Press.

DGECH (Direccion General de Estadistica y Censos)
1954 *Censo Nacional Agropecuario 1952.* Direccion General de Estadistica y Censos: Tegucigalpa, Honduras.

1968 *Censo Nacional Agropecuario 1965.* Direccion General de Estadistica y Censos: Tegucigalpa, Honduras.

1976 *Censo Nacional Agropecuario 1974.* Direccion General de Estadistica y Censos: Tegucigalpa, Honduras.

Durham, William
1979 *Scarcity and Survival in Central America: The Ecological Origins of the Soccer War.* Stanford, CA: Stanford University Press.

Hawkins, Richard
1984 Intercropping Maize with Sorghum in Central America: A Cropping System Case Study. CATIE: Turrialba, Costa Rica.

Horowitz, Michael, and Muneera Salem-Murdock
1987 The Political Economy of Desertification in White Nile Province, Sudan. In *Lands at Risk in the Third World: Local Level Perspectives*, edited by P. Little and M. Horowitz, 95–114. Boulder, CO: Westview.

IHMA (Instituto Hondureno de Mercadeo Agricola)
1987 Analisis y Propuestas para el Establecimiento de los Precios de Garantia para Granos Basicos. Tegucigalpa, Honduras.

Jones, Jeffrey R.
1982 Produccion y Consumo de lena en fincas pequenas de Honduras. Turrialba, Costa Rica: CATIE.

Larson, Donald
1982 The Problems and Effects of Price Controls on Honduran Agriculture (mimeo). Minneapolis, MN: Experience Incorporated.

Leonard, H. Jeffrey
1987 *Natural Resources and Economic Development in Central America.* New Brunswick, NJ: Transaction Books.

Little, Peter
1987 Land Use Conflicts in the Agricultural/Pastoral Borderlands: The Case of Kenya. In *Lands at Risk in the Third World: Local Level Perspectives,* edited by P. Little and M. Horowitz, 195–212. Boulder, CO: Westview.

Little, Peter, and Michael Horowitz
1987 Social Science Perspectives on Land, Ecology, and Development. In *Lands at Risk in the Third World: Local Level Perspectives,* edited by P. Little and M. Horowitz, 1–16. Boulder, CO: Westview.

Mintz, Sidney
1977 The So-called World System: Local Initiative and Local Response. *Dialectical Anthropology* 2(4):253–70.

O'Brien Fonck, Carlos
1972 *Modernity and Public Policies in the Context of the Peasant Sector: Honduras as a Case Study.* Latin American Studies Program Dissertation Series: Cornell University.

Ortner, Sherry B.
1984 Theory in Anthropology Since the Sixties. *Comparative Studies in Society and History* 26(1):126–66.

Painter, Michael
1987 Unequal Exchange: The Dynamics of Settler Impoverishment and Environmental Destruction in Lowland Bolivia. In *Lands at Risk in the Third World: Local Level Perspectives,* edited by P. Little and M. Horowitz, 169–92. Boulder, CO: Westview.

Parsons, James
1976 Forest to Pasture: Development or Destruction? *Revista de Biologia Tropical* 24 (Supplement 1):121–38.

Perez Brignoli, Hector
1982 Growth and Crisis in the Central American Economies. *Journal of Latin American Studies* 15:365–98.

SAEH/INCAP (Secretaria de Educacion Publica Direccion General de Educacion Primaria Servicio de Alimentacion Escolar de Honduras/Instituto de Nutricion de Centro America y Panama)
1987 *Primer Censo Nacional de Talla en Escolares de Primer Grado de Educacion Primaria de la Republica de Honduras, 1986.* Tegucigalpa, Honduras: SAEH/INCAP.

SAPLAN (Sistema de Analisis y Planificacion de Alimentacion y Nutricion)
1981 *Analysis de la Situacion Nutricional durante el Periodo 1972–1979.* Tegucigalpa, Honduras: Consejo Superior de Planificacion Economico (CONSUPLANE) [mimeo].

Schmink, Marianne, and Charles Wood
1987   The Political Ecology of Amazonia. In *Lands at Risk in the Third World: Local Level Perspectives*, edited by P. Little and M. Horowitz, 38–57. Boulder, CO: Westview.

Smith, Sheldon, and Ed Reeves
1989   *Human Systems Ecology: Studies in the Integration of Political Economy, Adaptation, and Socionatural Regions.* Boulder, CO: Westview.

Spooner, Brian
1987   Insiders and Outsiders in Baluchistan: Western and Indigenous Perspectives on Ecology and Development. In *Lands at Risk in the Third World: Local Level Perspectives*, edited by P. Little and M. Horowitz, 58–68. Boulder, CO: Westview.

Spooner, Brian, and H. S. Mann, eds.
1982   *Desertification and Development: Dryland Ecology in Social Perspective.* London: Academic Press.

SRN (Secretaria de Recursos Naturales)
1980   *Los Granos Basicos en su Aspecto Economico.* Tegucigalpa, Honduras.

Stares, Rodney
1972   *La Economia Campesina en la zona Sur de Honduras: 1950–1970.* Prepared for the Bishop of Choluteca: Choluteca, Honduras.

Stonich, Susan C.
1986   *Development and Destruction: Interrelated Ecological, Socioeconomic, and Nutritional Change in Southern Honduras.* Ann Arbor, MI: University Microfilms unpublished Ph.D. dissertation.

———

1988   Integrated Socioeconomic, Remote Sensing, and Information Management Procedures for Rural Development and Agricultural Policy Design. Paper presented at the Annual Meeting of the Society for Applied Anthropology. Tampa, FL. April [mimeo].

———

1989   The Dynamics of Social Processes and Environmental Destruction: A Central American Case Study. *Population and Development Review* 15(2):269–96.

———

1991a   Rural Families, Migration Incomes: Honduran Households in the World Economy. *Journal of Latin American Studies* 15(2) (in press).

———

1991b   Lands and People in Peril: Ecological Transformation and Food Security in Honduras. In *Harvest of Want: The Quest for Food Security in Central America and Mexico,* edited by A. Ferguson and S. Whiteford. Boulder, CO: Westview Press (in press).

United Nations World Commission on Environment and Development
1987   *Our Common Future.* Oxford, Eng.: Oxford University Press.

USAID (United States Agency for International Development)
1981   *Environment Profile of Honduras.* Tucson AZ: Arid Lands Information Center.

―――
1982   *Country Environmental Profile.* Virginia: JRB Associates.

―――
1989   *Environmental and Natural Resource Management in Central America: A Strategy for AID Assistance* (Prepared for the LAC Bureau by the Regional Office for Central America and Panama).

USDA (United States Department of Agriculture)
1985   *World Indices of Agricultural and Food Production, 1950–84.* Washington, DC: USDA.

―――
1987   *Livestock and Meat* (Foreign Agriculture Circulars); cited in Leonard 1987:216–17.

Warren, John P.
1984   The Natural Resources Management Project: A Status Summary. OET/AID/Honduras. Tegucigalpa, Honduras. [draft copy]

White, Robert
1977   *Structural Factors in Rural Development: The Church and the Peasant in Honduras.* Cornell University, unpublished Ph.D. dissertation.

Williams, Robert G.
1986   *Export Agriculture and the Crisis in Central America.* Chapel Hill, NC: University of North Carolina Press.

World Bank
1987 *World Development Report 1987.* New York: Oxford University.

―――
1988   *World Development Report 1988.* New York: Oxford University.

Agrarian Reform and the Food Crisis in Mexico

Notes

    1. This research was funded through the Sorghum and Millet Collaborative Research Support Project, Grant # AID/DSAN/XII-G-0149.

2. Although renting and sharecropping of ejido land is technically illegal, it has been common practice. Because of possible legal sanctions, however, many people are less than forthcoming in talking about land rental and sharecropping. Thus, these measures of total land access are good approximations, but not completely accurate.

3. The material style of life index was computed from a list of a large number of material goods that could be owned by households in the sample. This list included such items as a radio, iron, bicycle, motor vehicle, television, wardrobe, fan, refrigerator, and sewing machine. In past research, we have ordered these items into a Guttman Scale (see B. DeWalt, 1979). The scaling itself is thought to be meaningful because the scale indicates something about the priority attached to the items and therefore the order in which items are likely to be purchased. In order to get items to scale, however, many items are often eliminated. In this research, we chose to use a different approach to developing an MSL scale. The percentages of people owning each item in the communities indicates something about the difficulty and expense of acquisition. Thus, we weighted each item in inverse proportion to the percentage of individuals owning it (i.e., $1 = \%$ owning the item), then summed up the score for all of the items owned by the family. This insured that owning a vehicle (owned by very few families), for example, contributed more to the total overall score than owning a common item such as a radio (see Hayden and Cannon, 1984:30–32 for a similar approach).

4. The procedure most amenable to testing hypotheses about the equality of two means for variables measured on an interval or ratio scale is the T-test. This procedure tests the hypothesis that, in the population from which these samples were drawn, the means are equal. We looked at the separate variance estimates of the t value (a method appropriate when variances in the samples may be unequal), using a two-tailed test of significance (i.e., we did not predict a difference in means in one direction). These are the most conservative means of testing the differences between means.

5. The analysis of variance procedure tests the hypothesis whether observed differences in sample means can be reasonably attributed to chance (i.e., the population means are equal). We used the Scheffé multiple comparison procedure to compare the means of the anthropometric data. This method is conservative for pairwise comparison of means. That is, relatively large differences must be present before this procedure will indicate that the means are significantly different (see Norusis/SPSS Inc., 1990:195–98). We report the pairs of means that were identified as significantly different at the .05 level of significance.

6. Deciding the cut-off point for what is considered severe malnutrition varies in the literature. The percentages we have used correspond roughly to two standard deviations below the mean for weight for age, height for age, and weight for height. The percentage cutoffs we have used are widely used standards for international comparisons (Strauss, 1990:231).

7. By way of contrast, only .5 percent of two-year-old boys in the U.S. fall below 90 percent of the median height standard and only .6 percent of U.S. girls fall under 80 percent of the median weight for height. A 1985 rural survey of children in

the Cote d'Ivoire showed that 10 percent were stunted and 4.4 percent were below the median weight for height (Strauss, 1990:231–32). Data from communities in the highlands of Ecuador showed that about 55 percent of children were stunted (B. DeWalt et al., 1990:44).

8. The number of cases for the analysis for Table 4 differs depending on the health and nutrition indicator used. The data on proportion of household members sick and proportion of children who died is based on differences in the characteristics of households contained in the sample.

Because several of the households sampled had more than one child under five, we collected anthropometric data on all children under five in the household. Other analysts have handled the problem of having more than one child per household by selecting only one child for analysis or by averaging the anthropometric measurements of children in the household. Our desire was to utilize the actual data on all of the children in the various households. Thus, the anthropometric comparisons presented in Table 4 are based on an analysis using all of the children who were measured. In those instances where a household had more than one child under five, it is represented more than once in the comparisons.

References

Adelski, M. Elizabeth
    1987   *Ejidal Agriculture in Northern Sinaloa: Agricultural Resources, Production and Household Well-Being.* Unpublished Ph.D. dissertation, University of Kentucky.

Austin, James, and Gustavo Esteva, eds.
    1987   *Food Policy in Mexico: The Search for Self-sufficiency.* Ithaca, NY: Cornell University Press.

Barchfield, J.
    1979   *Land Tenure and Social Productivity in Mexico.* Madison, WI: Land Tenure Center Publication 121.

Barkin, David
    1982   El Uso de la Tierra Agrícola en México. *Problemas del Desarrollo* 47/48:59–85.

Barkin, David, and Billie R. DeWalt
    1985   La Crisis Alimentaria Mexicana y el Sorgo. *Problemas del Desarrollo* 61:65–85.

———
    1988   Sorghum and the Mexican Food Crisis. *Latin American Research Review* XXIII (3):30–59.

Barkin, David, and Blanca Suárez
    1986   *El Fin de la Autosuficiencia Alimentaria.* México: Editorial Océano y Centro de Ecodesarrollo.

Camara, F., and R. V. Kemper, eds.
1979 *Migration Across Frontiers: Mexico and the United States.* Albany, NY: Latin American Anthropology Group.

CIMMYT (Centro Internacional de Mejoramiento de Maíz y Trigo)
1980 *Planeacion de Tecnologias Apropiadas para los Agricultores: Conceptos y Procedimientos.* Mexico: CIMMYT.

Cornelius, Wayne
1976 *Mexican Migration to the United States: The Evidence from Sending Communities.* Cambridge, MA: Center for International Studies, Massachusetts Institute of Technology.

Couriel, Alberto
1984 Poverty and Unemployment in Latin America. *CEPAL Review* 24:39–62.

de Janvry, Alain
1981 *The Agrarian Question and Reformism in Latin America.* Baltimore, MD: Johns Hopkins.

DeWalt, Billie R.
1979 *Modernization in a Mexican Ejido: A Study in Economic Adaptation.* New York: Cambridge University Press.

———
1985a Mexico's Second Green Revolution: Food for Feed. *Mexican Studies/Estudios Mexicanos* 1:29–60.

———
1985b Anthropology, Sociology and Farming Systems Research. *Human Organization* 44:106–14.

———
1988 Halfway There: Social Science *in* Agricultural Development and the Social Science *of* Agricultural Development. *Human Organization* 47:343–53.

DeWalt, Billie R., and David Barkin
1987 Seeds of Change: The Effects of Hybrid Sorghum and Agricultural Modernization in Mexico. In *Technology and Social Change*, 2nd ed., edited by H. Russell Bernard and Pertti J. Pelto, 138–65. Prospect Heights, IL:Waveland Press.

DeWalt, Billie, Kathleen DeWalt, Jose Carlos Escudero, and David Barkin
1987 Agrarian Reform and Small Farmer Welfare: Evidence from Four Mexican Communities. *Food and Nutrition Bulletin* 9(3):46–52.

DeWalt, Billie R., and Pertti J. Pelto, eds.
1985 *Micro and Macro Levels of Analysis in Anthropology: Issues in Theory and Research.* Boulder, CO.: Westview Press.

DeWalt, Billie R., Jorge Uquillas, Kathleen M. DeWalt, William Leonard, and James Stansbury
    1990 *Dairy Based Production and Food Systems in Mejia and Salcedo.* Research, Extension, and Education Project Report #1. Lexington, KY: Nutrition and Agriculture Cooperative Agreement.

DeWalt, Kathleen M., Billie R. DeWalt, Jóse Carlos Escudero, and David Barkin
    1990 Shifts from Maize to Sorghum Production: Nutrition Effects in Four Mexican Communities. *Food Policy* 15:395–407.

Escárcega López, Everardo, and Carlota Botey Estapé
    1990 *La Recomposición de la Propiedad Social como Precondición Necesaria para Refuncionalizar el Ejido, en el Orden Económico-Productivo: Introducción a una Propuesta de Nueva Reforma Agraria.* Mexico City: Centro de Estudios Históricos del Agrarismo en México.

Esteva, Gustavo
    1987 Food Needs and Capacities: Four Centuries of Conflict. In *Food Policy in Mexico: The Search for Self-sufficiency,* edited by James Austin and Gustavo Esteva, 23–47. Ithaca, NY: Cornell University Press.

Garcia Sordo, Mario
    1985 Insuficiente Producción para satisfacer la demanda de proteínas de origen animal. *UnoMásUno* January 9, p. 8.

Gonzalez Casanova, Pablo
    1980 The Economic Development of Mexico. *Scientific American* 243:192–204.

Hardy, Chandra
    1982 Mexico's Development Strategy for the 1980s. *World Development* 10:501–12.

Hayden, Brian, and Aubrey Cannon
    1984 *The Structure of Material Systems: Ethnoarchaeology in the Maya Highlands.* SAA Papers #3. Washington, D.C.: Society for American Archaeology.

Hewitt de Alcantara, Cynthia
    1976 *Modernizing Mexican Agriculture.* Geneva, Switzerland: United Nationas Research Institute for Social Development.

IDB (Interamerican Development Bank)
    1986 *Economic and Social Progress in Latin America: 1986 Report.* Washington, D.C.: IDB.

_____
    1987 *Economic and Social Progress in Latin America: 1987 Report.* Washington, D.C.: IDB.

Meissner, Frank
1981 The Mexican Food System (SAM): A Strategy for Sowing Petroleum. *Food Policy* 6:219–30.

Norusis, Marija J., and SPSS Inc.
1990 *SPSS Base System User's Guide.* Chicago: SPSS Incorporated.

Pelto, Pertti J., and Gretel Pelto
1978 *Anthropological Research: The Structure of Inquiry,* 2nd ed. Cambridge and New York: Cambridge University Press.

Rama, Ruth, and Fernando Rello
1982 *Estrategias de las Agroindustrias Transnacionales y Política Alimentaria en México.* México City: UNAM, Facultad de Economía.

Rama, Ruth, and Raul Vigorito
1977 *El Complejo de Frutas y Legumbres en México.* Mexico City: Editorial Bueva Imagen.

Redclift, Michael
1981 Development Policy Making in Mexico: The *Sistema Alimentario Mexicano* (SAM). San Diego, CA: University of San Diego Working Papers in U.S.– Mexican Studies #24.

Reig, N.
1985 Las Tendencias Alimentarias a Largo Plazo en México: 1950–1984. *Problemas del Desarrollo* 61:9–64.

Sanderson, Susan R. Walsh
1984 *Land Reform in Mexico: 1910–1980.* Orlando: Academic Press.

Secretaría de Agricultura y Recursos Hidráulicos
1990 Programa Nacional de Modernización del Campo, 1990–1994. *Comercio Exterior* 40 (10):987–1008.

Shaner, W. W., P. F. Philipp, and W. R. Schmehl
1982 *Farming Systems Research and Development: Guidelines for Developing Countries.* Boulder, CO: Westview.

Solis, L.
1973 Mexican Economic Policy in the Post-War Period: The View of Mexican Economists. *American Economic Review* 61(3):11.

Strauss, John
1990 Households, Communities, and Preschool Children's Nutrition Outcomes: Evidence from Rural Cote d'Ivoire. *Economic Development and Cultural Change* 38:231–61.

World Bank
1986 *World Development Report, 1986.* New York: Oxford.

312 *Notes and References*

Yates, P. Lamartine
1981 *Mexico's Agricultural Dilemma.* Tucson, AZ: University of Arizona Press.

Unwanted Children as a Consequence of Delocalization in Modern Kenya

Note

1. The field research for this study was supported by a grant from the National Science Foundation. The Institute of African Studies, Nairobi University, Kenya, is thanked for my tenure there as a Research Associate (1984–85).

Particular gratitude is extended to Ridah M'Mbone Anyancia, Eannes M. Kaibe, Julius Kadima Lanya, John Ndung'u, and Solome Catherine Ouma, who were my assistants in data gathering and language acquisition (materials were collected in *Aabaluyia* dialects, *Ki Swahili,* and English). Additionally, Enock Lanya Mulama, Chief Nzoia Location; Gilbert Were, Assistant for Social Development; and Christopher Nyongesa, the Headmaster of Musemwa Primary School, and the many other officials that welcomed us are thanked.

To Dr. Janet Kilbride I extend my gratitude for her help in all phases of my professional and personal life while in the field. She provided intellectual stimulation to me, as she has done for many years, and in numerous ways collaborated in this project. Professors Poggie and Dewalt are thanked for their comments on an earlier version of this chapter.

References

Bronfenbrenner, U.
1974 Developmental Research, Public Policy, and the Ecology of childhood. *Child Development* 45, 1–5.

Bwibo, N.
1982 Battered Child Syndrome. In *Child Labor and Health,* edited by P. Onyango and D. Kayongo-Male. Nairobi, Kenya: Acme Press.

Demos, J.
1987 *Past, Present, and Personal: The Family and Life Course in American History.* New York: Oxford University Press.

Elkind, D.
1987 The Child Yesterday, Today, and Tomorrow. *Young Children* 42 (4):611.

Etienne, M., and E. Leacock
1980 *Women and Colonization: Anthropological Perspectives.* New York: Praeger Publishers.

Fraser, F., and P. Kilbride
1981 Child Abuse and Neglect—Rare But Perhaps Increasing Phenomena Among the Samia of Kenya. *International Journal of Child Abuse and Neglect,* 4:117–232.

Freeman, C.
1988 Colonialism and the Formation of Gender Hierarchies in Kenya. *Critique of Anthropology* 7 (3):33–50.

Garbarino, J.
1977 The Human Ecology of Maltreatment. *Journal of Marriage and the Family,* 29 (4):721–35.

Gelles, J., and C. Cornell
1985 *Intimate Violence in Families.* Beverly Hills, CA: Sage.

Gelles, J., and R. Lancaster
1987 *Child Abuse and Neglect: Biosocial Dimensions.* New York: Aldine and de Gruyter.

Johnson, O. R.
1981 The Socioeconomic Context of Child Abuse and Neglect in Native South America. In *Child Abuse and Neglect,* edited by J. Korbin, 56–71. Berkeley, CA:University of California Press.

Kayere, J.
1980 Rural Female Roles: Some Reflections. Seminar paper number 142, July, 1980, Institute of African Studies, University of Nairobi.

Kent, J.
1979 Helping Abused Children and Their Parents. *Families Today,* DHEW Publication no. (ADM) 79–815.

Kenyatta, J.
1938 *Facing Mt. Kenya: The Tribal Life of the Kikuyu.* London: Secker and Warburg.

Kilbride, P. L.
1980 Sensorimotor Behavior of Baganda and Samia Infants: A Controlled Comparison. *Journal of Cross-Cultural Psychology* 11 (2):131–52.

———
1986 Cultural Persistence and Socio-economic Change Among the Abaluyia: Some Modern Problems in Patterns of Child Care. *Journal of Eastern African Research and Development* 15:35–51.

Kilbride, P. L., and J. Kilbride
1990 *Changing Family Life in East Africa: Women and Children at Risk.* University Park, PA: Penn State University Press.

Kisekka, M.
　　1976　Sexual Attitudes and Behavior Among Students in Uganda. *The Journal of Sex Research* 12 (2):104–16.

Korbin, J.
　　1981　*Child Abuse and Neglect: Cross Cultural Perspectives.* Berkeley, CA: University of California Press.

Langness, L. L.
　　1981　Child Abuse and Cultural Values: The Case of New Guinea. In *Child Abuse and Neglect,* edited by J. Korbin, 13–35. Berkeley, CA: University of California Press.

LeVine, S., and R. LeVine
　　1981　Child Abuse and Neglect in Sub-Saharan Africa. In *Child Abuse and Neglect,* edited by J. Korbin, 35–56. Berkeley, CA: University of California Press.

Naroll, R.
　　1983　*The Moral Order.* Beverly Hills, CA: Sage Publications.

Nasimiyu, R.
　　1985　The Participation of Women in Bukusu Economy: The Situation at the End of the Nineteenth Century. In *History and Culture in Western Kenya,* edited by Simiyu Wandibba, 51–65. Nairobi, Kenya, Were Press for the National Museum of Kenya.

Onyango, P., and D. Kayongo-Male
　　1983　*Child Labor and Health.* Nairobi, Kenya: Acme Press.

Pelto, P.
　　1973　*The Snowmobile Revolution.* Menlo Park, CA: Cummings.

Pelto, P., and G. Pelto
　　1978　*Anthropological Research: The Structure of Inquiry.* Cambridge: Cambridge University Press.

Poggie, J., and R. N. Lynch, eds.
　　1974　*Rethinking Modernization: An Anthropological Perspective.* Westport, CN: Greenwood Press.

Segal, J.
　　1979　Child Abuse: A Review of Research. *Families Today* DHEW Publication no. (ADM) 79–815, 577–607.

Scheper-Hughes, N., ed.
　　1987　*Child Survival.* Boston: D. Reidel Publishing Company.

Strauss, M., and R. Gelles
　　1970　Physical Violence in Families. *Families Today* (2) DHEW Publication no. 79–815, 553–577.

Wagatsuma, H.
1981   Child Abandonment and Infanticide: A Japanese Case. *Child Abuse and Neglect,* edited by J. Korbin, 120–39. Berkeley, CA: University of California Press.

Wagner, G.
1949   *The Bantu of North Kavirondo,* vol. I. London: Oxford University Press.

———

1956   *The Bantu of North Kavirondo,* vol. 2. London: Oxford University Press.

Wallerstein, I. M.
1974   *The Modern World System: Capitalist Agriculture and the Origin of the European World Economy in the Sixteenth Century.* New York: Academic Press.

Worthman, C. M., and J. W. M. Whiting
1987   Social Change in Adolescent Sexual Behavior, Mate Selection and Premarital Pregnancy Rates in a Kikuyu Community. *Ethos* 15 (2):145–65.

"Practical History" and the Poarch Creeks

Notes

1. I extend my deep appreciation to the Poarch Creek Indians for the hospitality and cooperation they have extended to me for nearly twenty years. They have made my work possible.

2. Thanks to Dr. Elizabeth D. Purdum (my wife) for bringing this quotation to my attention.

References

Anderson, Terry
1978 Federal Recognition: The Vicious Myth. *American Indian Journal* (May 1978):7–19.

Boas, Franz
1889   On Alternating Sounds. *American Anthropologist* (old series) 2:47–53.

Fritz, John W.
1984   Federal Acknowledgment of the Poarch Band of Creeks; Proposed Findings. *Federal Register* 49(5):1141.

Gould, Stephen Jay
1988   Introduction to the Revised Edition, *In the Shadow of Man,* by Jane Goodall, v–viii. Boston: Houghton Mifflin Co.

Greenbaum, Susan D.
1985   In Search of Lost Tribes: Anthropology and the Federal Acknowledgment Process. *Human Organization* 44:361–67.

Hsu, Francis L. K.
1979   The Cultural Problem of the Cultural Anthropologist. *American Anthropologist* 81:517–32.

Kirk, Jerome, and Marc L. Miller
1986   *Reliability and Validity in Qualitative Research.* Sage University Paper series on Qualitative Research Methods, Volume 1. Beverly Hills, CA: Sage.

Lurie, Nancy Oestreich
1976   Comment. *Human Organization* 35:320–21.

Paredes, J. Anthony
1974   The Emergence of Contemporary Eastern Creek Indian Identity. In *Social and Cultural Identity: Problems of Persistence and Change.* Southern Anthropological Society Proceedings, No. 8., edited by T. K. Fitzgerald, 63–80. Athens, GA: University of Georgia Press.

_____
1976   New Uses for Old Ethnography: A Brief Social History of a Research Project with the Eastern Creek Indians, *or* How To Be an Applied Anthropologist Without Really Trying. *Human Organization* 35:315-20.

_____
1980   Kinship and Descent in the Ethnic Reassertion of the Eastern Creek Indians. In *The Versatility of Kinship: Essays presented to Harry W. Basehart,* edited by Linda S. Cordell and Stephen Beckerman, 165-94. New York: Academic Press, Inc.

_____
1992   Federal Recognition and the Poarch Band of Creek Indians. In *Indians of the Southeastern United States in the Late Twentieth Century,* edited by J. A. Paredes. Tuscaloosa,: University of Alabama Press.

Paredes, J. Anthony, and Sandra K. Joos
1980   Economics, Optimism, and Community History: A Comparison of Rural Minnesotans and Eastern Creek Indians. *Human Organization* 39:142–52.

Pelto, Pertti J., and Gretel H. Pelto
1976   Comment. *Human Organization* 35:321–22.

Schensul, Stephen L., J. Anthony Paredes, and Pertti J. Pelto
1968   "The Twilight Zone of Poverty": A New Perspective on an Economically Depressed Area. *Human Organization* 27: 30-40.

Speck, Frank G.
1947   Notes on Social and Economic Conditions Among the Creek Indians of Alabama in 1941. *America Indigena* 7:194-98.

1949   The Road to Disappearance: Creek Indians Surviving in Alabama: A Mixed Culture Community. *American Anthropologist* 51:681-82.

Stevens, Charles J.
1983   Demographic Variation and Ethnic Differentiation: A Comparative Demographic Analysis of the Poarch Creek Indians and their Neighbors in the 1900 United States Census of Selected Precincts of Escambia and Monroe Counties, Alabama. Unpublished Master's thesis, Department of Anthropology, Florida State University, Tallahassee, Florida.

Domain Analysis of Lost Scenes from Roanoke, WV

Notes

1. This article represents an expansion of an earlier treatment (Roberts and Carlisle, 1983) that was part of a comprehensive historical and architectural study (Carlisle, 1983) conducted in the Stonewall Jackson Lake project area in Lewis County, West Virginia, by the Section of Man (now the Division of Anthropology), the Carnegie Museum of Natural History. This work was performed as a cultural resource management study sponsored by the U.S. Department of Army, Pittsburgh District Corps of Engineers under contract number DACW59-81-C-0086. The authors wish to express their thanks to the Pittsburgh District of the Corps of Engineers for permission to publish information that first appeared in their report.

Figures 1, 2, and 3 as well as the elevation drawings in Plates 1 and 2 were drafted by Arden M. Bardol, Pittsburgh, Pennsylvania. Figure 1 is reproduced from Carlisle (1983: 4, Figure 1) and is based upon an earlier map that appeared in Gilbert/ Commonwealth, Inc. (1980: 10, Figure 1.1). Figure 2 is modified from Carlisle (1983: 8, Figure 3), which was in turn based upon Gilbert/Commonwealth 1980: 103, Figure 5.1, Sheet 14). Figure 3 is modified from Roberts and Carlisle (1983: 481, Figure 384). Table 1 represents a modification of Table 57 in Roberts and Carlisle (1983:484).

2. Until his untimely death in the spring of 1990, John M. Roberts was Andrew W. Mellon Professor Emeritus of Anthropology at the University of Pittsburgh. Jack's passing during the preparation of this manuscript was a tremendous loss to anthropology, to colleagues in the Department of Anthropology, and to his numerous collaborators. His coauthor for this article dedicates it to Jack Robert's memory and to the spirit of unquenched intellectual curiosity that characterized his work and the man himself. Acknowledgment is also made to Jack's wife, Marilyn S. Roberts, for her cooperation and support during the finalization of this manuscript.

References

Bastian, R. W.
1975   Architecture and Class Segregation in Late Nineteenth Century Terre Haute, Indiana. *The Geographical Review* 65:166-79.

Bauman, J. F., and T. H. Coode
1983   A Social History of Roanoke, West Virginia. In *Stonewall Jackson Lake, West Fork River, Lewis County, West Virginia. Architecture, History, Oral History, and Reconstructed Domains,* edited by R. C. Carlisle, pp. 12-65. A report prepared under the supervision of James B. Richardson III, principal investigator, by Carnegie Museum of Natural History, Section of Man, submitted to the U.S. Department of the Army, Pittsburgh District Corps of Engineers, Pittsburgh, Pennsylvania under contract DACW59-81-C-0086.

Canter, D. V.
1969   An Intergroup Comparison of Connotative Dimensions in Architecture. *Environment and Behavior* 1:37-48.

Carlisle, R. C., ed.
1983   *Stonewall Jackson Lake, West Fork River, Lewis County, West Virginia. Architecture, History, Oral History, and Reconstructed Domains.* A report prepared under the supervision of James B. Richardson III, principal investigator, by Carnegie Museum of Natural History, Section of Man, submitted to the U.S. Department of the Army, Pittsburgh District Corps of Engineers, Pittsburgh, Pennsylvania under contract DACW59-81-C-0086.

Chick, G. E., and J. M. Roberts
1987   Lathe Craft: A Study in "Part" Appreciation. *Human Organization* 46(4):305–17.

D'Andrade, R. G.
1978   U-Statistic Hierarchical Clustering. *Psychometrika* 43:59–67.

Fitzgibbon, J. E., J. Pomeroy, and M. B. Green
1985   Personal Construct Theory: A Basis for Evaluation of Landscape Aesthetics. *The Canadian Geographer* 29:267–70.

Gilbert/Commonwealth, Inc.
1980   *Historic Resources Evaluation, Stonewall Jackson Lake Project West Fork River, West Virginia* (two volumes). A report prepared under the supervision of John R. Kern, principal investigator, submitted to the U.S. Department of the Army, Pittsburgh District Corps of Engineers, Pittsburgh, Pennsylvania, under contract DACW59-78-C-0037.

Glassie, H.
1968   *Pattern in the Material Folk Culture of the Eastern United States.* Philadelphia, PA: University of Pennsylvania Press.

Higuchi, T. H.
1983   The Visual and Spatial Structure of Landscapes. Cambridge, MA: MIT Press.

Kemper, R. V., J. M. Roberts, and R. D. Goodwin
1983   Tourism as a Cultural Domain: The Case of Taos, New Mexico. *Annals of Tourism Research* 10:149–71.

Kniffin, F.
1936   Louisiana House Types. *Annals of the Association of American Geographers* 26:179–93.

Lowenthal, D.
1975   Past Time, Present Time. *Geographical Review* 65:1–36.

Mandler, J. M.
1984   Stories, Scripts, and Scenes: Aspects of Schema Theory. Hillsdale, NJ: Lawrence Erlbaum Associates.

Meinig, D. W.
1979   Symbolic Landscapes. In *The Interpretations of Ordinary Landscapes,* edited by D. W. Meinig, 164–92. New York: Oxford University Press.

Michael, R. L., and D. L. Grantz
1983   Descriptions of Surveyed Structures in the Roanoke, West Virginia, National Register of Historic Places District. In *Stonewall Jackson Lake, West Fork River, Lewis County, West Virginia. Architecture, History, Oral History, and Reconstructed Domains,* edited by R. C. Carlisle, pp. 65–477. A report prepared under the supervision of James B. Richardson III, principal investigator, by Carnegie Museum of Natural History, Section of Man, submitted to the U.S. Department of the Army, Pittsburgh District Corps of Engineers, Pittsburgh, Pennsylvania under contract DACW59-81-C-0086.

Pearce, S. R., and N. M. Waters
1983   Quantitative Methods for Investigating the Variables that Underlie Preferences for Landscape Scenes. *The Canadian Geographer* 27:328–44.

Price, E. T.
1964   Viterbo: Landscape of an Italian City. *Annals of the Association of American Geographers* 54:242–75.

Rapoport, A.
1969   *House Form and Culture.* Englewood Cliffs, NJ: Prentice-Hall.

———
1982   *The Meaning of the Built Environment: A Nonverbal Communication Approach.* Beverly Hills, CA: Sage Press.

Rickert, J. E.
1967   House Facades of the Northeastern United States: A Tool of Geographic Analysis. *Annals of the Association of American Geographers* 57:211–38.

Roberts, J. M., and R. C. Carlisle
1983   Remembered Buildings: A Reconstructed Cultural Domain. In *Stonewall Jackson Lake, West Fork River, Lewis County, West Virginia. Architecture, History, Oral History, and Reconstructed Domains,* edited by R. C. Carlisle, pp. 555–67. A report prepared under the supervision of James B. Richardson III, principal investigator, by Carnegie Museum of Natural History, Section of Man, submitted to the U.S. Department of the Army, Pittsburgh District Corps of Engineers, Pittsburgh, Pennsylvania under contract DACW59-81-C-0086.

Roberts, J. M., and G. E. Chick
1979   Butler County Eight Ball: A Behavioral Space Analysis. In *Sports, Games, and Play: Social and Psychological Viewpoints,* edited by J. H. Goldstein, 65–99. Hillsdale, NJ: Lawrence Erlbaum Associates.

──────
1987   Human Views of Machines: Expression and Machine Shop Syncretism. In *Technology and Social Change,* 2nd ed. edited by H. R. Bernard and P. J. Pelto, 302–27, 377–93. Prospect Heights, IL: Waveland Press.

Roberts, J. M., S. Morita, and L. K. Brown
1986   Japanese Sacred Places and Gods: Categories Elicited from a Conjugal Pair. *American Anthropologist* 88:807–24.

Solomon, R. J.
1966   Procedures in Townscape Analysis. *Annals of the Association of American Geographers* 56:254–68.

Taylor, S. M., and V. A. Konrad
1980   Scaling Dispositions Toward the Past. *Environment and Behavior* 12:283–307.

Tuan, Yi-Fu
1974   *Topophilia: A Study of Environmental Perception, Attitudes, and Values.* Englewood Cliffs, NJ: Prentice-Hall.

Anthropological Research Methods

References

Beebe, James
1987 Rapid Appraisal: The Evolution of the Concept and the Definition of Issues. In *Rapid Rural Appraisal,* edited by Grandstaff, et al. Khon Kaen, Thailand: Khon Kaen University Publ.

Behrens, Clifford A.
1989   Review of *Randomization Tests,* 2nd Ed., by Eugene S. Edgington (1987)

and *Assignment Methods in Combinatorial Data Analysis*, by Lawrence J. Hubert (1987). *Journal of Quantitative Anthropology* 1 (4):399–403.

Bentley, Margaret, et al.
1988   Rapid Ethnographic Assessment: Applications in a Diarrhea Management Program. In *Anthropological Studies of Diarrheal Illness*, edited by J. Coreil and J. D. Mull. Special issue of *Science and Medicine* 27 (1):107–16.

Bernard, H. Russell
1988   Research Methods in Cultural Anthropology. Beverly Hills, CA: Sage Publications.

Bernard, H. Russell, et al.
1986   The Construction of Primary Data in Cultural Anthropology. *Current Anthropology* 27 (4):382–96.

Borgatti, Stephen
1989, 1990   ANTHROPAC. Microcomputer Software Program. Columbia, South Carolina.

Chambers, Robert
n.d.   Running Notes on Participatory Mapping and Modelling. Unpublished manuscript.

DeWalt, Billie R., and David Barkin
1987   Seeds of Change: The Effects of Hybrid Sorghum and Agricultural Modernization in Mexico. In *Technology and Social Change*, edited by H. R. Bernard and P. J. Pelto. Prospects Heights, IL: Waveland.

DeWalt, Billie R., and Pertti J. Pelto
1985   *Micro and Macro Levels of Analysis in Anthropology: Issues in Theory and Research.* Boulder, CO: Westview Press.

Grandstaff, S. W., T. B. Grandstaff, and G. W. Lovelace, eds.
1987   *Rapid Rural Appraisal.* Proceedings of the 1985 International Conference. Khon Kaen, Thailand: Khon Kaen University Publ.

Johnson, Jeffrey C.
1990   *Selecting Ethnographic Informants.* Newbery Park, CA: Sage.

Kendall, Carl, et al.
1990   Exploratory Ethnoentomology: Using ANTHROPAC to Design a Dengue Fever Control Program. *Cultural Anthropology Methods (CAM) Newsletter* 2 (2):11, 7, 5.

Kleinman, Arthur
1980   *Patients and Healers in the Context of Culture.* Berkeley, CA: University of California Press.

Latour, Bruno, and Steve Woolgar
    1979 *Laboratory Life: The Social Construction of Scientific Facts.* Beverly Hills, CA: Sage Publications.

Marchione, Thomas
    1981 Ethnographic Study: Phase I. Field Manual. Infant Feeding Practices Study. Population Council/Columbia University/Cornell University. Unpublished technical paper.

Miles, Matthew B., and A. Michael Huberman
    1984 *Qualitative Data Analysis.* Beverly Hills, CA: Sage Publications.

Pelto, Gretel H.
    1984 Ethnographic Studies of the Effects of Food Availability and Feeding Practices. *Food and Nutrition Bulletin* 6 (1):33–43. (Based on field guide prepared for the Project on Infant and Young Child Feeding Practices in Cameroon.) Newton, MA: Educational Development Council.

————
    1990 (draft) Formative Research for Acute Respiratory Programmes: Guidelines for Ethnographic Studies. WHO/ Acute Respiratory Infections Programme. Unpublished technical paper.

Pelto, Pertti J.
    1970 *Anthropological Research: The Structure of Inquiry.* New York: Harper and Row.

Pelto, Pertti J., and Gretel H. Pelto
    1978 *Anthropological Research: The Structure of Inquiry,* 2nd Ed. Cambridge: Cambridge Univ. Press.

Plattner, Stuart, et al.
    1989 Ethnographic Method (Commentary). *Anthropology Newsletter* (30)1:23–30.

Rhoades, Robert
    1982 The Art of Informal Agricultural Survey. Training Document 1982 (2). Lima, Peru: International Potato Center.

Scrimshaw, Susan C. M., and Elena Hurtado
    1987 *Rapid Assessment Procedures for Nutrition and Primary Health Care.* Tokyo: United Nations University and UCLA Latin American Center.

Shaner, et al.
    1982 *Farming Systems Research and Development: Guidelines for Developing Countries.* Boulder, CO: Westview Press.

SYSTAT
    1988, 1989 SYSTAT Microcomputer Software and Manual. Evanston, IL: SYSTAT.

Trotter, Robert T.
    1988   Research Methods Training Requirements in Anthropology (Commentary). *Anthropology Newsletter* 29 (7):28.

Weller, Susan, and A. Kimball Romney
    1988   *Systematic Data Collection.* Beverly Hills, CA: Sage Publications.

Wellman, Barry
    1990   Integrating Textual and Statistical Methods in the Social Sciences. *Cultural Anthropology Methods (CAM) Newsletter* 2 (2):1–5.

White, Douglas, ed.
    1985, 1986 . . . 1990   *World Cultures* (electronic journal). Irvine, California.

Contributors

Lindsay H. Allen
Department of Nutritional Sciences
University of Connecticut
Storrs, CT 06269

Margaret E. Bentley
Department of International Health
School of Hygiene and Public Health
Johns Hopkins University
Baltimore, MD 21205

Ronald C. Carlisle
Transportation Planning Department
Michael Baker, Jr. Inc.
Airport Office Park, Bldg. 3
5th Floor, 420 Rosen Rd.
Coraopolis, PA 15108

Billie R. DeWalt
Department of Anthropology
University of Kentucky
Lexington, KY 40506

Kathleen M. DeWalt
Department of Behavioral Science
College of Medicine
University of Kentucky
Lexington, KY 40536

William W. Dressler
Department of Behavioral and Community Medicine
University of Alabama School of Medicine
Tuscaloosa, AL 35487

Philip L. Kilbride
Department of Anthropology
Bryn Mawr College
Bryn Mawr, PA 19010

Annette Kline
Department of Anthropology
University of Missouri
Columbia, MO 65211

Meenu Mathur
Operations Research Group
Baroda, India

J. Anthony Paredes
Department of Anthropology
Florida State University
Tallahassee, FL 32306

Gretel H. Pelto
Department of Nutritional Sciences
University of Connecticut
Storrs, CT 06269

Pertti J. Pelto
Department of Anthropology
University of Connecticut
Storrs, CT 06269

John J. Poggie, Jr.
Department of Sociology and Anthropology
University of Rhode Island
Kingston, RI 02881

Michael C. Robbins
Department of Anthropology
University of Missouri
Columbia, MO 65211

John M. Roberts (deceased)
Department of Anthropology
University of Pittsburgh
Pittsburgh, PA 15260

Barbara Rylko-Bauer
2825 E. Fulton
Grand Rapids, MI 49506

Dijouratie Sanogo
The Population Council
Dakar, Senegal

Susan C. Stonich
Department of Anthropology and Environmental Studies Program
University of California
Santa Barbara, CA 93106

Joseph Westermeyer
Department of Psychiatry and Behavioral Sciences
Oklahoma University Health Sciences Center
Oklahoma City, OK 73190

Index